THE PUBLIC SPHERE IN MUSLIM SOCIETIES

SUNY SERIES IN NEAR EASTERN STUDIES

Said Amir Arjomand
editor

THE PUBLIC SPHERE IN MUSLIM SOCIETIES

MIRIAM HOEXTER, SHMUEL N. EISENSTADT,
NEHEMIA LEVTZION

Editors

STATE UNIVERSITY OF NEW YORK PRESS

מכון ון ליר בירושלים

THE VAN LEER JERUSALEM INSTITUTE

معهد فان لير في القدس

Published by

STATE UNIVERSITY OF NEW YORK PRESS, ALBANY

For information, address
State University of New York Press,
90 State Street, Suite 700, Albany, NY 12207

Production, Laurie Searl
Marketing, Anne M. Valentine

Library of Congress Cataloging-in-Publication Data

The public sphere in Muslim societies / edited by Miriam Hoexter, Shmuel N. Eisenstadt, Nehemia Levtzion.
    p. cm.
   Includes bibliographical references and index.
   ISBN 0-7914-5367-7 (alk. paper) — ISBN 0-7914-5368-5 (pbk. : alk. paper)
   1. Islam and state. 2. Islam and justice. 3. Sociology, Islamic. 4. Islam—Essence, genius, nature. I. Hoexter, Miriam. II. Eisenstadt, S. N. (Shmuel Noah), 1923– III. Levtzion, Nehemia.

BP173.6 .P83 2002
306'.0917'671—dc21

2002021111

10   9   8   7   6   5   4   3   2   1

CONTENTS

Acknowledgments vii

Note on Transliteration ix

FOREWORD: THE RELIGIOUS PUBLIC SPHERE
IN EARLY MUSLIM SOCIETIES 1
    Dale F. Eickelman

INTRODUCTION 9
    Miriam Hoexter and Nehemia Levtzion

1 THE MIHNA (INQUISITION) AND THE PUBLIC SPHERE 17
    Nimrod Hurvitz

2 RELIGIOUS LEADERSHIP AND ASSOCIATIONS IN THE
PUBLIC SPHERE OF SELJUK BAGHDAD 31
    Daphna Ephrat

3 RELIGION IN THE PUBLIC SPHERE: RULERS, SCHOLARS, AND
COMMONERS IN SYRIA UNDER ZANGID AND AYYUBID RULE
(1150–1260) 49
    Daniella Talmon-Heller

4 THE PUBLIC SPHERE AND CIVIL SOCIETY IN THE OTTOMAN EMPIRE 65
    Haim Gerber

5 THE QĀDĪ'S ROLE IN THE ISLAMIZATION OF
SEDENTARY TRIBAL SOCIETY 83
    Aharon Layish

6 THE DYNAMICS OF SUFI BROTHERHOODS 109
    Nehemia Levtzion

7   THE *WAQF* AND THE PUBLIC SPHERE   119
        Miriam Hoexter

8   CONCLUDING REMARKS: PUBLIC SPHERE, CIVIL SOCIETY, AND
      POLITICAL DYNAMICS IN ISLAMIC SOCIETIES   139
        Shmuel N. Eisenstadt

      WORKS CITED   163
      LIST OF CONTRIBUTORS   185
      INDEX   187

Acknowledgments

The present volume is the outcome of a two-year workshop held at the Van Leer Jerusalem Institute, as part of a program on "Collective Identity, Public Sphere, and Political Order," under the auspices of the Van Leer Jerusalem Institute, the Swedish Collegium for Advanced Study in the Social Sciences in Uppsala, and the Max Weber Kolleg at Erfurt University.

The papers elaborated at the workshop were presented in their final form at an international conference held at the Van Leer Jerusalem Institute in October 1997. The participants of the workshop were joined at this conference by Professor Ellis Goldberg of the Center of International Studies, Princeton University, Professor Dale F. Eickelman of Dartmouth College, Professor Wolfgang Schluchter of the Max Weber Centre for Cultural and Social Study, Erfurt University and Heidelberg University, and Professor Bjorn Wittrock of the Swedish Collegium for Advanced Study in the Social Sciences in Uppsala.

The editors are grateful to the Van Leer Jerusalem Institute, and to its director, Dr. Shimshon Zelniker, for hosting the workshop. The Institute also covered the language editing and secretarial expenses connected with the production of the manuscript. A special note of appreciation goes to Evelyn Katrak, the language editor, to Sara Soreni, director of publications, and to Esther Rosenfeld for overseeing the preparation of the diskettes.

NOTE ON TRANSLITERATION

As the book is intended for a wide audience, including non-Middle East and Islam specialists, we used minimal transliteration for Arabic names and terms. All Arabic terms appear in italics, ` is used for the Arabic letter `*ayn* and ' for *hamza*. No sub- or superscripts are used, except in Aharon Layish's essay, where full diacritical transliteration is required because of the legal nature of the text. Turkish words and names were usually transliterated according to the system used in modern Turkish.

FOREWORD: THE RELIGIOUS PUBLIC SPHERE IN EARLY MUSLIM SOCIETIES

DALE F. EICKELMAN

The search for distinctive public spheres in premodern Muslim majority societies is a relatively recent undertaking. Until recently, historians and social theorists alike were deflected from considering such a possibility by conventional assumptions concerning the characteristics of "traditional" societies in general, and Muslim societies in particular. The contributors to this volume argue that "traditional" Muslim society had diverse and changing varieties of public spheres, the manifestations of which have been as far-ranging as the ideas and expression of Islamic civilization itself.

So pervasive was the impact of the early or "classical" formulations of modernization theory from the 1950s until the 1970s that they blocked more nuanced social and historical thought about the nature of the religious, educational, social, and economic structures in "premodern" societies. Thus, one leading modernization theorist in the 1960s saw the Muslim world as facing an unpalatable choice between a "neo-Islamic totalitarianism" intent on "resurrecting the past" or a "reformist Islam" that would open "the sluice gates and [be] swamped by the deluge."[1] In the late 1970s, assumptions about Islam's role in the development process remained similarly unnuanced: "In an industrializing nation, the gap between political and religious authority . . . becomes progressively greater," whereas "Islamic influence and control are strongest when maintaining the status quo in a backward community."[2] Such ideas have retained their vigor in some circles. In Ernest Gellner's *Conditions of Liberty*, the last book published during his lifetime, he reiterated his long-standing convictions about "Muslim society." He preferred the single, society, to the plural, societies, in writing about Islam because he regarded Islam as imposing "essential" constraints on the conduct and thought of those committed to it.[3]

Modernization theory framed not only the work of social theorists but also blocked historians from imagining the possibility that "traditional" empires, societies, and religious formations could be as dynamic as their presumed

1

"modern" counterparts. Thus, in both popular thought and in many historical analyses, a prevalent negative view of the possibilities of evolution of the Ottoman Empire discouraged consideration of possible continuities between the religious empire and the ensuing secular republic. Few considered the possibility that the former, even though demonized by early modernizers, may have contained many of the seeds for the development of the latter. Recent studies of the dynamics and demographics of Ottoman households, for example, show significant and gradually evolving continuities in the transition from empire to nation. There was no sharp break as asserted by reformers such as Mustafa Kemal Atatürk (1881–1938) and those influenced by the implicit and explicit assumptions of modernization theory.[4]

The notion of the public sphere, much like the narrower but more pervasive concept of civil society, reemerged as a key concept only in the past decade.[5] Some social theorists trace its origins to the eighteenth century. In Immanuel Kant's essay on the Enlightenment, for example, the notion of "public" is represented by the words of a writer appearing before readers independent of authoritative intermediaries such as preachers, judges, and rulers. "Public" thoughts and ideas presented in this manner are thus judged on their own merits. Implicit in this notion is the idea of a public space separate from both the formal structures of religious and political authority and the space of households and kin.[6] The notion is closely associated with the work of Jürgen Habermas, although his development of the idea is largely based on European societies and in the eyes of many is linked to the emergence of a certain form of bourgeois society and the "rational-critical" discourse possible within it.[7]

Habermas's approach to understanding the idea of the public sphere is closely tied to developments in Europe since the early sixteenth century. More directly useful for understanding the public sphere in other regions of the world—including premodern Muslim societies—is the approach of Eisenstadt and Schluchter.[8] In developing the notion of early modernities—note Eisenstadt and Schluchter's use of the plural—they stress that culture is created, contested, and in flux for both "traditional" and modern societies. Societies and civilizations develop not autonomously, but through a "continuous interaction between the cultural codes of these societies and their exposure to new internal and external challenges."

Such an idea is not entirely novel. Eisenstadt and Schluchter note that Max Weber's discussion of the role of sects in generating heterodoxies and movements of protest took account of the tensions internal and external to given social settings that gave rise to new cultural interpretations and practices. This understanding of the dynamics of "traditional" societies fits well with contemporary understandings of "classical" Muslim civilization. For example, a recent majesterial study of urban forms in Islamic countries argues that the urban process during the first four Islamic centuries was one of "adaptation and accretion rather than creation." This process resulted in highly complex and diverse forms generally adapted from preexisting Hellenic-Byzantine, Iranian, and other traditions.[9]

Nimrod Hurvitz (this volume) offers a strong historical analysis of a key incident in early Islamic history, the inquisition (mihna) of 833–848. His analysis foregrounds the contours of a religious public sphere. Hurvitz reminds us in the process that the existence of a religious public sphere involves not only a struggle over people's imaginations, but a contest over boundaries—in this case between the ruler and his subjects. In the fifteen years of the mihna, four successive caliphs supporting the scholastic theologians' faction among the ʿulama', decreed that Muslims had to accept the belief that the Qur'an was created in spite of intensely held popular support for the traditionalist view that it had always existed. This authoritarian imposition of doctrine through state violence and torture met fierce resistance and the effort was abandoned after 848. The result was to enlarge the space in which ʿulama' defined religious doctrine and set limits to a field of public action in which subsequent caliphs and other temporal rulers intervened only with caution, but generally left alone.

Hurvitz's narrative points to the existence of a religious public sphere offering a wide-ranging flow of "discursive social action" in which all members of the social community continuously observed one another, enforcing orthodoxy through informal consensus and an informal shared hierarchy of leaders of influence. The mihna sought to destroy the shared understandings and expectations of this religious public sphere but in the end failed to do so. As in the Buyid dynasty of tenth- and eleventh-century Iran and Iraq, recurring crises of royal authority coexisted with economic prosperity and an orderly social life made possible by shared understandings of trust, loyalty, and patronage. These understandings and networks of obligations implied a moral order distinct from state or royal authority that extended beyond the bonds of family, tribe, and loyalty.[10] These networks of obligations and their associated moral order imply the existence of a public sphere that is stable, but not static. This public sphere offered a framework for discourse and practice beyond shared households and immediate localities, and facilitated discussions of the common good and of boundaries of inclusion and exclusion. Similar arguments can be made for Cairo as depicted in the Geniza documents[11] and for the informal understandings and shared sense of community based on religious learning as portrayed by Michael Chamberlain for medieval Damascus.[12]

Daphna Ephrat's account of Seljuk Baghdad (this volume) also points to the existence of a religious public sphere in which a diversity of communities participated. This sphere was defined by the participation of Sufi orders, khanqahs, and intertwined networks of madrasas and madhhabs at the intersections of religious, political, and social life, largely distinct from formal, state-controlled institutions, and capable of maintaining the social order and preserving stability.

The network of understandings she describes was fixed and enduring in overall structure, but not without creative and occasional destructive tensions. The various *madhhabs* varied in their internal coherence and organization, and relation to political authority. In general, however, she argues that rulers refrained from taking a stand in theological controversies among the various schools and factions, intervening only when such disputes led to public disturbances. By the end of the eleventh century, inter-*madhhab* rivalries weakened, and the religious élite informally combined to set the tone for the public order. By the end of the twelfth century, however, Sufi orders began to replace the *madhhabs* in providing a pervasive framework for communal action and social affiliations, often cutting across ties of language, community, and class.

Both the *madhhabs* and the Sufi orders shared a common element. Ephrat writes of the "informality" of the traditions of learning and the enduring ties between masters and disciples in both institutions as a key to understanding how social action was legitimated. In a parallel fashion, Daniella Talmon-Heller (this volume) explores patterns of leadership within the Hanbali community in Syria under the Zangids and Ayyubids. In her case, the direct evidence for "popular" religious understandings and the full extent of understandings and practices in the public sphere is uncertain. Yet her account of the Hanbali community is made all the more dynamic and vivid by a fresh exploration of the available evidence.

The new approach she takes reminds me of a conversation in the early 1980s with Peter Brown, the historian of early Latin Christianity. I mentioned how surprised I was to find references in his *Cult of the Saints* to Moroccan saint cults of the twentieth century.[13] He replied that his reading of these ethnographic texts stimulated him to look in new ways at the sparse and often recondite evidence available to him for early Christianity. Similarly, the idea of the public sphere—in this case a religious public sphere—has allowed historians of premodern Muslim societies to make better sense of the underlying social and normative patterns embedded in often difficult source material.

The significance of "informal" ties for creating a stable religious public sphere becomes more salient when the concept of "institution" is taken at its root meaning—an accepted and socially legitimated means of accomplishing a task—rather than as a formal, chartered group "authorized" by some central authority. Seen in this light, the ties between master and disciple acquire a substance and concreteness as basic as that exemplified by such legally recognized institutions as *waqfs* or *madrasas*. In this respect, anthropologist Abdellah Hammoudi argues that the master-student tie in Sufism serves as the key metaphor and practice by which authority is legitimated throughout the Arab world in general, and Morocco in particular, to the present, notwithstanding the formal trappings of parliamentary and other representative institutions.[14]

Emendations and additions to the purportedly invariant and complete *shari`a* have occurred throughout Islamic history, particularly since the mid-nineteenth century. Muslim jurists have rigorously maintained the pious fiction that there can be no change in divinely revealed law, even as they have exercised their independent reasoning *(ijtihad)* to create a kind of de facto legislation.[15] In practice, however, this "independent" judgment was linked to a community of juridical peers and the shared norms and understandings of the community. As Haim Gerber (this volume) says of the public sphere in Ottoman society, the *shari`a* as practiced varied considerably from locality to locality because of these local understandings and judges, although appointed by the ruler, operated in a manner that was free from the intervention of the central government. Moreover, *qadis* exercised an influence that ranged beyond the *shari`a* itself, and could appeal to the whole of Islamic history and to popular usage to enforce an Islamic moral order as locally understood. Guilds, although recognized by the Ottoman administration, similarly operated in an autonomous manner, punishing infractions by their members, defining acceptable practice, and settling disputes. Pious foundations *(awqaf)* enjoyed a similar autonomy.

Aharon Layish's description of the role of the *qadi* in the process of sedentarization in modern Libya and the Judean desert shows structural parallels to Gerber's account. Again, he stresses that the *shari`a* as practiced developed outside the control of the ruler. *Qadis* were enjoined to enforce a codified statutory law—in the Judean desert: the Ottoman Family Rights Law of 1917, the Jordanian family laws of 1951 and 1976; and in Libya from 1972 onward, when the first codification of the law of personal status took place. Nonetheless, *qadis* still had a measure of autonomy with regard to noncodified elements of the *shari`a*, especially in matters of marriage and divorce. The contexts described by Layish are ones in which the implicit assumption is that tribal practice is removed considerably from the *shari`a*. *Qadis* in practice used their own discretion to bridge *shari`a* and social reality. Although this bridging is more pronounced in tribal settings such as Libya and Judea, *qadis* in settings as distinct as urban Saudi Arabia and Iran (where, however, judges apply a codified family law) employ a similar discretion.[16] Layish's discussion suggests that the role of *qadi* is a central one in creating a public sphere in a tribal society, and that the public sphere has expanded with Islamization since the nineteenth century. *Qadis* are appointed by the state, but they have a moral autonomy and their legitimacy in the eyes of the public is based on the perception that they operate in an autonomous sphere.

The complementary discussions by Nehemia Levtzion on Sufi orders and Miriam Hoexter (this volume) on *waqf* indicate the new ways in which historical evidence is analyzed in light of concepts such as the public sphere. Levtzion argues that in the eleventh century the roles of Sufi shaykh and *shari`a* scholar began to be seen as compatible. In some respects, the synthesis that he describes echoes Peter Brown's account of saints in early Latin Christianity.[17] Levtzion reminds us that beliefs held by the élite are significantly constrained by popularly prevailing ones—a point also raised in Hurvitz's discussion of the *mihna* and, more particularly, in Talmon-Heller's description of the role played by the general public in shaping religious practices.

In a masterful account that traces the changing form of Sufism over the centuries, Levtzion indicates how Sufi shaykhs and Sufi orders mobilized popular support, operating variously as a source of stability, as an outlet for personal and collective grievances, and as a means of articulating social and religious norms. For some, this pervasive popularity constituted a betrayal of the spiritual promise of Sufism. The late Fazlur Rahman went so far as to say that the popular mystical understandings of the twelfth and thirteenth centuries gave rise to charlatans and "spiritual delinquents."[18] Levtzion describes the major shifts of some Sufi orders toward more formal and hierarchical organization in the eighteenth century, allowing some orders to serve as vehicles for social and political change.

Notwithstanding these transformations, the common element in Sufi organizations before and after the "watershed" transformations of the eighteenth century was the tenacity of the master-disciple relationship and its potential for legitimating wider various forms of religious and political authority. As Levtzion emphasizes, Sufi orders reached out to a variety of constituencies—traders, townspeople, peasants, and people of varying social classes, regions, and economic condition—using not only *madrasa* Arabic but also the vernacular languages of the region. Ruling authorities were often deeply suspicious of the orders because of their autonomy and capacity for independent action, linking the local with much wider spheres of influence. In a remarkably parallel fashion, Vincent Cornell's work on sainthood in Morocco similarly indicates how saints or "pious ones" *(salihun)* involved not only a closeness to the Divine presence *(walaya)* but also the exercise of worldly authority *(wilaya)*. Saints embodied a just moral order, and both in action and as cultural metaphors set limits to the abuse of authority and contributed to the creation of Morocco's sharifian state.[19]

Finally, Miriam Hoexter's analysis of *waqf* suggests how this pervasive institution was multifaceted and voluntary, creating a public space that was independent from that of state authority. Her useful review of trends in *waqf* studies in recent years indicates their multiple dimensions for understanding everything from gender roles to the creation of public space, affirming a space for social and economic action situated between households and the ruling sphere alike and generating revenues to sustain autonomous institutions.[20]

One interesting issue that her study delineates is the pervasiveness of a tacit bargaining between rulers and society, generally but not exclusively through the `ulama'. "Tacit bargaining" in this case does not mean a direct ongoing contest between rulers and ruled, but a recognition of the widespread popular support for *waqf* as an institution and the implicit limits that it placed on the scope of royal authority. As Hoexter explains, rulers were major donors and used *awqaf* as an instrument of public policy. However, because of the rules of the institution, the ownership of endowed assets was withdrawn from the donor and placed (according to the Hanafis) in God. The rule of inalienability, the necessity to secure the authorization of a *qadi* for any transactions in *waqf* property (such as exchanges or long-term deals), and the community's vested interest in the institutions created by endowments gave rise to a continuous discourse, or tacit bargaining, between rulers and society. The administration of the largest endowments was controlled by the state, but even the state was subject to scrutiny and moral approbation.

Because of the proliferation of endowments and their prominence in the public space, this implicit discourse, or tacit bargaining, formed a major element of the public sphere. Much of this discourse was instigated by the community and the solution to problems involved a combined effort of the community, the `ulama', and the rulers. This ongoing discourse and the fact that rulers constructed a large number of endowments with their own funds, rather than simply using state revenues to build mosques or other public buildings, created a bond of shared values between rulers and society. This bond was based on the ideology and practice of *waqf*—serving the interests of the *umma* and defining the proper social order. It also contributed to legitimating the ruler in the eyes of society. In exploring this theme, Hoexter thus challenges an earlier widespread conception of a complete separation and estrangement between rulers and society—as embedded in the idea of "Oriental despotism." Creating and respecting *waqf* properties proved a ruler's concern for the needs and well-being of the *umma*.

The contributors to this book document the existence of a religious public sphere in premodern Muslim societies, one neither fixed in content or boundaries, but fluctuating significantly over different historical periods. The actors in these religious public spheres were not always united and the boundaries of this sphere were often permeable, but it was set apart from the sphere of royal authority and more diverse than a single household, extended family, or kin group. In most Western contexts, religion has been formally consigned to the private sphere. In Muslim majority societies, the boundary between public and private is often more blurred than in Western societies and rarely fixed.

Such blurring of lines—or, intermediate, connective spaces—reminds us of the impossibility of distinguishing sharply between public and private and point to more important continuities between one sphere and another. The result is to suggest new understandings of the role of religion in society. A long tradition of Western scholarship has recognized the role of the `ulama' in Muslim majority societies as intermediaries between royal authorities and localities. The notion of the religious public sphere expands and completes this picture and suggests the basis of autonomous moral authority on which this public sphere was based. It also suggests the ways in which this religious public sphere varied over time, linking diverse communities in a common social imaginary.

NOTES

1. Halpern 1963, 129.
2. Bill and Leiden 1979, 69.
3. Gellner 1994, 211.
4. Duben and Behar 1991.
5. For example, see Colas 1997.
6. See Chartier 1991, 23–28,
7. Calhoun 1992, 7.
8. Eisenstadt and Schluchter 1998, 5.
9. Wheatley in press.
10. Mottahedeh 1980.
11. See Goitein 1967 for a depiction of the complex and wide-ranging trade patterns based on such shared understandings.
12. Chamberlain 1994.
13. Brown 1981.
14. Hammoudi 1997.
15. See Eickelman and Piscatori 1996, 26, and Vogel 1999.
16. Vogel 1999; for Iran, see Mir-Hosseini 1999.
17. Brown 1981.
18. Rahman 1979, 185.
19. Cornell 1998.
20. Hoexter 1998b.

INTRODUCTION

MIRIAM HOEXTER AND NEHEMIA LEVTZION

The essays included in this volume were presented and discussed at an international workshop on the Public Sphere in Muslim Societies, held at the Van Leer Jerusalem Institute in October 1997. The workshop concluded two years of deliberations on the public sphere in general and its application to Muslim societies in particular, by a study group whose participants then presented their papers. They were joined by international scholars represented in this volume by Dale F. Eickelman. Their comments added substance to the project's aim to develop the concept of the public sphere in Muslim societies.

For the purposes of this volume we have adopted the definition of the public sphere put forward by Shmuel N. Eisenstadt and Wolfgang Schluchter. They define the public sphere as a sphere located between the official and private spheres. While both the official and the public spheres work for the common good, the public sphere recruits its personnel from the private sphere, not from the ruler's domain. The public sphere is thus autonomous from the political order, and "its influence rests on interpretations of the common good vis-à-vis the ruler, on the one hand, and the private sphere, on the other."[1] The concept of the public sphere adds a new dimension to the discourse on civil society. It shifts the emphasis from the political authorities to society and stresses the close connection between the autonomy of this sphere and the idea of the social order as promulgated in a specific society or culture without necessarily developing in the direction of Western political institutions.

The foreword and concluding chapter expand on the theoretical and comparative perspectives. The other chapters are case studies stretching from the ninth century to the twentieth. They certainly do not cover all periods or all regions of the Islamic cultural area; but they all refer to institutions that were central to Muslim societies during most periods and in most parts of the Muslim world. Each chapter deals with a specific period and region and treats specific aspects of the public sphere. Much of the discussion centers around issues, events or institutions connected with Islam. However, rather than a system of worship, confined to the private sphere,[2] the emphasis in all chapters

9

is on Islam as a regulator of the social order. We thus focused on the role of the *shari`a* as an autonomous civic force; the ensuing autonomy of institutions and social groupings based on the *shari`a* and their dynamics; the role of the community in the public sphere; and the nature of the interaction between the society and the ruling authorities. We have been inspired by the approach of Marshall Hodgson, who identified three religiously sanctioned institutions that held together all groupings of the *umma* (the community of believers) in the town: the *shari`a* laws, the *waqf* foundations, and the Sufi brotherhoods (*tariqa*, pl. *turuq*).[3] All three institutions figure prominently in the essays.

Umma and *shari`a* are central conceptions running through the discussion in virtually all the chapters included in the present volume. The *umma*—the community of believers—was accorded central importance in Islamic political thought. Not only were the protection and furthering of its interests the central concern of the ruler, the individual Muslim, and the `*ulama*'; the *umma*'s consensus (*ijma`*) on the legitimacy of the ruler as well as on details concerning the development of social and cultural norms was considered infallible. The community of believers was thus placed as the most significant group in the public sphere, and above the ruler (see Miriam Hoexter).

The *shari`a*—the sacred law, or the rules and regulations governing the lives of Muslims, derived in principal from the Qur'an and *hadith*[4]—was developed by *fuqaha'* (jurists) and was basically an autonomous legal system, independent of the ruler's influence. Above and beyond being a legal system, the *shari`a* embodied the values and norms of the social order proper to the community of believers and became its principal cultural symbol. The sacred nature of the *shari`a* is deeply entrenched in the public sentiment of Muslim societies. The sanction of the sacred law has contributed to the formation of a Muslim public opinion and endowed institutions and social groupings based on the *shari`a*—such as the *qadi*, the *mufti*, the schools of law (*madhahib*)— with a high degree of autonomy vis-à-vis the ruler. It has also accorded moral authority to the `*ulama*'—the *shari`a* specialists—who have asserted their position as authorized interpreters of the *shari`a* law and custodians of the moral values underlying the ideals of social order of the *umma*.

As Nimrod Hurvitz shows, the `*ulama*' secured themselves this role early in Islamic history. In his reinterpretation of the inquisition (*mihna*) he argues that already in the early ninth century the articulation of religious dogma was the domain of the `*ulama*'. The failure of the *mihna*, in which caliphs attempted in vain to enforce acceptance of the theological view of one faction of the `*ulama*', gave further substance to the division of responsibilities between the `*ulama*' and the rulers. It also secured the autonomy of the `*ulama*' in centuries to come.

The large measure of autonomy enjoyed by `*ulama*' in subsequent centuries—not only in matters of doctrine, but also in the exercise of their daily duties—is demonstrated in a number of papers. Daphna Ephrat relates that once an `alim in Seljuk Baghdad was appointed to teach in a *madrasa* endowed by a ruler, he enjoyed "academic freedom" in the admission of students and in all matters related to the content of his teaching. He could even influence the selection of his successor. The independence of the `ulama'—whether or not they held official positions—in the context of the Ottoman Empire is discussed by Haim Gerber. Although dependent on the ruler for his appointment, the *qadi* enjoyed a large measure of autonomy in the administration of justice in his court. In both substance and procedure, he followed the *shari`a* law and the ruler did not usually intervene in its day-to-day administration (see Ephrat, Gerber, and Aharon Layish). An in-depth analysis of the *qadi's* function is given in Layish's chapter. Discussing the role of the *qadi* in the process of sedentarization of tribal societies in Libya and the Judean Desert, he explains how the *qadi's* court became a distinct arena of the public sphere, free from the ruler's intervention. He demonstrates the measure of discretion of *qadis* in reconciling *shari`a* and custom, thus creating a favorable climate for members of a tribal society to apply to *shari`a* courts and eventually bringing tribal society within the orbit of normative Islam.

Ephrat, Layish, and Daniella Talmon-Heller articulate the broader public mission of the `ulama' and their ethic of public service, which consisted of providing guidance to the community concerning the proper norms of social, moral, and legal behavior. Indeed, their manifold functions—as judges, *muftis*, teachers, guardians of orphans, leaders of prayers, preachers—brought the `ulama' into daily contact with the people and made them natural leaders of public opinion and informal representatives of the community.

`Ulama' sometimes converted their charisma into social, economic, and even political power, and became leaders of autonomous organizations. Two categories of such organizations are represented in the present volume: the schools of law (*madhahib*) and the Sufi brotherhoods (*turuq*). As Ephrat and Nehemia Levtzion demonstrate, these organizations performed a variety of social functions and became major foci of communal life. They developed and restructured themselves according to their own dynamics, and their relative importance in the public sphere changed in the course of time.

Ephrat dwells on the change from factionalism and violent clashes among adherents of the different *madhahib* from the ninth century onward, to a spirit of cooperation and tolerance in the twelfth century. By that time the social importance of the schools of law had diminished, and their place as principal actors in the public sphere was gradually taken over by the Sufis. Only the Hanbalis retained a high degree of cohesive communal life in later periods. This is also illustrated in Talmon-Heller's study of a Hanbali community, whose members migrated from their villages in the region of Jabal Nablus to Damascus in the middle of the twelfth century, where they continued to lead their own organized community life, led by authoritative shaykhs. Under Zangid and Ayyubid rule she found no similar organization of community life among the adherents of the larger Shafi`i and Hanafi schools of law in Syrian cities. Relations between schools of law in that period were definitely less strained and violent than in Seljuk Baghdad.

The integration of Sufism into the mainstream of Islam in the eleventh and twelfth centuries was marked by the emergence of Sufi brotherhoods (*turuq*) as new social institutions, where disciples were inducted and trained by their masters. Gradually, Sufi brotherhoods also recruited lay people, and Sufism moved from the private to the public sphere. For six centuries, from the twelfth century to the eighteenth, Sufi brotherhoods were central to the life of the individual and the community. Levtzion analyzes the development of Sufi organizations and structures at different periods, as well as patterns of relationships between Sufi brotherhoods and the state, ranging from withdrawal and autonomy to dependency. In the eighteenth century, Sufi brotherhoods transformed into large-scale, cross-regional organizations. Brotherhoods penetrated into the countryside and mobilized the common people by addressing them in the vernacular language and articulating their grievances. As this process seems to have been associated with the decline of states, one may say that the public sphere created by the brotherhoods expanded at the expense of the official sphere.

The role of *waqf* foundations in the public sphere is discussed by Gerber and Hoexter. Throughout the premodern Islamic world, endowments were made by all strata of the Muslim population. They provided for the financing and maintenance of a host of public services and did so through an institution whose rules had remained, across the centuries, an integral part of the *shari`a*. Following Hodgson, Hoexter describes the *waqf* as a major tool through which the Islamic idea of the social order proper to the *umma* was implemented. She discusses the ideology underlying the Islamic endowment institution, its impact on the formation of the urban public space, its contribution to the crystallization of autonomous groups within the community of believers, and the nature of the discourse between the society and the ruling authorities generated by the *waqf*.

The role of the community in the public sphere and the nature of the interaction between the society and the ruling authorities are of central importance to an understanding of the dynamics of Muslim societies. They are discussed in virtually every chapter.

The community of believers exercised its influence in the public sphere in several ways. Gerber discusses the measure of autonomy of more or less structured organizations, such as professional guilds and neighborhoods. He and Hoexter dwell on the importance of endowments made by members of guilds and neighborhoods, groups of common origin, the *ashraf* (descendants of the Prophet), etc., in providing them an independent economic basis. Furthermore, they show how, through endowments, these groups enhanced group identification and social interaction among their members and became influential factors in the public sphere.

The concept of the public sphere may address also the role of the common people, or the uninstitutionalized community, and its participation in molding or changing social and normative practices. Talmon-Heller gives several examples of the active participation of the general public in twelfth- and thirteenth-century Damascus in the shaping of religious practices that became *sunna* for most believers. The community often succeeded in doing this in the face of initial strong opposition of `ulama' backed by the ruler. One of the most striking examples is that of saint worship and the visitation of tombs, which in turn contributed greatly to the growing popularity of devotional Sufism, as argued by Levtzion. Gerber shows how popular support contributed to the rise of the *shari`a* in the Ottoman Empire in the course of the fifteenth century, at the expense of the criminal law enacted by the state (*qanun*). The role of the community in the process whereby cash endowments were legalized in the Ottoman Empire (Gerber and Hoexter) is another case in point. All these examples point to the dynamics of a living tradition influenced to a large degree by public opinion. In addition, Gerber and Hoexter emphasize the variations in legal practice within the Islamic cultural area, influenced by local circumstances or resulting from different approaches to certain points of law prevalent among various local population. They also discuss some of the mechanisms that enabled the incorporation of changes in the *shari`a*: the *ijma`*—the consensus of the community of believers; the legitimization of custom (`urf, ta`aruf, ta`amul)—both general and local; and appealing to the best interests of the community of believers. The central position in the public sphere accorded to the community of believers in Islamic thought and practice is thus highlighted.

The importance of the *shari`a*—not only as a practical guide encompassing the moral values and norms of the public order proper to the *umma* but also as a symbol of cultural identity—and the central position of the *umma* in the public sphere were found to have been crucial factors affecting the relations between rulers and society.

While the ruler was devoid of authority to determine the norms governing the public sphere, his responsibility to uphold the *shari`a* was the condition for the legitimization of his rule. This responsibility implied an obligation on the part of the ruler to make sure that the public sphere in the territory under his control was construed in conformity with the basic moral norms and values of Islam, and that the law was administered according to the specific rules of the *shari`a*. The ruler's adherence to these norms and rules was the touchstone of his relations with the community under his control (see Hoexter).

To a large extent these principles determined the nature of the ruler's involvement in the public sphere. The rulers' degree of involvement in the public sphere and the nature of their relations with the community varied of course over the centuries and were largely dependent on their strength and the type of political regime.[5] Hurvitz shows how, as a result of the *mihna*, the space in which `ulama' defined the doctrine was enlarged and limits were set to future intervention of rulers in this field of action in the public sphere. Indeed, except in cases in which a ruler claimed special spiritual powers— that is, declared himself a *mahdi* (a divinely guided ruler who would restore Islam to its original perfection)—instances of personal involvement by rulers in matters of doctrine in periods subsequent to the *mihna* must have been very rare. Discussing Seljuk Baghdad, Ephrat dwells on the nature of rulers' intervention in the important ongoing debate between the schools of law (*madhahib*). The rulers kept aloof of the doctrinal debates; nor did they interfere in the formation or activities of social organizations based on *madhhab* adherence. Only when the rivalry between `ulama' and their supporters took a violent turn and public order was threatened did rulers step in to restore peace and order. Interestingly enough, as Ephrat shows, while preferring Hanafi or Shafi`i `ulama' in official positions, rulers often sided in such conflicts with their rivals, the Hanbalis—obviously because of their greater popular appeal and the large following they succeeded in mobilizing.

Rulers in all periods certainly issued decrees relating to the *shari`a*. However, as Hoexter points out, these decrees were not the result of a ruler's own discretion, nor was he involved in the preceding doctrinal debate. The ruler's decision was needed in order to clinch a lengthy discussion among the `ulama'; the decree was issued at the instigation of chief `ulama' and was always based on a legal opinion (*fatwa*) given by a chief *mufti*.

As part of their duty to uphold the *shari`a* in the territories under their control, rulers certainly cooperated with `ulama' in many ways. Talmon-Heller describes various aspects of such cooperation during a period in which Islam and *shari`a* were still in the process of taking root in the population and the orthodox doctrine was in danger of succumbing to various kinds of heterodox views, deviant groups, and eccentrics. She stresses the close cooperation of Ayyubid and Zangid rulers with `ulama' in enforcing Sunni orthodoxy (*ihya' al-sunna*) in their domains.

The personal piety or learning of a ruler, his public deference to revered `ulama' and to religion in general, and, *mutatis mutandis*, victories in the name of Islam certainly contributed to public legitimization of a particular ruler. Endowments by rulers and their entourages for public purposes had a similar effect on the attitude of the community to its rulers (see Hoexter and Gerber). They symbolized the adherence of the endowing ruler to the norms of good order inherent in the ideology of the *waqf*, created a bond of shared values between the ruler and the community, and contributed to public legitimization of the endowing ruler. Here, as in other cases, the role of the *shari`a* as a symbol of cultural identity is highlighted.

Moreover, the rules of the *waqf*—which withdrew ownership of the endowed assets from the endower and placed transactions relating to the endowed properties under the authorization of the *qadi*—the proliferation of endowments, and the community's vested interest in the institutions created and supported by *waqfs* brought about the active involvement of the `ulama' and the community in the way large foundations were administered, and generated a continuous discourse between community, the `ulama', and the rulers concerning major issues in the public sphere (Hoexter).

The picture that emerges from the contributions to this volume is that of a vibrant public sphere, accommodating a large variety of autonomous groups and characterized by its relatively stable yet very dynamic nature. The community of believers was the center of gravity around which activity in the public sphere revolved. Its participation in the formation of the public sphere was a matter of course; its well-being, customs, and consensus were both the motives and the main justifications for the introduction of changes in social and religious practices, in the law and policies governing the public sphere. The independence of the *shari`a* and the distribution of duties toward the community between the ruler and the `ulama', established very early in Islamic history, were crucial factors in securing the autonomy of the public sphere and putting limits on the absolute power of the ruler.

The implications of these findings for earlier theories as to the nature of relations between society and its rulers are discussed by Gerber and Hoexter. Gerber disputes the concept of the Ottoman Empire as a state of unbridled Oriental despotism. Hoexter challenges the idea embedded in the "Oriental despotism" thesis—the notion of a total separation and estrangement of the society from its rulers, and the latter's lack of concern for the community and its needs. Both point to the existence of a kind of social contract or a bond of shared values as the basis of state-society relations.

The absence of formal institutions in early Muslim societies has been the cornerstone of the thesis postulating a lack of civil society in premodern Muslim-majority societies and an extreme despotism on the part of the rulers. The papers that make up this volume demonstrate that formal institutions are not necessarily the only, and perhaps not even the most efficient way of securing an autonomous public sphere and mitigating the despotism of rulers. Indeed, informal relations and an ongoing discourse between society and its rulers governed the public sphere in Muslim societies. Social order, the dynamic participation of the community and its spokesmen in the public sphere, and discourse with the rulers rested on shared norms and values that created a bond of common cultural imaginary between ruler and society and placed limits on the absolute power of the ruler.

NOTES

1. Eisenstadt and Schluchter 1998, 10.

2. For theoretical discussions of the religious public sphere and the blurred boundaries between private and public spheres—see Eickelman, Eisenstadt, and Hoexter in this volume.

3. Hodgson 1974, vol. 2, 119.

4. Calder *EI²*.

5. See Arjomand 1999 on the relationship between types of political regime and the use of endowments as instruments of public policy.

CHAPTER ONE

THE MIHNA (INQUISITION) AND THE PUBLIC SPHERE

NIMROD HURVITZ

The term *public sphere* acquired its currency and importance in the framework of European historiography, which focused on the formation of a bourgeois society.[1] However, the concept can take on a more general meaning if we extend it beyond any specific temporal and geographic features such as the European bourgeoisie in the modern era. The theoreticians and historians who coined this term and used it in their writings refer to the public sphere as a social space in which discursive interactions between large segments of the public take place. In his exposition of the multiple meanings of the term *public*, Jürgen Habermas has emphasized that aspect of publicity in which the public functions as the "carrier of public opinion."[2] In a study of the French revolution, Roger Chartier has referred to the public sphere as "a space for discussion and exchange removed from the sway of state power."[3] The shaping of public opinion and autonomy from state influence are issues that need not be limited to the European experience. They are in fact also relevant to developments in Islamic societies. The concept of the public sphere can prove particularly useful in an exposition of the forces that shaped public opinion, laid the principles of religious discourse, and affected the efforts of scholars to maintain their intellectual independence.

In this chapter I will touch on these questions by focusing on a period of crisis that has been named by Muslim historians the *mihna* (inquisition). The *mihna* was initiated by the caliph al-Ma'mun in the year A.H. 218/ A.D. 833. Al-Ma'mun's sympathy towards the *mutakallimun* (scholastic theologians) moved him to attack their intellectual opponents, the *muhaddithun* (traditionists). Using the caliphal role of defender of the true faith of Islam, he interrogated individual `ulama' (scholars of religious sciences) with regard to their theological beliefs. The inquisitorial question touched on the created-ness of the Qur'an. Each `alim (sing. of `ulama') was asked if the Qur'an was created. Those who answered in line with al-Ma'mun and the *mutakallimun's*

17

point of view, that it was created, were released. Those that refused to state explicitly that it was created were put in jail, threatened, tortured, and even executed. Al-Ma'mun died four months after initiating the *mihna*, but the interrogations lasted fifteen years. Its administrators, after al-Ma'mun's death, were a group of *mutakallimun* influential in the caliphal court. The *mihna* was brought to a halt during al-Mutawakkil's reign (c. A.H. 234/ A.D. 848).

The unprecedented involvement of the rulers in the controversies of the `ulama', and their attempt to influence the articulation of theological doctrine, raises a number of questions. To what extent did the `ulama' actually have discursive autonomy during the first three centuries of Islam? What were the issues they discussed and what were the underlying premises of their discussions? How did the `ulama' shape public opinion—both within their own ranks and throughout the community? In other words, what modes of supervision and coercion did the `ulama' employ among themselves? I hope the ensuing analysis of the *mihna* will make it possible to sketch the contours and contents of the `ulama''s internal discourse in the early part of the third century A.H. and shed light on the contribution of the `ulama' to the public sphere in Islamic societies.

THE EXTENT OF THE `ULAMA''S DISCURSIVE AUTONOMY

The study of the *mihna* is relevant to the inquiry into the public sphere because it enables us to examine the extent to which the `ulama' were independent of the caliphs when forging Islamic doctrine. I would like to state from the outset that the present interpretation of the *mihna* differs from most accounts of this event.[4] In contrast to the predominant trend in modern historiography, which views the *mihna* as a clash between the caliphs and the `ulama' over spiritual authority, I view the *mihna* as the culmination of a controversy within the ranks of the `ulama'. During the last decades of the second century A.H. and the first decades of the third century A.H., the `ulama' were divided into two major trends, the proto-Sunni *muhaddithun* on the one hand and the *mutakallimun* on the other, each of which tried to shape Islam according to its own religious outlook. In the first stage of this struggle, the closing decades of the second century A.H. and the opening decades of the third century A.H., the *muhaddithun* placed tremendous pressure on the *mutakallimun*, refusing to associate with them or exchange religious ideas with them.[5] After decades of suffering at the hands of the *muhaddithun*, the *mutakkalimun* attained the active support of al-Ma'mun and implemented a new religious policy in which they interrogated, jailed, tortured, and even executed their opponents. I therefore view the *mihna* as the second phase in a decades-long struggle over the nature of Islam.

Al-Ma'mun's intervention in the affairs and debates of the `ulama' was a departure from the longstanding position of neutrality that previous caliphs had maintained.[6] However, according to my understanding of the mihna, al-Ma'mun did not claim to be the sole guide in the sphere of spiritual matters, and did not see himself as opposed to the `ulama'. Rather, as will be demonstrated, he identified a clash between two factions of the `ulama', in which he supported one of the sides and joined it. More specifically, the mihna was not perceived by its administrators as a challenge on the part of the caliphs against the `ulama' but as an alliance between the caliph and the mutakallimun against the ascending proto-Sunni muhaddithun.

Another aspect of the mihna that had a bearing on the question of the caliphs' relations with the `ulama' is the change that occurred during the mihna.[7] The mihna ought to be divided into two stages. During the first, which lasted only four months, al-Ma'mun initiated the interrogations and conducted them. Either he or his political representative in Baghdad, the governor Ishaq b. Ibrahim, questioned the `ulama' personally. After four months al-Ma'mun died. His four-months-old religious policy cannot be ascribed to his successors during the next fourteen years of the mihna. The next caliph, al-Mu`tasim, relinquished the position of interrogator, and from that point on, the mihna was run by the chief qadi, Ibn Abi Du'ad, who was a Mu`tazili.[8] He and a handful of pro-kalam (theology) qadis interrogated and tortured the mihna's victims, while the caliph neither put an end to the policy nor participated actively in it. As a result, shortly after the mihna was instigated by al-Ma'mun, the caliphs receded to the background and it took on the features of a struggle of the muhaddithun against the mutakallimun.

An important aspect of this reinterpretation of the mihna is the history of the relations of the `ulama' and the caliphs in the early `Abbasid era. The prevalent view, which assumes a history of subdued tensions, has lately been challenged by M. Q. Zaman. In his analysis, Zaman writes about the superiority of the `ulama''s spiritual status over that of the caliphs. The `ulama' are described as being competent, while the caliphs attempt to acquire such competence;[9] the `ulama' "are the locus of religious authority," while the caliphs aspire to gain such authority.[10] Following Zaman's analysis, I would like to emphasize the status of `ulama' as the spiritual authorities of the Islamic community and argue that by the second century A.H., the `ulama' were sitting securely at the top of the Islamic spiritual hierarchy. The `ulama' were by far the most important participants in legal or theological discussions; they compiled the canonic collections of traditions deriving from the Prophet (hadith), made the legal decisions, and articulated doctrine. Perhaps the most important feature of their spiritual authority is that it was recognized by the caliphs themselves. Abu Yusuf's introduction to the Kitab al-Kharaj serves as a fine example of the `ulama''s widely recognized spiritual supremacy.[11]

In Abu Yusuf's opening statement of the Kitab al-Kharaj, he presents himself as more knowledgeable than the caliph, Harun al-Rashid: "The Commander of the Faithful, may Allah strengthen him, has requested me to compose

for him a comprehensive book. . . . A book for him to study and act upon."[12]
According to this remark, Abu Yusuf wrote, and the caliph studied his writings.
A few pages later, this subtle hierarchy of religious knowledge and spiritual
authority is reiterated: "Yea, I have written for you what you have commanded,
and have expounded and explained it to you. Learn it, ponder it and re-read it
until you remember it."[13] Abu Yusuf's conception of his own intellectual superiority comes across quite clearly in this remark. He knows and explains, while
Harun al-Rashid listens, reads, and studies. He concludes in the authoritarian
tone of classroom teacher: "Learn it, ponder it, and re-read it."

Abu Yusuf's tract is full of comments about the ruler's wisdom. Nevertheless, as we read the introduction we can discern that he considered himself
superior to the ruler in spiritual and religious matters. Abu Yusuf creates an
implicit dichotomy between the spiritual and the sociopolitical spheres. He
places the ruler at the top of the political one, but political clout does not
entail religious knowledge nor spiritual authority. Furthermore, it does not
ensure the best rewards in the world to come. On the Day of Judgment the
caliph's social and political standing will be of no importance. Says Abu
Yusuf: "He [Allah] judges people on the Day of Judgment, according to their
actions and not according to their status."[14] In the final analysis religious and
spiritual uprightness will determine the caliph's fate in the next world, and
these depend on his knowledge and understanding of religious and spiritual
matters, which he can acquire from such scholars as Abu Yusuf. This view was
not limited to Abu Yusuf. We have every reason to believe that Harun al-
Rashid read this introduction and agreed with its premises. On the basis of
this example, as well as others, I conclude that the caliphs did not consider
themselves to be competing with the `ulama' for spiritual authority. There
was a clear division of labor and responsibility, and the caliphs did not
infringe on the `ulama''s status as the community's spiritual guides.

The mihna and its background, according to my understanding of this
event, reveal that for the most part the caliphs were reluctant to get involved
in doctrinal controversies and incapable of imposing their will in the rare
instances they did interfere. The reluctance of the early `Abbasid caliphs to
intervene in the elaboration of doctrine, and the failure of those that tried,
reveal the strength of the `ulama''s hold in this arena. They articulated doc-
trines, determined the principles of religious discourse, and decided on the
reputation and standing of religious leaders. One of the most valuable insights
to be acquired from the mihna is that the `ulama' had vast areas of intellectual
maneuvering in which they were practically unchallenged.

CONTROVERSY WITHIN AUTONOMY:
DETERMINING ISLAMIC RELIGIOUS DISCOURSE

Autonomy hardly implies harmony. A prevalent notion about the `ulama'
that needs to be rectified relates to their unity. Most accounts of the mihna

describe the `ulama' as a unified body that opposed the rulers and strove to attain an agreed-upon political aim. This is hardly the case. `Ulama' is a label that refers to learned individuals who were members of a number of intellectual and ideological movements. Each of these movements was busy debating other groups of `ulama', articulating its own theological doctrine, jurisprudential outlook, views on Qur'anic exegesis, and other contested issues. Not only were the `ulama' splintered into numerous intellectual and ideological groups and movements, they did not establish any overall organization. As a consequence, they could not reach an agreed-upon decision or lead a concerted struggle against the rulers.

Islamic doctrine is, in large part, the outcome of the controversy between these trends and groups; their ability to persuade one another or defeat one another in the battle for public opinion determined the Islamic belief system. Barring ideologies that jeopardized the regime, such as certain Shi`i and Khawarij sects, the rulers did not intervene in the struggles that took place between these groups. In the course of their internal debates, the `ulama' of the formative period decided on the issues of contention, determined the means of proof, articulated the beliefs, and wrote the books that would become canonic in Islam.

In the letter that set the *mihna* rolling, al-Ma'mun is clearly conscious of these rivalries between the different strands of the `ulama'. He is also painfully aware that the faction he supports, the *mutakallimun*, is losing out to the *muhaddithun* in the battle for public opinion. He begins his discourse on the *muhaddithun* by describing the incompetent masses whom they lead astray. The "lower strata of the commonality," he lashes out, are incapable of comprehending religious truths.[15] He then shifts his focus to the intellectual leadership of the masses, those people who "consider themselves adherents of the *sunna*."[16] Al-Ma'mun is clearly disturbed by the success of these self-styled "adherents of the *sunna*" and dedicates a large part of his letter to outlining how they arrived at this position and how they abuse it.

These self-styled "adherents of the *sunna*" have consolidated their social and spiritual position by winning over influential groups among the people, one such group being individuals "who lead an ascetic life." The ascetics' tendency to support the self-styled "adherents of the *sunna*" has enhanced the latter's position and placed them in a position of "leadership and [won them] a reputation of probity."[17] Furthermore, "their testimony had been accepted because they [the ignorant ones or the people of false belief] have declared them [those who claim to be the people of truth] to be veracious witnesses, and the prescriptions of the Book have been put into effect through [those who claim to be the people of truth]."[18]

The meaning of this comment is not quite clear. Al-Ma'mun makes the point that his opponents enjoy the standing of religious authorities. What does he mean, however, by "testimony"? My understanding of the term is in the context of *hadiths* and the developing `ilm al-rijal—a branch of knowledge concerning information about *hadith* transmitters.[19] Since one of the crucial aspects of a *hadith* is its transmitters, the "testimony" that al-Ma'mun mentions may be the evidence touching on the trustworthiness of the transmitters of *hadith*. In other words, al-Ma'mun is complaining that it is his opponents who determine what is authentic and what false in the vital field of *hadith* due to their ability to determine who are "veracious witnesses." Alongside that, because they have become the authoritative interpreters of the Qur'an, it is they who put the "prescriptions of the Book . . . into effect." In other words, al-Ma'mun is linking his initiation of the *mihna* with his opinion that the self-styled "adherents of the *sunna*" have come to dominate the religious scene of Islam.

Like al-Ma'mun, Hanbali sources describe the *mihna* as part of a debate between two factions that have opposing views about theology. On the surface stood the inquisitorial question: was the Qur'an created? But the powerful undercurrent that raised this question to the surface was the profound disagreement over the status of theology. In the course of Ibn Hanbal's interrogation—a rare record of a direct exchange between the *muhaddithun* and *mutakallimun*—we come across such remarks by Ibn Hanbal as: "Give me anything from the Book of Allah or the *sunna* of his messenger."[20] Such a remark is a reaction to his interrogators' efforts to draw him into a theological debate. Ibn Hanbal's refusal to participate in the debate and his insistence on remaining within the confines of scripture indicate that he does not think his opponents' conclusions constitute articles of faith. Ibn Hanbal insists that his interrogators should base their opinions on the Qur'an and *sunna*, the sanctified sources of Islam. In other words, Ibn Hanbal and his *mutakallimun* interrogators were debating the very principles of theological inquiry.

Ibn Hanbal's obstinacy stretched Ibn Abi Du'ad's patience to its limits; at a certain point the chief *qadi* retorted: "And you, do you limit yourself to the Book of Allah or the *sunna* of his Messenger?"[21] Ibn Hanbal replied: "Of what is Islam made besides the Book and the *sunna*? You have invented (*ikhtara'ta*) a personal opinion and interpreted an interpretation which you propagate [lit. to which you call] to the people."[22]

Ibn Hanbal's reply does not address Ibn Abi Du'ad's accusation. It merely emphasizes the dichotomy of scripture and personal opinion. Theological investigation falls under the rubric of personal opinion. Ibn Hanbal is willing to accept theological truisms if, and only if, they are clearly stated in the Qur'an and *sunna*. However, he is unwilling to consider the results of theological investigation as theological truth, precisely because they do not derive directly from a sanctified text. If a particular theological problem has to be investigated, it means that it did not appear in a clear manner in the texts. Consequently, the conclusions of such an investigation cannot be considered an article of faith. From this point of view, personal opinion—which is the human imagination that concocts theological questions, the human faculties of reason that answer these questions, and the human vanity that embraces these answers and promotes them to the status of absolute truth—cannot be put on a par with scripture. Ibn Hanbal was concerned with demarcating the sphere of articles of faith, not with proving his own opinion correct. He ignored Ibn Abi Du'ad's impatient accusation because he thought it did not matter how he or his opponents built their arguments. By definition, the whole discussion, including Ibn Hanbal's own opinion, could not be treated as a component of faith.

In contrast to Ibn Hanbal, who was not concerned whether a believer understood the articles of faith, al-Ma'mun thought that comprehension of the articles of faith is the most important aspect of belief. In his first *mihna* letter, al-Ma'mun writes: "For there can be no good works except after sure faith, and no sure faith except after fully apprehending the true nature of Islam."[23] For a *mutakallim* such as al-Ma'mun, true Islam hinges on apprehension. It is not enough to follow the ordinances of Islamic law and morality. If believers do not understand what they are doing and why they are doing this, if they do not use their minds, then their faith is incomplete. The contrast between the *muhaddithun* and *mutakallimun* is stated by the Mu`tazili al-Jahiz:

> And the traditionists (*ashab al-hadith*) and the masses (*wa'l-`awamm*) are those that follow blindly (*yuqallidun*) and do not infer (*wa-la yuhassilun*), and they do not choose, [yet] blind acceptance is objectionable according to rational reasoning, and forbidden by the Qur'an (*manhi `anhu fi al-Qur'an*), as you can see they [traditionists] have reversed (`*akasu*) the matters, and violated norms. We have no doubt that he who examines and investigates and compares is in the better [position] to understand and arrive at the truer argument.[24]

Al-Jahiz is pointing here to the heart of the matter. He contrasts blind following with rational reasoning. Blind following, which he ascribes to the *muhaddithun*, means relying on scripture without straying off into the terrain of theological speculation. To some extent, Ibn Hanbal would agree with this description of the *muhaddithun*. However, whereas he would feel that to "follow blindly" the scripture is to take the right path, al-Jahiz assumes that this is "forbidden by the Qur'an." Al-Jahiz argues that "rational reasoning" is the utmost expression of belief, whereas Ibn Hanbal believes that true doctrine is in the canonized books of Islam and cannot be uncovered by rational speculation.

Although Ibn Hanbal and Jahiz discuss the *mihna* from contrasting points of view, and although each of them tries to promote his understanding of the event, both of them associate the *mihna* with the debate over theological proof. Despite their disagreement over the status and importance of theology, they agree that it is their disagreement over what constitutes an article of faith that lies at the foundations of the *mihna*. Al-Ma'mun's harsh denunciation of his opponents' inability to handle theological subtleties is in line with Ibn Hanbal's and al-Jahiz's view of the *mihna*'s causes.

The sources that describe the *mihna*, be they Hanbali or Mu`tazili polemics, emphasize two crucial points. First, the *mihna* was a consequence of a debate over the standing and importance of theological investigation. It seems clear to writers of both persuasions that the inquisitorial question only opened a door that led to a much wider and more meaningful issue: the nature and standing of theology. Second, the debate was between two camps of `ulama'. Most caliphs, including some of those that reigned during the *mihna*, were either too ignorant of and disinterested in such matters or too smart and politically savvy to get involved in the cross fire of the `ulama'. It was the `ulama', knowing enough and caring greatly about Islamic religiosity, who battled among themselves over the premises of religious discourse.

DISCOURSE INTO POWER

The violent religious policy of the court and the *mutakallimun* was not merely a reaction to the debates that raged over the nature of theology. It was also a response to the heavy price that the *mutakallimun* had paid in the period preceding the *mihna*.

Al-Ma'mun's criticism of the self-styled Sunnis in his first *mihna* letter hints at these persecutions. One of his most important observations is that in the years preceding the *mihna* an aggressive campaign was waged against his allies. This point is raised in several parts of the letter, though in a somewhat obscure manner. In his descriptions of the self-styled "adherents of the *sunna*," Al-Ma'mun points out two of their characteristics: First, they falsely believe themselves to be "people of divine truth."[25] With this, I presume, al-Ma'mun could live. The second characteristic, his enemies' assertion "that all others are people of false beliefs, infidelity and schism,"[26] was much more difficult to put up with. These accusations, which the *muhaddithun* aimed at their intellectual opposition, indicate that the *muhaddithun* were intolerant of interpretations of Islam other than their own, and that they played a zero-sum game: either a scholar accepted their religious outlook or he was excluded from the scholarly milieu and, in certain instances, from the Islamic community altogether. In more concrete terms, al-Ma'mun's remark refers to a protracted campaign on the part of the self-styled Sunnis, who accused their intellectual and ideological rivals of infidelity (*kufr*).

Al-Ma'mun was outraged by the self-styled Sunnis' conduct, and in his fury he wrote that they are "the tongue of Iblis, who speaks through his companions and strikes terror into the hearts of his adversaries, the people of God's own religion."[27] Here, as before, al-Ma'mun divided the Islamic community into two factions. The bad guys, whom al-Ma'mun labels self-styled "adherents of the *sunna*" and I identify as *muhaddithun*, are described as "the tongue of Iblis." The good guys, to whom al-Ma'mun belonged and I identify as the *mutakallimun*, are described as "the people of God's own religion." The new piece of information that al-Ma'mun adds to this dichotomy is a reference to the terror that the companions of Iblis (i.e., the *muhaddithun*) struck in the hearts of "the people of God's own religion." This is a dramatic accusation and a key to understanding the *mihna's* background. What did al-Ma'mun have in mind when he used the word "terror"?

I believe that when al-Ma'mun accused his opponents of terrorizing his allies, he was referring to the attempts by the *muhaddithun* to marginalize and discredit the *mutakallimun* and exclude them from the professional milieu and even from the overall Islamic social fabric. The *muhaddithun* used two forms of sanctions. First, they put up social barriers between the *mutakallimun* and the rest of the community. For example, there were pronouncements by proto-Sunni `ulama' that prohibited marriage or praying behind theological deviants.[28] Second, they applied professional sanctions against the *mutakallimun*. By resorting to a mechanism of supervision known as `ilm al-rijal, they succeeded in weeding out from the circles of *hadith* transmitters the followers of various theological and political trends—Qadaris, Murji'is, Shi`is, and Khawarij.[29] For example, around the end of the second century A.H., they discredited numerous Qadaris such as Mu`adh b. Hisham (d. 200/815), `Abad b. Mansur (d. 152/769), and Thaur b. Yazid (d. 155/774), and in some cases brought to their eviction from the ranks of *hadith* transmitters.[30] After marginalizing scholars that ascribed to theological and political ideas that clashed with evolving Sunni ideas, the *muhaddithun* were able to shape the pliant religious doctrine of Islam.

According to our present state of knowledge it seems that the first books on `ilm al-rijal were composed during the first decades of the third century A.H.[31] However, scholars that have studied the development of `ilm al-rijal have observed that expertise in this field and the circulation of information about transmitters of *hadith* began in the second century A.H. In his monumental study, *Muslim Studies*, I. Goldziher writes:

> Only when the invention of partisan and tendentious traditions had prevailed did anxious theologians pay closer attention to the informants of each saying with a view to making the validity of the hadith dependant on their quality. It seems to have been in the time of Ibn `Awn (d. 151), Shu`ba (d. 160), `Abdallah b. Mubarak (d. 181) and others of their contemporaries that criticism of the authorities begins.[32]

The founders of this branch of knowledge, which examines transmitters of *hadith* critically, died in the middle of the second century A.H., suggesting that criticism of transmitters was circulating between experts in the first half of the second century A.H. Much in line with this periodization that Goldziher offers, G. H. A. Juynboll assumes that "the starting date of systematic *rijal* criticism in Islam" was at about 130/747.[33]

The information that *hadith* critics collected about transmitters was of various kinds: biographical details (birth, death, teachers, disciples); intellectual ability (memory or loss of memory, the branches of knowledge mastered (*hadith*, *fiqh*, and `*ilm al-rijal*); theological beliefs; and jurisprudential approach. Clearly, anyone who mastered this field of knowledge had tremendous power in his hands because he could determine the professional reputation of each and every scholar and bring about his expulsion from the ranks of the scholarly community.

A brief glance at three scholars who died before the *mihna* was initiated can give us an idea of how `*ilm al-rijal* experts discussed the theological beliefs and jurisprudential outlook of their colleagues.

Abu Yusuf (d. 182), the chief *qadi* under Harun al-Rashid, was Ibn Hanbal's first teacher. Nothing about Abu Yusuf's behavior seems to have bothered Ibn Hanbal when he began his career. Later in his life, however, Ibn Hanbal was not very comfortable with this biographical detail and he remarked: "Abu Yusuf is the first (teacher) on whose authority I wrote *hadith* and I do not transmit on his authority."[34] Ibn Hanbal distanced himself from his teacher because of Abu Yusuf's jurisprudence: "Abu Yusuf is truthful (*saduq*) but it is inappropriate to transmit anything on the authority of the pupils (*ashab*) of Abu Hanifa."[35] These remarks give us some idea of the scrutiny that each scholar underwent. But more important, they reveal the danger of being affiliated with the *ahl al-ra'y* (adherents of private opinion) who were often associated with the *ashab* of Abu Hanifa.[36] For certain scholars, even those who had been his students, Abu Yusuf's jurisprudence was reason enough to marginalize him retrospectively.

Another problematic teacher was `Ali b. Hashim al-Burayd (d. 179).[37] Al-Burayd was known to have Shi`i sympathies. Some scholars, among them Ibn Hanbal, considered this a problem but were willing to transmit on his authority. Others thought his Shi`i sympathies went too far and, as a result, included his name in the *Kitab al-Majruhin*, a book that surveys problematic transmitters and elaborates their faults.[38] Another teacher whose ideological affiliation was problematic was Abu Mu`awiyyah (d. 185/195), the leader of the Murji'a in Kufa.[39]

The biographical dictionaries, which furnish us with information about these three scholars as well as thousands of others, drew information from numerous contributors. They are the written residue of ceaseless oral exchanges. `*Ilm al-rijal* constituted a constant flow of information that was verified and put to use in a manner that determined the professional relations between scholars. It is safe to assume that every scholar contributed to it, that every scholar was scrutinized by it, and that it touched on every issue that was deemed relevant to a scholar's career. These discussions, in which scholars examined their colleagues, constituted a field of internal discourse, and served as a means of ensuring that unacceptable beliefs would not enter the belief system of Islam. If new beliefs were introduced, the scholars who embraced them knew they risked exclusion from the scholarly community. I would therefore conclude that `ilm al-rijal was a highly effective means of shaping the belief system of the `ulama' and, as a consequence, the opinions and beliefs of the public. Al-Ma'mun realized that the muhaddithun's control of `ilm al-rijal was the reason behind the mutakallimun's defeat in the battle over public opinion and thus initiated the mihna.

CONCLUSION

Historians of the early `Abbasid era have noted that during that period the relations between the caliphs and the `ulama' were, for the most part, untroubled. Some of these historians assume that behind the serene façade lurked hidden tensions, while others emphasized the cooperation between the caliphs and the `ulama'.[40] The revisionist interpretation of the mihna presented here is close to the latter. It assumes that the caliphs and `ulama' acquired for themselves a hold on different spheres of influence and that both sides understood that the articulation of religious dogma was the domain of the `ulama'. In light of this division of influence and the cooperation between the caliphs and `ulama', it is argued that the mihna is the outcome of religious clashes between different trends of thought among the `ulama', and much less so, a consequence of the caliphs' will to shape doctrine.

This interpretation emphasizes factional strife among the `ulama' and the efforts of each trend to forge public opinion. It assumes that the articulation of doctrine by the `ulama' was not a serene process since it was accompanied by confrontations between the varying ideological movements. Therefore, to understand the mihna and the dynamics within the public sphere, it is crucial to uncover how the different factions of `ulama' built their power and how they used it.

Power in `ulama' circles, was based on control of `ilm al-rijal. This was the medium by which scholars determined the status of their colleagues, and in some cases it was used to exclude scholars from the scholarly community. It was a fascinating system of self-supervision, in which every scholar was both supervisor and supervised. As details about scholars were passed by word of mouth, scholars who accumulated this knowledge and were considered authoritative experts in this field, had in their hands a devastatingly powerful tool. One of the consequences of this activity was the exclusion of whole groups and ideological trends from the community of believers.[41]

`Ilm al-rijal was an effective tool for the shaping of public opinion. It determined the standing of scholars, and as a consequence the validity of the ideas they propounded, as well as the reception and dissemination of these ideas within the whole community. Historically, caliphs and their officials did not participate in this arena, as their opinions carried no weight in such matters. Against this background, the mihna can be perceived as an attempt to diverge from this policy of nonintervention and to retaliate against the effects of `ilm al-rijal, by supporting its victims. However, the caliphs failed, and their unsuccessful intervention in `ulama' politics backfired on two levels. The first, it probably served as a warning sign to future caliphs and led to the decrease of their involvement in the partisan politics of the `ulama'. The second, the mutakallimun, whom the court supported throughout the mihna, were dealt a decisive political blow from which they never recovered. Though their doctrine and intellectual tradition were kept alive two or three centuries after the mihna, their leaders rarely acquired political influence after this episode. As a consequence, the hold of the `ulama' on doctrinal aspects of the Islamic public sphere was strengthened, and within the `ulama', the burgeoning Sunni element also grew stronger.

NOTES

I would like to thank the participants of the workshop "The Public Sphere in Muslim Societies," held at the Van Leer Jerusalem Institute, for their remarks and comments.

1. Habermas 1989, Calhoun 1994, Chartier 1991.

2. Habermas 1989, 2.

3. Chartier 1991, 20

4. For a general overview of mihna see Hinds, EI²; on the interrogation of Ibn Hanbal during the mihna see Patton 1897; on the controversy over the createdness of the Qur'an see Madelung 1974; for a survey of modern historiography of the mihna see Nawas 1994.

5. For a survey on Sunni attitudes toward kalam see Pavlin 1996. On the pre-mihna era see idem. 105–106. For a short remark on the tensions between the mutakallimun and muhaddithun see Pines 1996, 74. On this subject see also below.

6. Crone and Hinds 1980, 93, observe that there were no confrontations between the caliphs and the `ulama' in the early `Abbasid period, although they believe a confrontation was in the cards during that period. Zaman 1997, 102, 105, points out that up to al-Ma'mun, `Abbasid caliphs did not challenge the authority of the `ulama'.

7. The caliphs' change in attitude toward the mihna is noted in Zaman 1997, 112.

8. On Ibn Abi Du'ad see K. V. Zettersteen and Ch. Pellat, EI²; for an interesting presentation of his contribution to the Mu`tazila see Ibn al-Nadim (d. end of fourth century A.H.; tenth century A.D.) 1970, 409. For an argument that he was not a Mu`tazili see Van Ess 1992, 481.

9. Zaman 1997, 105.

10. Ibid.

11. For a similar reading of Abu Yusuf's (d. 182/798) tract see Zaman 1997, 91–101.

12. Abu Yusuf 1969, 35.

13. Ibid., 39

14. Ibid., 37.

15. al-Tabari (d. 310/923) 1987, 200.

16. Ibid., 201.

17. Ibid., 202.

18. Ibid.

19. For a more detailed presentation of `ilm al-rijal see below.

20. Ibn Ahmad, Salih (d. 266/880) 1981, 56, 59, 60; Ibn Ishaq, Hanbal (d. 273/886) 1977, 49; for a Mu`tazili description of this interrogation see al-Jahiz, Abu `Uthman `Amr b. Bahr (d. 255/869) 1979, vol. 1, 292–96.

21. Ibn Ishaq, Hanbal 1977, 51; Ibn Ahmad, Salih 1981, 56.

22. Ibn Ishaq, Hanbal 1977, 51; a similar reply appears in Ibn Ahmad, Salih 1981, 56.

23. al-Tabari 1987, 203.

24. al-Jahiz 1979, vol. 1, 298.

25. al-Tabari 1987, 202.

26. Ibid.

27. Ibid., 203.

28. Ibn Ahmad, `Abdallah (d. 290/903) 1986, 103–106.

29. For a statistical study of the decline in sectarian transmitters of Prophetic traditions see Melchert 1992. On the pressure that was placed by the *muhaddithun* upon the *mutakallimun* see the remarks by the Mu`tazili writer al-Jahiz 1979, vol. 3, 283–89. Even though al-Jahiz and al-Ma'mun do not mention `ilm al-rijal, the practices that they attribute to the *muhaddithun* and their consequences fit this label.

30. On all three see Ibn Hajar al-Asqalani (d. 852/1449) 1984. For Mu`adh b. Hisham see vol. 10, 196–97; for `Abad b. Mansur see vol. 5, 104–105; for Thaur b. Yazid see vol. 2, 33–35.

31. Juynboll 1983, 164, 165.

32. Goldziher 1971, 135.

33. Juynboll 1983, 20.

34. al-Khatib al-Baghdadi (d. 463/1072) 1966, vol. 14, 259.

35. Ibid., 259, 260.

36. Abu Hanifa and many of his disciples were reputed to have embraced theological ideas of the *mutakallimun*.

37. Al-Khatib al-Baghdadi 1966, vol. 12, 116, 117; Ibn Hajar al-`Asqalani, Ahmad b. `Ali 1984, vol. 1, 63.

38. Ibn Hibban, Muhammad (d. 354/965) 1976, vol. 2, 110.

39. Ibn Hajar al-`Asqalani 1984, vol. 9, 120–22.

40. On hidden tensions see Crone 1980, 77; On cooperation see Zaman 1997, 12.

41. Melchert 1992.

CHAPTER TWO

RELIGIOUS LEADERSHIP AND ASSOCIATIONS IN THE PUBLIC SPHERE OF SELJUK BAGHDAD

DAPHNA EPHRAT

During the eleventh century emerging social associations and institutions developed in Islamic societies to disseminate religious knowledge (`ilm), apply the Islamic religious law (the shari`a), and harness mysticism. During this century, a period often called the "Sunni revival," the four Sunni schools of law (the madhahib, sing. madhhab) were consolidated, the nuclei of the Sufi brotherhoods were formed, and the religious sciences colleges (madaris, sing. madrasa) and Sufi centers for devotion and learning (khawaniq, sing. khanqah, or rubut, sing. ribat), were founded. These developments took place against the background of the `Abbasid caliphate's disintegration—a process that began as early as the late ninth century—and the subsequent rise to power in the early eleventh century of a new Turkish sultanate, the Great Seljuks.[1]

This chapter, in seeking to evaluate the significance of religious leadership and associations in the public sphere, addresses several questions: to what extent did the religious leadership and the groupings that grew up around it enjoy autonomy vis-à-vis the central authorities, that is, develop and restructure according to their own dynamics, independent of the official sphere? Did the political rulers intervene in religious matters at all? Were the madhahib the nuclei of public sphere arenas and the focus of solidarity for local communities? What were the bases of solidarity that bound members of the legal schools together? Did the character and operation of religious association as an arena of public sphere undergo changes over time? These questions will be dealt with in the particular context of Seljuk Baghdad (from the Seljuk conquest of the city in 1055 to the dissolution of the Great Seljuks' empire in the mid-twelfth century). Significantly, the city of Baghdad, which more than any other Islamic city suffered from the upheavals and instability of this century, featured prominently in the madhahib's process of consolidation and the development of the madrasa into its "mature" form. Indeed, the madaris founded in Baghdad in the late eleventh century represented a new form of organization. For the first time schools were founded on the large Islamic endowments (waqfs) that had been given in perpetuity for the teaching of the law according to one of the four Sunni madhahib (the Shafi`i, Hanafi, Hanbali, and Maliki). The substantial waqfs endowed by the founders, often the Seljuk viziers and sultans, paid the salaries of the teachers and stipends for students, thereby increasing the new schools' attraction.[2]

Eleventh-century Baghdad, it is also important to note, was a city in which all four Sunni law schools were represented, and which retained its position as a major religious and intellectual center, a magnet for aspiring students, even as its central political and economic role was eroded. As the seat of the `Abbasid caliphs and representatives of the Seljuk sultans, the caliphal city remained a major center of government as well.

THE `ULAMA' AND THE OFFICIAL SPHERE

Historians of medieval Islamic societies have largely agreed that with the emergence of the Seljuks as the new ruling elite in the central lands of Islam, patronage and sponsorship of Sunni religious institutions and the religious scholars, the `ulama', reached unprecedented heights. This policy was nowhere more clearly revealed than in the foundation of madaris on substantial endowments, and the employment of their graduates as religious and civil officials. Given their traditional status in Islamic societies and the nature of the ruling elite during this period, the choice of the `ulama' as benefactors of state patronage should not seem surprising. Deriving their moral authority and their standing from the shari`a, they were the sole civilian elite that could bridge the gap between the alien Turkish military elite and the indigenous population. Moreover, the `ulama' could legitimize the Seljuk regime by enjoining obedience on the local population, as well as by performing a host of tangible and intangible services for the government. The heterogeneous character of their socioeconomic background and networks, and their close ties with the urban populace, further strengthened the position of the `ulama' as a "glue," intermediaries between the rulers and their subjects. For the `ulama' came from, or had representatives in, all segments of the society, including the ruling elite.[3]

The `ulama' of Seljuk Baghdad appear in our sources as administrators of mosques, schools, and orphanages—functions that put them in control of great corporate wealth. Occasionally, they also acted as patrons of local groups and spokesmen of the populace. They were, on several levels, a powerful political presence, taken very seriously by the political rulers, who sought their advice and support. Their ties with the urban populace took a variety of forms. As teachers they instructed the general Muslim community in the fundamentals of their religion. As qadis they administered religious law; as muftis they expounded this law by issuing fatwas (legal opinions). As pious and charismatic leaders they considered themselves responsible for correct Islamic behavior. As a group they shared an ethic of public service, providing educational, religious, and legal guidance for the Muslim community. Phrases such as "he informed the people" (afada al-nas), "the people derived benefit from him" (intafa`a al-nas bihi), and "he educated the people with fatwas" (`arafa al-nas bi'l-fatwa) appear frequently in the biographies of `ulama' of this period.[4] Accounts of `ulama' deeply dedicated to public service further convey the impression of a group closely linked to the urban populace and playing a vital role in daily community life. Many `ulama' are praised for their generosity to the poor. They are reported to have supported the needy from their own pockets or given them a portion of their income, and to have collected the poor tax (zakawat) and alms (sadaqat) and distributed the money to their poor followers (ashab).[5]

In the view of several scholars, while enhancing the position of the `ulama' in the public sphere, state patronage—primarily through the foundation of madaris and employment of their graduates—sowed the seeds for the creation of a religious establishment incorporated into the governmental apparatus and dependent on the military ruling elite. To fulfill their religious and social roles, the `ulama' depended not only on the central government for protection against external enemies but also on gifts and endowments supplied by the military elite, who controlled and manipulated the main resources of the society. The underlying assumption here is that the madaris were state instruments intended to control institutions of learning that would give the political rulers influence over the `ulama'.[6]

An inquiry into the pattern of appointment to lucrative posts—qadis in the main courts, teachers (mudarrisun, sing. mudarris) in the great colleges—and the prerogatives of their holders, is one way to assess the autonomy of `ulama' placed at the head of the religious institutions vis-à-vis the political rulers. To be sure, in theory, it was the political rulers—Seljuk sultans and their viziers—who appointed the qadi and the mudarris, paid their salaries, and dismissed them at will. However, the pattern of appointment, if there was any definite pattern, seems to have depended on personal ties between an individual patron and a particular religious scholar, rather than on ties of patronage binding the `ulama' as a group to the official sphere.[7] Moreover, the biographies of the appointees reveal that in practice these appointments confirmed an existing leadership rather than created a new one. A considerable number of scholars who taught in the madaris of Seljuk Baghdad and served as qadis in the city's courts had already acquired renown as great scholars of religious law in their time; these included the heads of the schools of law and the chief qadis of Baghdad and its environs. In fact, appointments to the posts of qadi and mudarris may even have been subject to the decision of the holders of these positions, who would naturally recommend their most qualified and closest disciples. Whether or not mudarrisun and qadis actually nominated their own successors, our sources attest that many disciples who were closely associated with their masters did eventually succeed them in their positions.[8] Yet the involvement of the `ulama' in the appointment process could go beyond mere suggestions regarding which of their disciples were appropriate for teaching or judicial positions. In their endeavor to further their control over such important sources of patronage, the most reputable and powerful scholars passed their positions on to their own sons and relatives. This phenomenon of inherited high-ranking religious posts, already apparent in the late eleventh century, became more evident in the course of the subsequent century, the period that initiated the decline of the Seljuk Empire. Members of the ruling elite continued to build and endow *madaris* and assign scholars to religious institutions. However, as a result of the growing weakness of the central authorities, the ties of patronage between the rulers and the `ulama' loosened and Baghdadi `ulama' came to enjoy greater freedom in the choice of their successors and the administration of the religious institutions in general.[9]

Once a scholar was appointed to the post of teacher of the law in the *madrasa* he seemed to enjoy complete freedom in the admission of students, the sequence and method of all instruction, and the choice of treatises. Although the *madrasa* was founded for the teaching of the traditional religious and legal sciences (to the exclusion of the so-called "ancient," rational sciences), what a professor taught was not closely regulated. He would teach what he knew, and there are no examples of a trustee (*nazir, mutawalli*)—the administrator of the *waqf* by which the *madrasa* was founded—complaining about the study content or reprimanding or dismissing a *mudarris* because he taught the "wrong books" or in the "wrong way." Thus, there were teachers who, in their partiality to the rationalist fields, would teach them under the guise of the traditional Islamic sciences or through the ancillary subject of the popular sermon (*wa`z*), which in the Shafi`i *madaris* bore a theological message of a rationalist Ash`ari message. We can learn about such attempts primarily from accounts of the objections of the Hanbalis, who headed the movement of "the people of *hadith*" (*ahl al-hadith*).[10]

Although more dependent than the *mudarris* on the political rulers for his employment and status, the *qadi* enjoyed no less freedom in the administration of the *shar`i* court and the judicial procedures than did the *mudarris* in the instruction of the law in the *madrasa*. The sultan would appoint the *qadi* over the *shar`i* court while exercising "administrative" justice in the civil court (the *mazalim*) personally or through his agents. The law administered in the *qadi*'s court, as well as the rules of evidence and procedure, were those laid down in the *shari`a*. The *qadi* enjoyed full freedom in the administration of the *shar`i* law; there is no evidence of members of the ruling elite intervening in the application of the law. Held in a mosque, in his residence, or in some other duly appointed place, the *qadi*'s court was concerned primarily with family lawsuits and matters of personal status: the settlement of litigation, the execution of testaments, and matters of inheritance, escheat, and transfer of property. Taken together, the *qadi's* roles and prerogatives made him a crucial figure in the public sphere of Seljuk Baghdad. Apart from his strictly judicial functions, the *qadi* was responsible for the administration of the affairs of orphans, widows, and others legally incapacitated. Moreover, the chief *qadi* (*qadi al-qudat*) was usually entrusted with the "general supervision" (*nazar `amm*) of pious endowments, in particular in mosques, and the estates of orphans and other persons, as well as with the supervision of officials in the legal administration, notably the market inspector (*muhtasib*). His supervision of the mosques sometimes included the power to nominate the preacher of the Friday sermon (*khatib*) and leader of the public prayer (*imam*), though in Baghdad the *khatib*ship was often secured for the Hashimites, descendants of the clan of Muhammad. With regard to the administration and supervision of the endowments supporting *madaris*, there were a variety of practices during the Seljuk period. If the founder had not appointed a controller-supervisor of the endowment (*nazir*), the chief *qadi* administered the *waqf* directly; if, however, as happened in Seljuk Baghdad, each of these endowments had its private controller, the chief judge merely exercised general supervision over the administration of the *waqfs*.[11]

Due to the prestige and public respect enjoyed by the chief *qadi*, and the *qadis* in general, they occasionally acted as envoys and mediators. Already in 433/1041 the caliph, al-Qa'im, sent the famous *qadi* Abu al-Hasan al-Mawardi as his envoy to the Seljuk chieftain Tughril Bey to inquire into conditions in the domains conquered by the Seljuks or the object of their future expansionist intentions.[12] After the establishment of Seljuk rule in Baghdad, leading `ulama'—chief *qadis*, in particular—were sent by the caliphs to intercede with state officials who overstepped their authority in Baghdad or oppressed the local population. For example, in 495/1101, when strife between the Baghdadi populace and the head of the local police (*shihna*) broke out, the caliph sent ad-Damaghani, the chief judge, to intercede.[13] In addition, chief *qadis* came to be involved in the contraction of marriage alliances between the houses of the caliph and the sultan, a matter that had significant political implications. Still, the most significant political role of the chief *qadi* was his participation in the oath-taking ceremony (*bay`a*), which confirmed the appointment and authority of a new caliph, at the side of the vizier, the head of the army, and other high military dignitaries. Following the conquest of Baghdad by the Shi`i Buyids (in 945) and throughout the Saljuk period, the chief *qadi* maintained this prerogative.[14]

If not through official appointment to high-ranking positions, was it through the incorporation of the `ulama' into the official sphere that the political rulers created and dominated a religious establishment? My investigation has shown that apart from the `ulama' assuming offices in the *qadi*-ship—a special category between religious scholarship and governmental service—the number of religious scholars who entered state bureaucracy as chancery and fiscal officials was relatively small. Thus, the `ulama' of Seljuk Baghdad were far from being entirely integrated into the official sphere.[15] Rather, the overwhelming majority of the Baghdadi `ulama' during this period were not employed by the state and did not hold any official religious or administrative positions. Among them were hundreds of *hadith* transmitters and teachers of the law in a variety of educational forums, who lived on individual donations and gifts or sustained their teaching activities with other professions (notably trade), and the *muftis*, who acted independently of all outside powers, especially governmental power. *Muftis* were not appointed by the state, their authority was based on their reputation as learned and pious men, their opinion had no official sanction, and a layman might resort to any scholar he knew and in whom he had confidence. During the Seljuk period the individual soliciting the *mufti* for his legal opinion remunerated him; but many *muftis* performed the service without charging a fee, especially when they had other means of support.[16]

Doubts about whether to associate with the government at all, which had characterized their predecessors under the `Abbasids, continued to disturb many `ulama' during the Seljuk period and probably increased as a result of the nature of the ruling elite and the growing ties of patronage between the political rulers and the `ulama'. Such reoccurring phrases as "to pursue worldly success" (*talab al-dunya*), "to meddle in worldly matters" (*dahkhl fi ashghal al-dunya*), or "to mingle with the people of the world" (*khalt abna' al-dunya*) convey the criticism and disrespect felt toward `ulama' who associated with men of wealth and power. In contrast, refusal to accept the financial patronage of the rulers, and abstention from any connection with them, became a source of pride, respect, and prestige. In their competition for public esteem many `ulama' thus placed a high value on separating themselves from the moral corruption that tainted the state's acts. Indeed, even those who benefited from state patronage by accepting paid positions, such as that of *qadi*, distanced themselves from the political rulers and from court life. At the same time, in their endeavor to draw themselves closer to the urban population, these religious and civil officials would use the endowments and gifts supplied to them to assume the role of patrons and benefactors of the people.[17]

It may thus be argued that in the long run, rather than increasing their dependence on the political rulers, state patronage allowed the `ulama' to carry out their social roles independently of the official sphere. They enjoyed autonomy not only in the institutions related to the application and transmission of Islamic religious law but in the public sphere of Seljuk Baghdad as a whole. Moreover, due to their centrality in the public sphere, the `ulama'— both those who benefited from state patronage and those who refused any endowments or gifts from the rulers—could put pressure on the political authorities to enforce the norms of the Islamic community (the *umma*) laid down in the *shari`a*, of which they were the acknowledged interpreters.

THE *MADHAHIB* AS ARENAS OF PUBLIC SPHERE

By the twelfth century the four Sunni legal schools, the *madhahib*, had been consolidated as networks of masters and disciples, united on the ideological level by their adherence to the doctrines of their school's founder and tied together socially by a variety of personal ties.[18] By that time Baghdad had become a major scene in the process of the crystallization of the Hanafi, Shafi`i, and Hanbali schools, both as legal bodies and as social networks. Members of these three legal schools dominated the application of religious law and transmission of the religious and legal sciences, though prominent representatives of the Maliki and Zahiri schools were still present in the city.[19] Most Shafi`i scholars in Seljuk Baghdad were transients and immigrants, drawn to the city primarily from Iran, as were many `ulama' of the Hanafi school. In contrast, the Hanbali school in Baghdad during this period was dominated by native-born `ulama'.[20]

Except for the `ulama' of the Hanbali school of theology and law, which was often identified with the theological stream of *ahl al-hadith*, references to the theological inclinations of `ulama' of the different legal schools are rare. What we do know, however, indicates that for the most part Ash`ari theology, which was often regarded as a compromise between rationalism and traditionalism, appealed to the Shafi`is, while those who inclined toward Mu`tazili rationalist theology were more likely to be Hanafis.[21]

Another difference among the Baghdadi *madhahib* relates to the kind of offices their scholars held and to their consequent relationships with the political rulers. Nearly a third of the Shafi`i and Hanafi scholars held paid civil and religious offices, often as professors in the *madaris* founded by the political rulers for legal scholars of the two schools, as well as various positions in the judiciary. The Shafi`is, who gained power under the vizierate of Nizam al-Mulk, predominated in the office of the *mudarris*. But after his death (in 1092), and up to the mid-twelfth century, the Hanafis were the most favored. The Hanbalis, who normally refrained from seeking the financial patronage of the political rulers, largely controlled the professorships in the great mosques as well as the *khatib*ships, positions that were not subsidized by the state.[22]

That by the twelfth century the majority of the Baghdadi `ulama', and probably those of other Islamic cities as well, belonged to one or another of the legal schools is evidenced by the growing number of scholars who are referred to in biographical dictionaries by their affiliation (*nisba*) to a *madhhab*. However, there is as yet no way of estimating what percentage of lay persons identified

themselves with a specific school, nor of estimating exactly what this affiliation meant. Did they look to its scholars for guidance on proper Islamic conduct, its witnesses to register contracts and marriages, and its judges to
mediate disputes? Did they have customs, leaders, and patrons of their own?[23]
Nor do we know much about the internal structure of the *madhahib*. Circles of
teachers and their students, along with legal functionaries such as deputies,
notaries, and clerks in the service of the *qadis*, probably made up the core of
the schools. It is also possible that from this core membership the law schools
branched out to include a larger number of people who adhered to them on
the basis of birth or the traditional membership of their quarter; they may
have prayed in the same mosque, studied in the same Qur'anic school or
madrasa under the teachers of their respective *madhahib*, even married each
other. Bab al-Basra is a good example of a quarter associated with a particular
school of law. Yet, though generally considered to be the Hanbali section of
town, members of all legal schools taught or studied in the quarter's mosques
as a matter of routine.[24] Only when attempts were made to preach Ash`arism
in the mosque of al-Mansur—the stronghold of the Hanbali community—did
it become an arena of conflict between the religiously defined factions.[25]
Moreover, people tended to settle in quarters according to common professional pursuits and/or geographical origins.[26] The issue of the various schools
as social organizations in specific residential quarters is thus complex, and the
resulting picture unclear.

In trying to evaluate the extent to which the legal schools in Seljuk
Baghdad became the organized bodies in which society was structured, however, a distinction should be made among the three legal schools dominating
religious learning in the city. The difference between the *madhahib* in terms of
geographical origins, theological inclinations, and office holding must have
affected the networks of social relations into which the schools' `ulama'
entered, and consequently their status and roles in the public sphere.

Since there are few biographical dictionaries of Hanafis, it would be difficult to describe any general features of this school in Baghdad. The many
Shafi`i biographies, however, convey the portrait of an exclusive, elitist group
of legal scholars, immersed in intensive study and transmission of the law in
their study circles, teaching mosques, and *madaris*. It is also important to bear
in mind that the majority of Shafi`is in Baghdad came from elsewhere, prima-
rily the provinces of eastern Iran. Some settled in Baghdad and gained a reputation in their own small scholarly groupings, others moved to other Islamic
cities or returned to their hometowns. To judge from the letter sent by al-Shirazi, the leader (*imam*) of the Shafi`is in Baghdad, to the Seljuk vizier (cited
below), the school remained a minority community, unable to put down roots
in the caliphal city and attract a large local following. The inclination of
some leading `ulama' of the school toward Ash`arism, and even more important, their financial patronage by the political rulers primarily through the

foundation of *madaris*, certainly did not contribute to their popularity, serving instead as a pretext for their criticism by the Hanbalis and their followers. Naturally, the acceptance of paid religious and civil positions by many scholars of both the Shafi`i and Hanafi schools involved a certain degree of association with the political rulers. In contrast, only rarely do we find any references in their biographies to their association with other social groups, such as merchants or the common people.

Hanbalism—a school of law and theology—was the most localized and inclusive of the Baghdadi schools.[27] Preserving the old, informal style of scholarly association, the school was open to a relatively large number of part-time scholars, from various professional and social "classes," committed to the study and transmission of the Prophetic traditions. From its circles of masters and disciples, Baghdadi Hanbalism thus reached out to include a community of followers from among the unlearned people to become a genuinely popular movement.

Driven primarily by religious motives, Hanbali preachers and theologians sought a remedy for the decline of the `Abbasid caliphate and its capital by insisting on morality and individual action to combat religious and social unwarranted innovations *(bid`a)*. It was this view of Islam's glorious past, as well as the distance many kept from the government, that helped their movement gain many supporters.[28] Phrases such as "he guided the people" (*sada al-nas*), "the people adhered to him" (`akafa al-nas bihi), and the "Sunni gained victory with him" (*intasara bihi ahl al-sunna*), which appear in biographies of Hanbali `ulama' as a matter of course, convey the impression of a group highly regarded by the populace and cultivating a large following.[29] Since they avoided the patronage of the political rulers, the Hanbalis depended on personal support among the school's adherents to finance their activities and help the needy. Shaykhs with private means and wealthy patrons and supporters of the school founded educational institutions and provided financial support to teachers and students. Among the most generous benefactors of the Baghdadi Hanbalis was the wealthy merchant Shaykh al-Ajjal Abu Mansur b. Yusuf. Upon his death, a group of Hanbalis went to his grave, rubbed their cheeks against it, and cried: "O Master! . . . Whom do we have who will assist the Muslims after you? In whom shall we seek refuge after seeking it in God?"[30] Designed to cater for the everyday needs of the school's followers, such patronage undoubtedly reinforced the social identity and unity of the Hanbali school. Hence the importance of investigating the informal social practices that lie beyond the organizational forms.

Several historians have suggested that the foundation of the *madrasa* as a formally organized college for a particular school of law might have lent the *madhahib* a greater unity and identity, thereby contributing to their process of consolidation. United hitherto by the international system of scholarly connections, the legal schools found a new mode of organization for their legal

instruction, religious propaganda, and political action.[31] Obviously, this interpretation of the social effect of the establishment of *madaris* is at odds with
the view—frequently repeated in the literature—describing the transmission
of religious lore as a highly personal process, one dependent entirely upon the
relationships between individual shaykhs and their disciples.[32] Given this primary characteristic of the transmission of `ilm, scholarly groupings that con-
stituted the core of the *madhahib* constructed their identities and loyalties
around renowned shaykhs, rather than around educational institutions.[33] The
situation in Seljuk Baghdad seems to have conformed to the latter description; the *madaris* had not yet come to monopolize or even dominate religious
learning. Nor were the new schools centers around which scholarly networks
were formed and crystallized. Rather, the transmission of Islamic learning and
the social ties that grew up around it took place in a variety of study circles
(*halaqat*, sing. *halqa*) convened wherever a celebrated shaykh sat.[34] It is noteworthy that the `ulama' of the Hanbali school, the most coherent *madhhab* of
all, were the last to adopt the *madrasa* as a teaching institution, and even when
they did, most of the school's teaching and preaching activities continued to
take place outside the *madrasa*. As for the Shafi`is, given the absence both of
traditional, well-established Shafi`i forums in Baghdad, and a large following
amongst the Baghdadi urban populace, the *madaris* founded for them probably
played a role in establishing and ensuring the position of their *madhhab* in the
city. The Shafi`is and their local followers would rally around their *madaris*,
thereby stressing their *madhhab* affiliation in the face of threat and danger—
notably when the Hanbalis mobilized their following to wage a struggle against
the Shafi`is following the latters' attempt to preach Ash`arism in their *madaris*.
In a letter sent by al-Shirazi (the schools' leader) to the caliph's vizier Fakhr al-
Dawla on one of these occasions, he complained, "[The Shafi`is] are but a
small community, which enjoys neither sufficient followers nor governmental
support to challenge their opponents. They therefore gather in their *madrasa*
[the Nizamiyya *madrasa*], which was erected to serve their small community as
a home (*dar*) and a place of refuge (*malja'*) in good and bad times."[35]

Indeed, it was primarily on shared theological and moral concepts that the
ties of social solidarity among the adherents of a *madhhab* were based, rather
than, as one might have expected, on legal interpretation per se.[36] This further
explains why the Hanbalis achieved greater coherence. While within the other
legal schools there was still dissension between the rationalists (*ashab al-ra'y*, or
Mu`tazilites), and the traditionalists (*ahl al-hadith*), the Hanbalis formulated a
rather uniform position in matters of theology, dogma, and morality. Consequently, Hanbali preachers and theologians succeeded in becoming the dominant force in the movement for the restoration of Sunnism from its beginning
in the late tenth century.

Thus, the Hanbalis, who were relatively removed from the ruling elite
and its resources, developed to a greater extent than the other *madhahib* in

Seljuk Baghdad a social organization around their networks of masters and disciples. This is not to say that the Shafi`i and Hanafi schools did not develop
and restructure according to their own dynamics, or that their scholars did
not play significant social roles as teachers, *muftis*, and *qadis*, as well as patrons
and leaders of local groups.[37] Still, given their association with the political
rulers, the elitist nature of their scholarly networks, and the theological dissension within their ranks, they did not develop into social organizations similar to that of the Hanbalis in Seljuk Baghdad.

THE DYNAMICS OF RELIGIOUS FACTIONALISM

During the eleventh century the city of Baghdad still suffered from the severe
religious factionalism whose origins can be traced back to the time of the
"inquisition" *(mihna)* in the early ninth century. By the tenth century the
Hanbalis had become the most vigorous and dynamic sub-faction among the
Sunni population of Baghdad. At the heart of the conflict between the Hanbalis and their rivals in the caliphal city was the old disagreement between *ahl
al-hadith* and *ahl al-ra'y* over the status of rational investigation. Fearing that
rational inquiry into divine revelation would detract from the perfect
integrity of the simple original faith, the Hanbalis led the movement of *ahl al-
hadith*, which insisted on finding *hadith* solutions to legal and theological
questions whenever possible. Hence, in addition to taking it upon themselves
to persecute the Shi`a, Hanbali popular leaders and theologians were occu-
pied in fighting rationalism of all shades, trying to enforce their rigid orthodoxy on Baghdadi society, and honing the boundaries between the religiously
defined groups. During the second half of the eleventh century the Hanbalis
of Baghdad fought against the Ash`aris, deriving their support primarily from
among the city's lower classes.[38]

One of the most violent attacks of this kind occurred when the famous
Ash`ari theologian and preacher Abu Nasr al-Qushayri al-Nishapuri arrived
in Baghdad on his way to the *hajj* in 469/1076 and preached in the Nizamiyya
madrasa, mixing theological remarks with his sermon. Mobilizing the masses,
a group of Hanbalis waged a merciless war against the Shafi`is, accusing them
of leaning toward Ash`arism. The riots were so violent that they are described
in the sources as a *fitna* (lit. civil strife, rebellion). As the *fitna* intensified and
a member of the Shafi`i school was killed, the Shafi`is fled to the Nizamiyya
and closed its gates.[39] One poet, a witness to the violent riots, wrote to Nizam
al-Mulk pleading with him to put an end to the *fitna*. "Order and security in
the city have crumbled," the poet warned, ". . . the soldiers are fighting one
another . . . and the people of Baghdad are oppressed and their honor has been
trampled."[40] The vizier then ordered that the Ash`ari preacher be removed
from his lectern in the Nizamiyya and sent back home.[41] Again, in 475/1082,
the Ash`ari theologian al-Bakri, who had previously accused the Hanbalis of

heresy, was prevented by order of the vizier from preaching Ash`arism in the mosque of al-Mansur.[42] Several years later, in 484/1091, while visiting Baghdad, Nizam al-Mulk convened a group of Hanbalis to inquire into the theological debate between the Shafi`i and Hanbali schools regarding the Divine attributes. Ibn al-Jawzi, the Hanbali historian, responded to the accusation by the Shafi`is of the Hanbali anthropomorphization of God (tashbih, tajsim): "Those who associate with the political rulers and seek worldly benefits (talab al-dunya) have no right to fight us over theological questions."[43]

These and similar accounts raise the question of the intervention of the political authorities in the internal debates between the religiously defined factions in Seljuk Baghdad. In contrast with several `Abbasid caliphs before them, Seljuk sultans and their viziers rarely participated in religious life; they knew very little about theological and legal controversies and did not strive to define Sunnism according to a centrally espoused dogma.[44] After all, as an alien political elite, the Seljuks could not raise similar religiously based claims to authority in religious matters. Indeed, except for one effort to exert religious control during the vizierate of Amid al-Mulk al-Kunduri, who in 1048 charged all proponents of Ash`ari theology in Nishapur with being heretical innovators, the Seljuks refrained from taking a stand in matters of local religious authority.[45] In other words, they did not strive to change the balance of power of the local factions. In a similar vein, Nizam al-Mulk's preference for the Shafi`is as candidates for religious and civil offices was not intended to establish the Ash`ari "middle-road" orthodoxy, as has been asserted.[46] Nor was this preference designed to encourage the rivalries between the religiously defined factions in Baghdad, thereby strengthening the position of the central government vis-à-vis the `ulama'.[47]

The main objective of Nizam al-Mulk and other members of the ruling elite was to put an end to, or at least reduce, the turmoil caused by debates among the local factions over proper creed and behavior. Hence, only when such debates involved large segments of the population posing a threat to public order, did the rulers step in to restore peace and order. On such occasions, they usually acted in favor of the religious faction that had already gained the largest local following. This may explain why, while patronizing the Shafi`is, Nizam al-Mulk took the side of the Hanbalis, their rivals in Baghdad, yielding to their demand to frustrate any attempt to preach Ash`arism in the city's madaris and mosques.

During the last decades of the eleventh century, though still constituting a source of factionalism and causing occasional riots, the struggle against rationalism seems to have lost the vigor it had early in that century and consequently, its centrality in the public sphere. Simultaneously, a trend toward cooperation between `ulama' of different schools of law and thought began to develop. In the unstable milieu created by the breakdown of the `Abbasid caliphate and the rise to power of an alien Turkish elite of military lords, there were `ulama' who sought to maintain a unified Islamic community by delimiting a commonly accepted Sunni form of Islam and acting as a unified group. One of the most telling accounts attesting to collaboration for a common cause is that describing how al-Sharif Abu Ja`far, the head of the Hanbali faction, and Abu Ishaq al-Shirazi, the leader of the Shafi`i faction, struggled together against the spread of immorality, which was regarded as the reason for the great inundation of the year 464/1071. Mobilized by their shaykhs, the Hanbalis gathered in al-Qasr Mosque and called al-Shirazi and his followers to join them in their struggle against prostitution, the charging of interest, and the drinking of wine. The two shaykhs demanded that the caliph, al-Qa'im, destroy the brothels and uproot the other iniquities of the local population. At the same time, a letter was sent to the Seljuk sultan informing him of this demand.[48]

The creation of a commotion by people or groups with common interests distinct from those of the `ulama' was another cause for collaboration between `ulama' of different schools. This was the case when in 473/1080 the cloth merchant 'Abd al-Qahir al-Hashimi became leader of the local *futuwwa* (association of young men, *fityan*). Having proclaimed himself the chief secretary (*katib*) of the *fityan*, he tried to control membership in the association by issuing a certificate of admission to each new member and even attempted to extend his leadership over *futuwwa* organizations in other Muslim cities. Urged by a group of Hanbalis, the caliph's vizier ordered the head of the police (*shihna*) to subdue the leader (*ra'is*) of the *fityan*. Several *fuqaha'* from different schools then issued a legal opinion ordering the *fityan* to end their disturbance (*fasad*).[49] While reflecting the fear of leading `ulama' that the association might become a source of factionalism and public disorder, this sole account of their attitude toward local popular forces may also testify to their endeavor to control the public sphere in the face of emerging rival groups.

In the course of the twelfth century the spirit of tolerance among members of the *madhahib* grew, and their popular activism began to fade away. A more equal distribution of remuneration by the political rulers among the schools contributed to the reduction of tensions among them and to a mutual recognition of legitimacy. The foundation of educational institutions for the instruction of the Qur'an and the *hadith* (*dar al-Qur'an* and *dar al-hadith*) during the late twelfth century stressed the shared traditions of the legal schools. Finally in 631/1232–1233 the Mustansiriyya *madrasa* was founded in Baghdad, comprising four *madaris* for the teaching of the law according to the four *madhahib*. Although the *madaris* remained open to their own adherents, the advent and spread of the multiple-system *madrasa* undoubtedly reduced the tensions among the schools and added a sense of unity among Sunni `ulama'.[50] However, given the weakness of the political authorities during the twelfth century, and the Seljuks' noninterference in religious matters, the growing tolerance among the *madhahib* must have stemmed from a change in the internal dynamic of the `ulama' themselves.

By the time the multisystem Mustansiriyya *madrasa* was founded in Baghdad, the debates over proper Islamic creed and behavior among the factions, named after the legal schools and led by their shaykhs, had faded away. Consequently, affiliation with the legal schools became increasingly formal, confined to the legal context. This change in the character and operation of the *madhahib* must have changed their position and role in the public sphere of Baghdad. Though leading `ulama' within one or another of the *madhahib* continued to provide a variety of religious and social services for the Baghdadi Muslim community, at the end of the twelfth century the legal schools were no longer the leading factor in providing social affiliation and identity, and in creating a basis of factionalism.

CONCLUSION

While focusing on the character and operation of religious leadership and associations in Seljuk Baghdad, this chapter has attempted to foster an understanding of the forces and dynamics of the public sphere in Islamic societies of the post-`Abbasid era. At first glance, Baghdad was governed by an alien elite of military lords who, in their endeavor to establish their position in the caliphal city and ensure the obedience of its populace, tried to gain influence over the `ulama' at the head of religious institutions and associations. However, a closer examination of the triangle formed by the rulers, the ruled, and the `ulama' yielded a much more complex picture. Religious leadership and `ulama'-led associations were little affected by the policies of the Seljuks. Indeed, even `ulama' who were incorporated into the official sphere carried out their religious and social roles independently of the political authorities. Being the sole group that could legitimize the alien regime, and as mediators between the rulers and the ruled, the position of the `ulama' vis-à-vis the political authorities in the city's public sphere was enhanced. Though lacking formal organization and means of coercion at their disposal, leading `ulama' (the Hanbalis in particular) played a major role in the organization and shaping of communal life and became the foci of associations. The character of religious leadership and associations underwent changes in the course of the Seljuk period. At the heart of this process was the transformation of the legal schools from social solidarity groups into rigid professional bodies engaged in rigorous instruction and application of the Islamic religious law. By granting equal remuneration to the *madhahib*'s scholars in order to reduce the tensions among them, the rulers played a role in this process. But changes in the character and operation of religious leadership and association resulted from the changing dynamics within this group of `ulama' itself.

In the late twelfth century a new religiously based social organization—the Sufi (mystic) brotherhoods, the *turuq*—assumed importance in the Baghdadi public sphere. Their beginnings had been modest, as religious and social life orbited around shaykhs who led an ascetic and exemplary life, refusing any worldly benefits. Significantly, authors of biographical dictionaries speak more about the outstanding *zuhd* (piety, asceticism) of these men than about their learning. They were endowed with *baraka* (divine blessing), performed miracles *(karamat)*, and turned their residences *(rubut)* into centers of public preaching and distribution of charity as well as of pilgrimage to seek divine blessing.[51] Obviously strong links existed between a shaykh's activities and his recognition in society; the more he provided for the spiritual and nonreligious needs of the common people, the more they gathered around him; the larger his following became, the more he was admired. Eventually, in the course of the thirteenth century, the Sufi brotherhoods were to replace the *madhahib* as the most significant religiously based and led social organizations in the public sphere.[52]

NOTES

1. For a perception of the eleventh century as a transitional period during which new forms of organization of religious and social life were laid see especially the introductory remarks and articles by Bosworth 1973, Bulliet 1973, Laoust 1973, and Mottahedeh 1973. See also Hodgson 1974, vol. 2, esp. 3, 8–9.

2. The most important works on the *madrasa* are Makdisi 1961; 1971; 1981a.

3. This is in concordance with the observations of Lapidus, who has offered us perhaps the most significant interpretation of the role and status of the `ulama' in the later Middle Ages. Lapidus 1967, chapters 4 and 5; 1969, esp. 52–60. For a different interpretation see Bulliet 1972. Bulliet describes the `ulama' of tenth-eleventh-century Nishapur as a civilian elite with "class" interests separate from those of other social categories, such as merchants and landowners. Made up of a small number of local families, this elite succeeded in guaranteeing its continuity by heredity. The different interpretations of the role and status of the `ulama' must be related, at least to some extent, to the different political conditions in these cities. In contrast to Mamluk cities of the high Middle Ages, medieval Nishapur was placed under relatively indirect political control. Consequently, a "patriciate" evolved that enjoyed a greater degree of freedom and autonomy.

4. For examples see Ephrat 2000, 136–37.

5. Ibid.

6. Watt 1968, 75–76 was the first to point out that education in the Nizamiyya *madrasa* (the most important *madrasa* of all) was designed to create an "orthodox bureaucracy." Bulliet 1972, 73–75, claims that the Nizamiyya *madrasa* became a vital instrument of the policy of its famous founder, Nizam al-Mulk, in controlling what Bulliet labels the "patriciate" of Nishapur; and Leiser 1986, 18, notes that one of the reasons for founding *madaris* "was the desire of the ruling authorities to dominate, to a considerable degree, the religious elite." Regarding the use of the *waqf* of the *madaris* as a political tool see also Arjomand 1999.

7. The most telling example of such close association is that between Nizam al-Mulk and the celebrated al-Ghazali. Upon the death of his master, the Shafi`i Ash`ari scholar al-Juwayni (known as Imam al-Haramayn) in 478/1085, al-Ghazali went to Nizam al-Mulk's court at Isfahan and was sent by order of the vizier to occupy the

chair of law in the Nizamiyya *madrasa*. Nizam al-Mulk inclined to Shafi`ism and, like al-Ghazali, was born and raised in a small village in eastern Iran. For the ties between al-Ghazali and Nizam al-Mulk see especially the biography of the former by al-Subki (d. 771/1370) 1966–1967, vol. 4, 101–20. Abu Bakr al-Khujandi (d. 552/1157), another *mudarris* in the Nizamiyya *madrasa*, also had close relationships with political figures. His biographer relates that he was so closely associated with them that "in the respect he gained he was more like a vizier than like an `alim." Ibid., vol. 6, 134.

8. For details see Ephrat 2000, 121–22.

9. Ibid., 122–23.

10. See for example the story below about the preaching of the Ash`ari al-Qushayri in the Nizamiyya *madrasa*.

11. For a general discussion of the prerogatives of the *qadi* under the Seljuks see Lambton 1968, 213, 227ff.; 1988, 72ff.

12. Ibn al-Athir (d. 631/1233) 1965–1967, vol. 10, 28.

13. Ibid., 117–18. One of the main functions of the *shihna* was to carry out the decisions of the *qadi*'s court when coercive force was necessary. On the office of the *shihna* see Lambton 1968, 244.

14. See Saadeh 1977, 255–58.

15. Of the total number of 121 `ulama' whose religious or administrative positions are indicated in their biographies, only twelve held purely administrative positions. See Ephrat 2000, figure 6.1 (in chapter 6).

16. For the position of the *mufti* during the Seljuk period see Makdisi 1981a, 197–200.

17. The piety and generosity of the Shafi`i jurist and vizier Abu Shuja` al-Rudhrawari (known as Zahir al-Din), as related by Ibn Khallikan, serves as a good example: "He never left his house without having first read a portion of the Qur'an, paid the required alms-tax on all his property, and gave generous alms anonymously. After receiving a note informing him of a widow with four needy children, he ordered one of his servants to provide them with clothing and food. He then removed his own clothes and vowed neither to dress nor warm himself until the order was carried out." Ibn Khallikan (d. 681/1282) 1970, vol. 5, 137.

18. Studies on the consolidation of the legal schools up to the twelfth century include: Laoust 1959; Makdisi 1963; 1981a, 3–9; Bulliet 1972.

19. During the eleventh century the Maliki school had its main centers in North Africa and Spain. In this century the Zahiri school's importance gradually waned in Baghdad, and by the beginning of the subsequent century, it had disappeared completely from the city (the last representative of the school died in Baghdad around 475/1082). Its extinction in Baghdad, the cultural center of the Muslim world, marked a crucial phase in the process by which only the four schools that have survived down to our time remained. For the history of the Zahiri school in Baghdad see Makdisi 1963, 278–79.

20. See Ephrat 2000, figures 2.2–2.7 (in chapter 2).

21. Ibid.

22. See ibid., figure 6.1 (in chapter 6).

23. For historians who have tried to show that the schools of law were indeed meaningful social organizations in tenth to fifteenth-century urban Islamic societies, see Lapidus 1969; Bulliet, 1973; Makdisi 1981b. For a different interpretation see

Chamberlain 1994, 2. It was the elite household, according to Chamberlain, that constituted the prime, if not sole, meaningful social framework in the high medieval Middle East.

24. The most important mosque in Bab al-Basra, frequently mentioned in the sources as a meeting place for instruction and other scholarly pursuits of `ulama' of all three legal schools, was the Friday mosque of al-Mansur. See Makdisi 1961, 4–6.

25. See, for example, the story below about the preaching of the Ash`ari theologian al-Bakri.

26. For example, according to al-Ya`qubi (d. 897/1491) 1892, 248, the entire area surrounding Bab al-Sham was inhabited by people from Balkh, Marv, and Bukhara. For other examples see Makdisi 1959, 180–82.

27. Of the total number of 176 native-born `ulama' in Seljuk Baghdad whose legal school affiliation is indicated in the sources, 91 were Hanbalis, compared with 38 Shafi`is, 24 Hanafis, 5 Malikis, and 2 Zahiris. See Ephrat 2000, figure 2.7 (in chapter 2).

28. For the Hanbalis in Baghdad during the Seljuk period see Makdisi 1963; 1973; 1981b.

29. See, for example, the descriptions of public demonstrations led by the Hanbali scholar Ibn al-Wafa' in Ibn Rajab (d. 796/1393) 1952–1953, vol. 1, 52.

30. Ibn al-Banna' (d. 471/1078) 1956, part. 3, no. 100, 26.

31. See, for example, Lapidus 1988, 165–66. Makdisi, 1981a, esp. 1–3, makes a clear distinction between schools of law and colleges of law. However, he too presents a parallel and interrelated development of the two types of institutions.

32. Tibawi 1962 was the first to note that, for all the establishment of endowed and structured institutions of learning, Islamic education remained essentially informal, flexible, and linked to persons rather than to institutions. Most recently, Berkey 1992 has provided us with an extremely detailed and illustrative description of the informal character of Islamic education in Mamluk Cairo.

33. This is in line with Mottahedeh 1980, which represents the most comprehensive study of the creation of networks of informal, personal ties (defined by family, ethnic origins, or sectarian homogeneity, or by a shared professional background) in the Buyid and early Seljuk periods. Taking over the role of formal and stable institutions, these networks constituted the nucleus of the social structure in the post-`Abbasid era.

34. For details see Ephrat 2000, 69–71. As Chamberlain 1994 has shown, even at a later period the madaris played a marginal role as far as the transmission of `ilm and the social relationships among the `ulama' were concerned. Chamberlain 1994, esp. 69–90—referring to the period 1190 to 1350—stresses the marginality of the madrasa in the world of the `ulama'. The madrasa, Chamberlain asserts, was essentially a center for financial patronage, and, as such, had many uses that had nothing to do with education and the forging of relationships among the religiously learned.

35. Sibt b. al-Jawzi (d. 654/1256) 1968, 187–88.

36. Bulliet 1972 and 1994, focusing on the `ulama' of medieval Nishapur, is probably the most important contribution toward the understanding of the meaning of affiliation to the legal schools and the source of conflicts between them. See his concluding remarks in Bulliet 1994, 110–11.

37. For example, Abu Hamid al-Isfahani (d. 406/1016), who at the beginning of the eleventh-century instituted the Baghdadi method or system (tariqa) of Shafi`i law,

is said to have been deeply committed to the spread of religious learning (nashr al-'ilm) and other community services. People used to bring him their payments of the poor tax (zakawat) and alms (sadaqat) so that he could distribute the money. Besides distributing a monthly allowance to his poor followers (ashab), he donated money for the pilgrimage caravans. Eventually, "he became a leader in religious and worldly matters" (intahat ilayhi riyasat al-din wa'l-dunya). See Ibn al-Jawzi (d. 597/1200) 1940, vol. 7, 277. Abu Ishaq al-Shirazi, the leader of the Shafi'is in Baghdad up to his death in 467/1083 and the first mudarris in the Nizamiyya madrasa is also said to have combined the two leaderships. See Sibt b. al-Jawzi 1951, part. 8, vol. 1, 83.

38. See especially Makdisi 1963; 1973; 1981b.

39. Sibt b. al-Jawzi 1968, 187.

40. Ibid.

41. Ibid., 188; and see also Ibn al-Jawzi 1358/1940, vol. 8, 305–306.

42. Sibt b. al-Jawzi 1968, 217–18; Ibn al-Jawzi 1358/1940, vol. 9, 3–4; Ibn al-Athir 1965–1967, vol. 10, 124–25.

43. Ibn al-Jawzi 1358/1940, vol. 9, 484.

44. Chamberlain 1994, 167–78, makes the same observation with regard to the Mamluk authorities in high medieval Damascus. His examination of the contest over correct belief in Damascus during this period allows a great advance of our understanding of the relationships between the scholarly and ruling elites in pre-Ottoman Islamic societies.

45. Al-Kunduri's official ban forced hundreds of Ash'aris out of their posts and put many of them on the road to exile. For a detailed account of this episode see Bulliet 1973, 80–85.

46. Watt 1968, 75–76, was the first to point out that by supporting Ash'arism, the Great Seljuks played a significant role in the process of Sunni revivalism. This view has been disputed by Makdisi 1973, 155–68, who argues that the renewed activity of Sunni Islam was independent of the Seljuks and Ash'arism.

47. For a different view see Laoust 1973, 175–85.

48. Ibn al-Jawzi 1940, vol. 8, 272; Ibn al-Athir 1965–1967, vol. 10, 99; Ibn Kathir (d. 774/1372) 1966, vol. 12, 105.

49. Ibn al-Jawzi 1940, vol. 8, 326–27.

50. For the foundation of the various educational institutions see Makdisi 1971, 83.

51. For the proliferation of rubut in Baghdad and their consolidation as Sufi centers where a variety of educational and social activities took place see Amin 1965, 239–41. See also Jawad 1954.

52. For the proliferation of the Sufi brotherhoods see Levtzion in this volume.

CHAPTER THREE

Religion in the Public Sphere: Rulers, Scholars, and Commoners in Syria under Zangid and Ayyubid Rule (1150–1260)

DANIELLA TALMON-HELLER

At least five tracts composed around the middle of the thirteenth century criticize the people of Damascus for preferring superogatory public prayers to the obligatory daily prayers: a manual for the inspector of public morality (*muhtasib*), polemical works against unwarranted innovations (*bida`*), and legal responsa (*fatwas*). The tracts mention *salat al-tarawih*—long nocturnal prayers held during the second half of Ramadan—the celebration of *laylat al-nisf min sha`ban*—the night of the fifteenth of the month of Sha`ban, perceived as a time of judgment and mercy—and *salat al-ragha'ib*—a prayer said on the first Friday night of Rajab, on which it was also customary to fast and to light candles in mosques.[1]

Of the three practices it was *salat al-ragha'ib* that was attacked most vehemently, the main argument against it being the lack of evidence that the Prophet ever performed it or approved of it.[2] Scholars' endeavors to stop this popular practice failed. They themselves admit that mosques were full and brightly lit on the night in question. One of the leading polemicists against *salat al-ragha'ib* quotes contemporary *imams* complaining, as it were, that they were actually forced to lead the prayers—commoners (*al-`amma*) were so keen on performing them. A decree issued under the pressure of the `*ulama*' by the Ayyubid ruler al-Malik al-Kamil (615/1218–635/1238) banning this prayer in 632/1235, must have been disregarded, as five years later one of the prominent scholars of Egypt and Syria at that time, `Izz al-Din al-Sulami, was still engaged in denouncing the prayer.[3] Apparently, people refused to give up what they thought to be a correct and meritorious act of religious devotion, in spite of scholarly reservations. Finally, the sultan permitted it anew, receiving authorization from the *mufti* Ibn al-Salah al-Shahrazuri (d. 643/1245), a scholar who was known to approve of a variety of modes of piety.

Al-Shahrazuri had simply labeled the prayers *bid`a hasana* (welcome innovation), admittedly on basis of a "weak" *hadith* (that is, a tradition deriving from the Prophet supported with a not very reliable chain of authorities). He explained that he would rather see the crowd praying than doing anything else.[4] Hence, as a result of pressure from below, the questionable prayers were legitimized through the orthodox mechanism of *ifta'* (the issuance of a legal opinion), and a sultanic decree.

The whole episode offers us an opportunity to reexamine the complex relationships and interactions between four participants in the public sphere of medieval Muslim societies: rulers, scholars, the common people, and the religious law. The following study is an attempt to do so, focusing on religious life in the public sphere in Syria, from its unification by Nur al-Din b. Zangi (549/1154) until the Mongol conquest and Mamluk occupation (658/1260).[5] Two points will be stressed: the contribution of commoners and rulers to the shaping of religious norms, and the pious atmosphere prevalent in the public sphere.

Michael Chamberlain, who studied the inner dynamics of Damascene society between 1190 and 1350, claims that the rulers of Damascus usually refrained from taking a stand in matters of religion, and whenever they did step in, it was to end riots and secure peace and order, not to reestablish orthodoxy or to enforce a doctrine.[6] This chapter argues that Zangids and Ayyubids did take a stand in matters of doctrine and of popular practice, and played an active role in all types of religious institutions of their times.

Contemporary historians quote Nur al-Din (d. 569/1174) making a commitment to defend religion against anything opposed to it, and to "the spread of religious knowledge, the refutation of innovation and the manifestation of religion in all these lands."[7] Both he and Saladin (570/1174–589/1193) were dedicated to *jihad* against Shi`is and Franks, referred to within the wider framework of *ihya' al-sunna*—the revivification of Sunni Islam in face of enemies from within and without.[8] Their successors adopted this program, and implemented it (albeit with varying degrees of enthusiasm), pursuing various lines of action. It should be noted that most Ayyubid princes enjoyed a thorough religious education to begin with, and some of them even had justified scholarly pretensions.[9] Saladin was a firm supporter of Ash`ari theology.[10] Al-Malik al-`Adil (592/1196–615/1218) opted for the strict enforcement of Muslim prohibition of liquor, moral laxity and non-*shar`i* taxes (to the degree that in his days Damascus was said to be "clean and pure");[11] al-Malik al-Mu`azzam (615/1218–624/1227) vigorously advanced the position of his adopted Hanafi school of law;[12] al-Malik al-Ashraf (626/1229–635/1237) nurtured a somewhat populist public veneration of the Prophet and took to the persecution of dissenters from what was considered to have been the Prophet's proper path.[13]

Most of them tended to intervene in cases of socioreligious conflict: tension between Hanbalis and Shafi`is[14] and between Sufis and anti-Sufis,[15] quarrels between two Hanbali factions,[16] or opposition to established leadership inside the Jewish community.[17] As we saw above, even the liturgy in the mosques was not beyond their sphere of influence.

More often than not, `ulama' and rulers cooperated in order to strengthen what may be labeled the mainstream Sunni camp: shar`i-minded and para-doxically inclusive of Ash`ari theology, moderate Hanbali theology, and moderate Sufism.[18] Radical Hanbali theologians, ecstatic and antinomian Sufis, religious skeptics, Shi`is, so-called zanadiqa (heretics),[19] and plebeian claimants to prophecy were doomed to marginalization, if not punished in a more severe manner.

A dramatic example is the assembly (majlis) that convened in the citadel of Aleppo to decide the fate of the prominent Sufi and theosophist Yahya b. Shihab al-Din al-Suhrawardi. Al-Suhrawardi was accused of deliberately vio-lating the shari`a (inhilal), holding heretical theological views and treading the path of the pagan philosophers. The faylasuf (Arabic word for philoso-pher) was regarded as a threat to the authority of the `ulama', thereby threat-ening the political establishment as well. Al-Malik al-Zahir of Aleppo (582/1186–613/1216) was well inclined toward him, but `ulama', and following them Saladin, al-Zahir's father and superior, ordered his execution. Graced with making the choice of the method of his own execution, al-Suhrawardi starved to death in the citadel of Aleppo.[20]

The execution of a scholar was an extremely rare event under the gener-ally tolerant Ayyubids, but an unfavorable attitude toward those suspected of philosophical inclinations was to spread in their domains, easy to detect in the discourse of contemporary biographers and chroniclers. Some such sus-pects were barred from teaching, or banished from town.[21] An acclaimed scholar of law and theology, Sayf al-Din al-Amidi (d. 631/1233), was accused of incorrect theological beliefs and slack practice. He lost his positions in madaris in Cairo and Damascus, on the orders of al-Malik al-`Adil and al-Malik al-Ashraf.[22]

The provocative Hanbali scholar `Abd al-Ghani al-Maqdisi may be located on the other end of the intellectual spectrum. A majlis that convened in the citadel of Damascus in the presence of the local governor in 596/1199 turned into an investigation of his theological beliefs by hostile Shafi`i jurists. `Abd al-Ghani was accused of teaching gross anthropomorphism (tajsim) in his lec-tures, and pronounced an "innovator." The governor sentenced him to exile, and ordered that the pulpit upon which he used to teach be demolished. In addition to that, the Hanbalis lost the privilege of prayer behind an imam of their own in the great mosque.[23]

Shi`is were more vulnerable. Shortly after the conquest of Aleppo in 541/1147, Nur al-Din warned the local religious authorities that if anyone dare to pronounce the Shi`i version of the call to prayer, he would be thrown from the minaret, head down. Eleven years later, when Nur al-Din lay severely ill, the Shi`is did dare again. Unfortunately for them, Nur al-Din recuperated and immediately enforced the proper Sunni call to prayer again. As far as we know, no Shi`i muezzin climbed to the top of that tower.[24]

The most important representative of antinomian Sufism in Syria during Ayyubid times, `Ali b. Abi al-Hasan al-Hariri (d. 645/1247), had spent a few years in prison. Finally he was banished from Damascus, along with the Qalandar dervishes. He and his jama`a (group, community) of young people— a mixed crowd of ahdath (rabble, in this case) and members of Damascene elite families—were accused of moral laxity, negligence in prayer and scandalous attire. Their expulsion marks the disappearance of heterodox Sufism from Damascus for some thirty years, as far as we know.[25]

We know even less about uneducated, non-establishment charismatic figures that appeared on the Syrian scene once in a while. Sources tell us mainly about their persecution, if they mention them at all. One of them was an `ajami (foreigner) who appeared in Damascus claiming to be `Isa b. Maryam (Jesus). He is said to have "corrupted [the belief of] a multitude of the commoners" (afsada jam`an min al-`awamm). In compliance with a fatwa that sentenced the man to death, the governor of Damascus ordered his crucifixion in 595/1199.[26] A "crazy prophet," known for his power to grow fruit out of season, made similar claims to prophethood in the late 630s/1230s. Many villagers followed him until he chose to retreat to the village of Sifsaf.[27] A Maghribi who showed up in the village of Mashghara in the province of Damascus shortly before the death of Nur al-Din (569/1174) and declared himself a prophet, caused much more trouble, and was treated accordingly. His rural followers rebelled against their landlords and fled to the mountains. They were tracked down by the army in Northern Syria during the month of Ramadan 570/1175 and killed in a cruel manner.[28]

For mainstream `ulama', however, it was a period of unprecedented prosperity, particularly in Damascus and Aleppo. Dozens of new religious institutions were established and hundreds of posts became available for men of religious training. Numerous well-known teachers and aspiring students from other Muslim countries visited these cities and often remained in them, to become teachers and religious functionaries, or to serve in the state administration.[29]

In our sources, rulers are depicted—whether by way of faithful recording or by way of skillful reconstruction (probably both)—as careful to demonstrate deference toward the authority of the mufti, the qadi, and the shari`a.[30] Nur al-Din is said to have insisted upon strictly enforcing shar`i regulations concerning hearing witnesses in court and limitations on punishment, to the extent that contemporaries in Mosul complained of an increase in crime in their locality.[31] More specifically, when he undertook the reconstruction of the great mosque in Aleppo, and the work involved demolishing a nearby market owned by a religious endowment, he first consulted a *mufti*.[32] Sibt b. al-Jawzi, a contemporary of al-Nasir Yusuf (648/1250–658/1260), the last Ayyubid to have had ruled over Damascus and Aleppo, claims that al-Nasir governed "according to the regulations (*qawanin*) of the religious law."[33]

In the period that stretches between those two rulers, Saladin had a *qadi* certify that he used his private money to purchase from the *bayt al-mal* (the treasury) property that had been Frankish prior to his reconquest of Jerusalem, before endowing it as *waqf*.[34] Al-Malik al-`Adil listened to the moralizing of `Abd al-Ghani al-Maqdisi, who made bold and even violent criticism of any sign of moral laxity in Damascus, as defined by the strictest Hanbali standards.[35] Al-Malik al-Ashraf, who was eager to keep a sandal considered to be the Prophet's, waited until its holder bequeathed it to him upon his death (restraining himself from getting possession of it in other ways), and finally placed it in a public institution—the *dar al-hadith*—so as to make it accessible to all.[36] The puritan *qadi*, *mufti*, and *khatib* `Izz al-Din al-Sulami (d. 660/1262) ruled against the interests of the military elite twice, but was heeded nonetheless. In the first case he disqualified the `itq (manumission) of high-ranking Egyptian mamluk emirs. Reluctantly, they went through the ceremony again, this time "performed in a *shar`i* manner." He spoke out again in Aleppo, before a meeting of the members of the military and scholarly elite, convened in the face of the Mongol threat of 657/1259. The issue under debate was raising money for the defense of the city, and al-Sulami held that the people should be asked to finance the army only if the soldiers had already sold their silver and gold.[37] One must not conclude that freedom of speech in politico-religious matters was unrestricted: an earlier conflict between `Izz al-Din al-Sulami and the political authorities ended with his dismissal from the pulpit of the Great Mosque of Damascus, his imprisonment, and finally—his exile from the city. On that occasion he had used his Friday sermon to attack the ruler's lenient attitude toward the sale of arms to the Franks, and the territorial concessions that he had agreed to make.[38]

To end this survey of pious behavior let us take a look at the conduct of al-Malik al-`Adil in 596/1200, as it offers a fine example of a well-publicized show of respect toward the religious law, and of the intricate reciprocal relationship between rulers and `ulama'. In the course of securing his domination over the confederation his brother Saladin left behind, al-Malik al-`Adil disinherited Saladin's ten-year-old grandson from the sultanate of Egypt. He then brought together a group of *fuqaha'* and asked for their legal opinion regarding the right of a minor to rule. They issued a legal opinion asserting that he was unfit. The chronicles do not speculate on their motives. They do tell us that Malik al-`Adil's address to the emirs began with the words: "You have heard the decree of the `ulama'," and ended with a demand for their oath of alliance.[39]

Respect aside, the livelihood of thousands of scholars depended on state pensions and *awqaf* endowed by rulers, or by members of their families, in favor of *madaris*,[40] assemblies for scholarly disputation (*majalis al-'ilm*),[41] and the composition and dissemination of religious literature.[42] Patronage was selective, of course, and was used to enhance the position of certain groups, or to divide power. Affiliation with the "right" school of law at the right time, and proper familial ties, seem to have been major factors in determining an 'alim's chances of finding favor with a patron.

Once in control of Syria, Saladin replaced Hanafis by Shafi'is in the senior religious posts of chief *qadi*, head of Sufi lodges (*shaykh al-shuyukh*), *khatib*, and *nazir* (inspector) of the great mosque. Shafi'is continued to hold those posts throughout the Ayyubid period, except under al-Malik al-Mu'azzam (615/1218–624/1227), who promoted members of his adopted Hanafi *madhhab*. Less prestigious posts, those of the *muhtasib* and the assistant to the chief *qadi*, were usually given to Hanafis, as were many positions in *madaris* and on diplomatic errands.[43]

Of major relevance to the central themes of this chapter is the fact that Ayyubid rulers extended their patronage to institutions of religious education and learning intended for the community of believers in general, thus benefiting in particular 'ulama' of lower rank and laymen. They endowed Qur'anic schools for children (*makatib*),[44] Sufi lodges (*khawaniq*),[45] shrines (*mashahid* and *maqamat*) and sacred relics, mosques, public assemblies of exhortation (*majalis al-wa'z*), and gatherings for *hadith* recitation.

A series of public recitations of the *Musnad* of Ibn Hanbal (d. 241/855) by Hanbal al-Rusafi (d. 604/1207) from Baghdad were supported by al-Malik al-'Adil, and honored with his presence. Al-Rusafi was merely a minor functionary at one of the mosques of his home city, one "accustomed to a poorman's diet of oats," who happened to be the last person to have heard the entire *Musnad* from a well-known deceased scholar, and took to the road in order to pass it on. Although the text he recited—a compilation of *hadith* classified according to its transmitters, rather than by subject matter—can hardly be considered as ideal for popular consumption, a multitude of laymen showed up, rubbing shoulders with the sovereign and his entourage and with all the leading scholars of Damscus.[46]

Rulers contributed to the establishment, upkeep and growth of shrines, established throughout Syria during the twelfth and thirteenth century. Some were built on recently "rediscovered" ancient graves of prophets and *sahaba*, others on the graves of popular scholars, shaykhs, and martyrs. The initiative for the inauguration of new sites came from men and women of diverse social standing, military and civilian functionaries and members of their household, and common folk in the towns and villagers (often inspired by dreams).[47] Once erected, sites were preserved and continued to develop thanks to *awqaf* dedicated by rulers or members of the elite, and contributions of goods and labor offered by local residents and visitors.

The story of *Mashhad Ruhin* in northern Syria is a fascinating example. A clerk in the administration of al-Malik al-Zahir of Aleppo (582/1186–613/1216) happened to find himself at the site of what was then a deserted sanctuary, considered to be the grave of Quss b. Sa`ida (an early Arabian monotheist), on one of his business trips. Miraculously cured of a lingering disease, he thereon decided to dedicate his time and money to the rehabilitation of the sanctuary. After some time al-Malik al-Zahir paid him a visit, and endowed the site with the revenues of a nearby village. His heir provided for the salaries of caretakers. A cistern, a bath-house, and a *khan* were endowed by an emir, a daughter of some other emir, and the supervisor of the *waqf*, while a wall was added on by villagers.[48] It should be noted that in twelfth century Syria, personal pilgrimage *(ziyara)* to graves of holy men, and to shrines built to honor them or their relics, was hardly controversial. Most scholars allowed prayer, Qur'an recitation, *dhikr* (Sufi litany), votive offerings of oil and lamps, and service to other pilgrims in *mashahid*.[49] They themselves often sought the *baraka* (blessing) of such sites and recognized the possibility of encountering a mystical, or at least a highly emotional religious experience at them.[50] Yet while it is clear that rulers and scholars visited sanctuaries and played a role in the intensification of the cult of saints and pilgrimage to holy sites, they did not take the lead. Here, as in the case of the superogatory prayers, they joined in, or were led in, perhaps so as not to abandon the arena and let popular forces control it unchecked. Only in Mamluk times, particularly with the advent of *mawalid* (communal celebrations of the birthdays of saints), do we hear of vehement attacks on practices and excesses related to the cult of saints, but even then, outright denial of the legitimacy of grave visitation is rare.[51]

An arena more securely controlled by `ulama', though by no means exclusively by them, was the mosque. Mosques were a favorite construction project of the Ayyubids, especially of al-Malik al-Ashraf. Seven out of fourteen religious institutions he had founded between 626/1229 and 635/1237 were mosques, three of them Friday mosques.[52] Yet mosques and mausolea with a prayer niche (sometimes even an *imam*) were also established by members of the urban elite, emirs and their wives, and even by shop owners and artisans who constructed or renovated small mosques with their own hands.[53] An uncommonly detailed and vivid account of such a project depicts a group of Hanbalis who had emigrated from villages around Nablus, then under Latin occupation, and resettled on Jabal Qasyun on the outskirts of Damascus. It will be discussed below.

But first we should pause to scrutinize our sources for information that may allow us to assess how accessible mosques were to laymen in towns and villages, and to what extent laymen indeed frequented them. Historiographic and epigraphic evidence tells us that a thick network of mosques was spread over Syria already in the sixth/twelfth century. Ibn ʿAsakir (d. 571/1176), the city's leading historian and geographer, lists 420 mosques in Damascus and its suburbs. A list prepared by the later Ibn Shaddad (d. 684/1285) includes 660 mosques in Damascus, sixty-one of them in the suburbs.[54] Aleppo could boast of about two hundred mosques at that time; smaller towns and many villages of one or two.[55]

Direct information on mosque attendance in towns or villages is rare in our sources. Some chroniclers mention in passing that the great mosque (jamiʿ) in a certain town or village was full for the Friday prayer.[56] Ibn Jubayr, the Maghribi traveler who visited Damascus in 580/1184, gives a lively description of gatherings in and around the great mosque of Damascus: people came and went the whole evening, some strolling along, some talking with friends, others reading. According to him, standing there, one could get the impression that any ordinary evening was the twenty-seventh of Ramadan.[57]

Prayer was but one of several activities conducted in the mosque. People assembled in mosques for the recitation (qiraʾa) and for the study (taʿlim) of Qurʾan. According to Ibn Jubayr's estimate, some five hundred men took part in a daily reading of a few short suras in the Friday Mosque of Damascus, and received a small allowance for it. Similar information can be found in Ibn Shaddad's historical-geographical work, written ninety years after Ibn Jubayr's Rihla. He mentions children, among them orphans, who recited "Say: He is Allah, the One!" (the short sura 112) every evening.[58] On Fridays, Qurʾan recitation was also held in khawaniq. Again, commoners took part. This can plainly be deduced from the bonus offered at the khanqah al-Sumaysatiyya to those who prayed for its founder at the end of the reading: loaves of white bread.[59] In the village of Busra (in the Hawran) a well-known exegete, Abu al-ʿAbbas al-Harbi (d. 600/1204), would explain Qurʾanic passages after prayers.[60] Another scholar, ʿAli b. Muhammad al-Sakhawi (d. 643/1245), claimed that thousands of people read the Qurʾan from cover to cover under his direction.[61] The pious and emotional ʿAbd al-Ghani al-Maqdisi (d. 600/1203) read hadith in the jamiʿ of Damascus on Thursday nights and on Fridays, moving the audience to delightful tears.[62] Half a century earlier his uncle, Shaykh Ahmad b. Qudama, had read hadith to villagers in the vicinity of Nablus,[63] and there are numerous other examples of such popular classes that were held in central and in peripheral mosques.

On top of all that activity, relics and sacred objects—such as the original copy of the Qurʾan, supposedly sent by the Caliph ʿUthman to Syria,[64] the skull of Yahya b. Zakariyyaʾ (John the Baptist),[65] or a few lines in the handwriting of ʿAli b. Abi Talib[66]—were kept in mosques, as repositories of divine blessing for the faithful. Thus, Muslims of diverse levels of religious learning could and did engage in the devotional and educational activities carried out in the precincts of the mosque, whether patronized "from above," or initiated "from below."

Similar things may be said about *majalis al-wa`z*—assemblies for public exhortation that were held on weekdays, or on special occasions, in mosques and in the courtyards in front of them, but also in cemeteries and various other open spaces. Chroniclers and biographers agree that their audiences were large and heterogeneous, composed of "the great and the humble," the young and the elderly, rulers and commoners, scholars and Sufis.[67] The preachers who delivered those sermons in Syrian towns in the Ayyubid period (and reached posterity in the writings of their contemporaries) were almost uniformly established scholars. They had acquired their preaching skills from respectable teachers, together with other branches of religious learning.[68] Often they had close relations with rulers, who graced their sermons with royal patronage and presence, and sometimes even dictated the subject matter.[69]

Sibt b. al-Jawzi (d. 654/1256), a grandson of the famous Baghdadi preacher and scholar Ibn al-Jawzi (d. 597/1200), was known as the most prominent *wa`iz* of his times. He settled in Damascus in 1206, and until his death fifty years later, Damascenes spent their Saturdays listening to his sermons (except when he traveled to preach elsewhere in Syria and the Jazira).[70] People refrained from work on those days. Some men and women, eager to secure themselves a good seat, even would spend the night before the assembly in the proximity of the Great Mosque, engaging in devotional practices. Sometimes only the *musalla* (a vast enclosure for special communal prayers) could accommodate the multitude.

According to Sibt b. al-Jawzi himself, in 607/1210 for example, he spoke in front of an audience of thirty thousand people, including the governor of Damascus and its dignitaries. Hundreds of youths, moved deeply by his words, repented, or at least made the symbolic gesture of clipping their *nasiya* (forelock) in public.[71] The pile of hair from the heads of penitents reminded him of a story told on the authority of Abu Qudama al-Shami a third/ninth century *ghazi* (raider), and he narrated it to his audience. A brief version of the rather lengthy story goes as follows. On his way to the Byzantine front, Abu Qudama met a woman who begged him to take her long beautiful hair and plait it into a rein for his horse, going to battle *fi sabil Allah* (for God). Abu Qudama hesitated, but could not resist her desperate insistence. Months later, he discovered that she had also sacrificed her husband and two sons for the sake of holy war.

This wonderful and terrible tale inspired the people, and filled them with religious emotion. The crowd surrounded Sibt b. al-Jawzi and escorted him to the *musalla*, where he continued his preaching. At the end of the day they were all on their way to raid Frankish territory.[72]

Sibt b. al-Jawzi was again asked by al-Malik al-Mu`azzam to rouse the people to *jihad* in 616/1219 (after the fall of Damietta to the Franks).[73] In 626/1229 al-Malik al-Nasir Dawud sponsored a sermon against the concession of Jerusalem to the Franks in a contract his brother, al-Malik al-Kamil, signed with the German emperor Frederick II. Somewhat apologetically Sibt b. al-Jawzi complied, and at the explicit request of the ruler of Damascus reduced "all the people of Damascus" to tears.[74] A few years later he led a rally of support for al-Malik al-Ashraf, then combating Jalal al-Din Mingburnu Khwarizmshah in Eastern Anatolia, and was just as effective.[75] Safely back, al-Malik al-Ashraf urged Sibt b. al-Jawzi to propagate his favorite work on prayer and its merits (the Maqasid al-Salat of the contemporary `Izz al-Din al-Sulami) through one of his sermons.[76] No doubt he, like many others, had appreciated the mobilizing power of the topics that Sibt b. al-Jawzi addressed—jihad, martyrdom, Sunni revival, and personal piety—and of the assemblies themselves, as powerful manifestations of unity and consensus within the public sphere.

Indeed, relationship between groups with conflicting theological views and between the four schools of law, were less strained, definitely less violent, than in `Abbasid or Seljuk Baghdad (discussed earlier in this volume). Subdivisions of the community of faithful continued to exist of course. Groups whose particular religious affiliation was contested, to some degree or other, by the majority, often had the advantage of a higher degree of organized communal life, self-conscious identity, group solidarity, and self-help. Religious leadership of such groups tended to be more involved in the lives of their followers, in matters both sacred and mundane.[77] That, as is well known, was typical of non-Muslim minorities, particularly of the Jews,[78] but Muslim minority groups exhibited similar characteristics. In twelfth and thirteenth century Syria the Hanbalis stood out in this respect, as I intend to show now.

In the middle of the twelfth century 160 men, women, and children left their villages in Mt. Nablus (Palestine), then under Frankish occupation, to journey to Muslim-ruled Damascus. They all shared an affiliation with the Hanbali school of law, and a trust in a local religious leader, Shaykh Ahmad b. Qudama. Upon their arrival in Damascus they enjoyed the hospitality of local Hanbalis. During the summer of 555/1160 Shaykh Ahmad visited what was to become the community's new abode on Mount Qasyun on the outskirts of Damascus. After the landowner had showed him the site of an ancient mosque on the spot, Shaykh Ahmad went down to the river, performed the ritual ablutions, and returned to symbolically establish a mosque: he laid several stones on the place of the qibla (niche pointing toward Mecca), prayed and blessed the place. Only then did he order his people to begin construction work on the site. Working together, in an organized manner, they built their own homes and a mosque.[79]

Some forty years later, the people of that neighborhood undertook the establishment of a Friday Mosque. This ambitious project, however, was completed only after the governor of Damascus and the ruler of Irbil established awaqf to help finance the works.[80] By then, Shaykh Ahmad's son, Abu `Umar, had inherited his father's formal roles of imam, khatib, and religious instructor, and his informal functions of intercessor with God, arbitrator in cases of inner strife, and pleader for his people at the courts of the rulers. It should be noted that this last function was probably not a particularly demanding one, as on the whole the relationship between the Hanbalis and Nur al-Din, and later with the Ayyubids, was good, and they were well integrated into Syrian society.

When Abu `Umar's time came, other members of the community, either from among the emigrants or from the local Hanbali families, assumed leadership. Thus, for several generations to come, there was a continuous line of persons enjoying religious and secular authority in the community, to secure its marked Hanbali identity, shared performance of religious rites, and strong internal social bonds.[81]

I have not found evidence pointing toward similar organization of community life among the more numerous adherents of the larger Shafi`i and Hanafi schools of law in Damascus, or in other Syrian cities. Nor did the scholars who were considered to be the heads of those schools (ru'asa' al-madhhab) function like their Hanbali colleagues; they were mainly busy with scholarly work, writing, and teaching, and not with catering to the everyday spiritual and mundane needs of a community of believers.[82] Other minority groups, such as Sufis and small heretical groups that appeared from time to time on the margins of society, as we have seen earlier, seem to have resembled the Hanbalis in this respect. But this is an issue that deserves further study.

CONCLUSION

Rulers, scholars, and commoners contributed to the construction of religious life in the public sphere in twelfth-thirteenth century Syria. Zangid and Ayyubid sultans and princes supported a wide range of religious institutions—majalis al-`ilm, madaris and khawaniq, majalis al-wa`z, mosques, mashahid, and makatib—thereby nurturing various types of devotion and learning. They served not only as patrons (who selected their clients with care), but also as arbitrators. Rather than maintaining a "laissez faire attitude towards civil society,"[83] they pursued a quite consistent policy of supporting mainstream Sunnism and suppressing its rivals (referred to as ihya' al-sunna and imatat al-bida` by contemporaries).

Rulers cooperated closely with `ulama', bolstering their role as guardians of the religious law, and as propagators of Islamic norms in wider social circles. In their capacities as khatibs, qadis, muftis, and jurisconsults, as well as prayer leaders, popular preachers, reciters of the Qur'an, and humble transmitters of hadith in mosques, cemeteries, open public spaces, and the courts of rulers, `ulama' secured the place of the shari`a as the symbol of the proper social order in the public sphere.

The air of piety, advocated by the `ulama and supported by the religious elite, seems to have been truly popular, and shared by members of society at large. Moreover, Muslims of different social strata, with or without proper religious education, participated in the ongoing process of the formation of religious belief and practice. Thus, what puritan `ulama'` might have defined as bid`a (and the modern scholar might label as "popular religion"), gradually became sunna for most believers.[84] The outcome of the debate over salat al-ragha'ib discussed at the beginning of this chapter, the construction of mosques, mausolea, and shrines with the resources of individuals that did not belong to ruling military or scholarly elites, and the promotion of the cult of saint, are indicative of both phenomena.

NOTES

This paper is based upon parts of my "Society and Religion in Syria from the Reign of Nur al-Din to the Mamluk Occupation (1154–1260)," Ph.D. diss., The Hebrew University of Jerusalem, Jerusalem 1999 (in Hebrew). I am grateful to Nehemia Levtzion for his helpful comments, to Michael Cook of Princeton University for revising my English, and most of all, to Miriam Hoexter, for her invaluable editing.

1. Ibn al-Athir (d. 637/1239) 1939, vol. 2, 150; Abu Shama (d. 665/1268) 1990, 124–261; al-Sulami (d. 660/1262) in al-Subki (d. 771/1370) 1971, vol. 8, 251–55; al-Nawawi (d. 676/1277) 1999, 34–35. About the prayers see Kister 1971, 206–207; Wensinck EI and EI²; Fierro 1992, 224–26; al-Albani 1960–1961, 29–30, and Lazarus-Yafeh 1981, 39.

2. Other arguments being that it was wasteful and extravagant, that people were misled into believing that it was a sunna (rather than an optional pious deed), that there were numerous shortcomings in specific details of its liturgy, and, notwithstanding, that it was prohibited to single out certain days for special worship. I am inclined to regard these claims as an expression of a deeply conservative impetus, engaged in the ongoing struggle against change and innovation (rather than seek for some hidden political motivation).

3. Al-Subki 1971, vol. 8, 210. In another case, al-Malik al-Kamil demanded that members of all four schools of law perform the evening prayer in the Great Mosque of Damascus together rather than separately, as had been the norm (Abu Shama 1947, 166).

4. Abu Shama 1990, 196, 209, 215; al-Albani, 1960–1961, 14–18.

5. For a concise history of the Ayyubid confederation see Cahen EI²; for a full account see Humphreys 1977. Recent studies of twelfth- and thirteenth-century Damascus and Aleppo include the works of Gilbert 1980; Pouzet 1986, Chamberlain 1994, Morray 1994; Mouton 1994 and Eddé 1999.

6. Chamberlain 1994, 168–72.

7. He is also quoted rating the rulers' duty of protecting religion above that of securing the roads against thieves and robbers (Abu Shama 1991, vol. 1, 363, 372, 377).

8. An ideology promoted by `Abbasid caliphs under Buyid rule at the beginning of the eleventh century and picked up by Seljuk sultans half a century later: see Makdisi 1973; Humphreys 1989, 166; Ephrat 2000, 2–3.

9. Al-Malik al-Mu'azzam was especially learned, as noted by Ibn Wasil (d. 697/1298) 1972, vol. 4, 208–18. So was al-Malik al-Mansur prince of Hama (587/1191–617/1220): see Hartmann *EI²*. See also Humphreys 1989, 167; Chamberlain 1994, 49, 169–70.

10. Madelung 1985, 159.

11. Sibt b. al-Jawzi (d. 654/1256) 1954, vol. 8, 640; Humphreys 1977, 146.

12. Pouzet 1986, 69.

13. Humphreys 1977, 209–13.

14. Ibn Kathir (d. 774/1373) 1932, vol. 13, 38–39; Dhahabi (d. 748/1348) 1984, vol. 21, 463; Ibn Wasil 1977, vol. 5, 142.

15. Sibt b. al-Jawzi 1954, vol. 8, 690.

16. In the time of Nur al-Din: Ibn Tulun (d. 953/1546) 1949, 36; under al-Malik al-'Adil: Sibt b. al-Jawzi 1954, vol. 8, 469.

17. Goitein 1970, 109 and 1971, 406.

18. See an elaboration of this argument in Talmon-Heller 1999, 159, 165.

19. For the terminology regarding heresy and the treatment of heretics in medieval Islam see Kraemer 1982; Lewis 1993; Pouzet 1986, 256–57.

20. The case of al-Suhrawardi appears in several variations, in most contemporary and later biographical dictionaries, the earliest source being *al-Bustan* (Cahen 1937–1938). See in some detail Ibn Khallikan (d. 681/1282) 1972, vol. 6, 268–74; Dhahabi 1984, vol. 21, 207–11. Suhrawardi's theosophy and fate have attracted a number of modern scholars, see bibliography in Ziai *EI²*.

21. See for example Ibn al-'Adim (d. 660/1262), 1988, vol. 3, 1325; Abu Shama 1947, 216; Sibt b. al-Jawzi 1954, vol. 8, 427.

22. Ibn Khallikan 1972, vol. 3, 293–94; al-Subki 1971, vol. 8, 306. See also Ibn al-Athir 1939, vol. 2, 148–49 for instructions for the *muhtasib* dealing with similar cases.

23. Abu Shama 1947, 16; Ibn Rajab (d. 795/1392) 1953, vol. 2, 22–24.

24. Ibn al-'Adim 1968, vol. 2, 294, 308–10.

25. Dhahabi 1985, vol. 23, 224–28; Ibn Kathir 1932, vol. 13, 173–74, 148; Humphreys 1977, 209–10; Bosworth 1976, 114. For information on the Qalandariyya see Karamustafa 1994, 39–44, 52.

26. Abu Shama 1947, 16.

27. See Bosworth 1976, 113.

28. There are at least three versions of this story (Cahen 1937–1938, 140–41; Ibn al-'Adim 1968, vol. 3, 25–26; Ibn Kathir 1932, vol. 12, 291).

29. Elisséeff 1949; Gilbert 1977, 70–76 and 1980; Humphreys 1989, 164–65.

30. A recent study of *qada'* in Syria in a slightly later period confirms those findings, suggesting that there existed an efficient judicial system, entirely determined by Islamic law (Jokisch 1999, 514).

31. The local *shihna* (head of police force) complained that *al-zu'ar wa'l-mufsidin wa-qutta' al-tariq qad kathuru* (Abu Shama 1991, vol. 1, 376). See also ibid., 363–64, 373.

32. Ibn Shaddad (d. 684/1285) 1953, 32.

33. Sibt b. al-Jawzi 1954, vol. 8, 785.

34. Frenkel 1992, 66.

35. Ibn Rajab 1953, vol. 2, 13–14.

36. Sibt b. al-Jawzi 1954, vol. 8, 713. Chamberlain suggests that he was simply too weak to act against the `ulama' (Chamberlain 1994, 49).

37. Al-Subki 1971, vol. 8, 216; Ibn Kathir 1932, vol. 13, 215.

38. Al-Subki 1971, vol. 8, 243; Humphreys 1977, 266.

39. Ibn Kathir 1932, vol. 13, 22.

40. That was Ibn al-Jubayr's impression: Ibn Jubayr (d. 614/1217) 1907, 275. It is thoroughly documented in all studies of the period. See in particular the detailed works of Humphreys 1989 and 1994, providing qualitative and quantitive data on patronage in Damascus.

41. See examples in Abu Shama 1991, vol. 1, 327; Ibn Wasil 1972, vol. 4, 213.

42. Saladin ordered an Ash`ari `aqida (creed) from a Shafi`i scholar (Abu Shama 1992, vol. 2, 302); al-Malik al-Mu`azzam financed a large compilation of Hanafi law and the teaching of Hanafi works (Sibt b. al-Jawzi 1954, vol. 8, 427, 647; Pouzet 1986, 68); Al-Malik al-Ashraf sponsored the reading of the Maqasid al-Salat of `Izz al-Din al-Sulami (see below).

43. See several examples in Pouzet 1986, 75–76, 66; Eddé 1999, 366, 617; Humphreys 1994, 38–39.

44. Elisséeff 1972, 138.

45. See the testimony of Ibn Jubayr 1907, 275. Khawaniq probably accommodated elite and lower-class mystics and ascetics; a few were designed for women. We actually have very little information on this subject.

46. Ibn al-`Adim 1988, vol. 6, 2972–82. On the continuous value of the oral transmissions of written texts in later medieval Islamic culture see Ephrat 2000, 68–69.

47. For some interesting examples see Ibn Shaddad 1991, 131, 152–55; Abu Shama 1947, 108; Ibn al-`Adim 1988, vol. 1, 467, vol. 7, 3381–82, RCEA vol. 10, 66; Sauvaget 1941, 131; Humphreys 1994, 38.

48. Ibn al-`Adim 1988, vol. 1, 466; Sourdel 1953; Eddé 1999, 433.

49. Abu Shama 1947, 75; al-Nawawi 1999, 94; al-Sulami 1996, 325, 330. See also Taylor 1998, chapters 5 and 6, for a nuanced discussion of scholarly attitudes.

50. See also autobiographical notes in Abu Shama 1992, vol. 2, 128; Ibn al-`Adim 1988, vol. 1, 462–66, vol. 7, 3440, vol. 9, 4062, vol. 10, 4419, 4621.

51. See Taylor 1998, 64–65.

52. Humphreys 1977, 211–12; Ibn Shaddad 1953, 59–60; 1956, 87; Gilbert 1977, 137.

53. Morray 1994, 49, 94; Ibn al-`Adim 1988, vol. 6, 2908; Abu Shama 1947, 29, 157; RCEA vol. 9, 32; vol. 10, 40, 142, 156, 183.

54. Gilbert 1977, 80; Ibn Shaddad 1956, 91–166; Pouzet 1986, 143.

55. Ibn al-`Asakir (d. 571/1176) 1995, vol. 2, 288–321; Ibn Shaddad 1953, 59–93. For other towns and villages see Talmon-Heller 1999, 36–39. On the close links and cultural continuum between towns and adjacent villages in the medieval Middle East see Lapidus 1969, 54–57.

56. Ibn al-`Adim 1988, vol. 10, 4416; Ibn al-`Asakir 1995, vol. 2, 321; Drory 1988, 95; Talmon-Heller 1994, 112.

57. Ibn Jubayr 1907, 266. Ramadan 27th (laylat al-qadar) is held to be the night of the first Qur'anic revelation and a time of judgment.

58. Ibid., 271–72, 291; Ibn Shaddad 1956, 81–83.

59. Ibn Jubayr 1907, 289–90.

60. Ibn al-`Adim 1988, vol. 2, 764.

61. Sibt b. al-Jawzi 1954, vol. 8, 759–60.

62. Dhahabi 1984, vol. 21, 452. For more on the transmission of knowledge to commoners in Ayyubid and early Mamluk Damascus see Leder 1997.

63. Ibn Tulun 1949, 27.

64. Al-Harawi (d. 611/1215) 1953, 5; Ibn Jubayr 1907, 268.

65. Ibn Shaddad 1991, 123, 459, 461; al-Harawi 1953, 4.

66. Ibn Shaddad 1991, 131–32.

67. Abu Shama 1947, 104, 195. On popular preaching (as opposed to the official sermon delivered by the *khatib* in the Friday mosque) see Pedersen 1948, 234–36; Pedersen 1953; Swartz 1982; Makdisi 1990, 173–75, 182–87; Berkey 2000; Talmon-Heller (forthcoming).

68. Although medieval didactic literature sometimes attacks uneducated *wu`az* who spread unauthorized and incorrect religious learning (as stressed by Berkey 2000, 54–55), historical sources read for this study make no mention of sermons that communicated an unorthodox religious opinion, or a politically rebellious message. Quite the contrary.

69. Dhahabi 1985, vol. 23, 97; Ibn Rajab 1953, vol. 2, 194–95.

70. Ibn Kathir 1932, vol. 13, 58; Sibt b. al-Jawzi 1954, vol. 8, 701.

71. Ibid., 530; Abu Shama 1947, 48–49. On the *nasiya* see Goldziher 1967, vol. 1, 227.

72. Sibt b. al-Jawzi 1954, vol. 8, 545. For a detailed account of this sermon and a few other sermons see Talmon-Heller (forthcoming).

73. This bid was unsuccessful, however (Sibt b. al-Jawzi 1954, vol. 8, 604; Abu Shama 1947, 17).

74. Sibt b. al-Jawzi 1954, vol. 8, 654; Ibn Wasil 1972, vol. 4, 245; Humphreys 1977, 203. On propaganda for *jihad* against the Franks see Sivan 1968, 142–50. On earlier *qussas* and *wu`az* who promoted holy war see Pedersen 1948, 232; Berkey 2000, 57.

75. Sibt b. al-Jawzi 1954, vol. 8, 662.

76. Al-Subki 1971, vol. 8, 239.

77. Useful definitions of a "religious community" may be found in Weckman 1986–1987, and in Marshal 1994.

78. For an exposition of this theme see Goitein 1971, introduction and 42–43; Cohen 1997, esp. 80–81.

79. Ibn Tulun 1949, 37.

80. Abu Shama 1947, 29; Sibt b. al-Jawzi 1954, vol. 8, 510. RCEA vol. 9, 241–44, vol. 10, 90.

81. Sourdel 1972; Talmon-Heller 1994, 107; 1999, 80–83.

82. For biographical entries on prominent Shafi`i and Hanafi scholars see al-Subki 1970, vol. 7, 132–36; Sibt ibn al-Jawzi 1954, vol. 8, 630; Ibn Abi al-Wafa' (d. 775/1373) 1993, vol. 1, 337, vol. 3, 467; Abu Shama 1947, 167.

83. Janet Abu-Lughod's assessment of most medieval Muslim political authorities (Abu Lughod 1987, 162).

84. See Jonathan Berkey's thought-provoking discussion of *sunna* and *bid`a* in Berkey 1995, 40–41, 49–50.

CHAPTER FOUR

THE PUBLIC SPHERE AND CIVIL SOCIETY IN THE OTTOMAN EMPIRE

HAIM GERBER

One of the more popular topics in historical sociology in recent years has been that of civil society or, more precisely, the attempt to trace autonomous aspects in earlier societies. Strong impulses in this direction have been the globally felt drive toward democratization and, more recently, the democratization of Eastern Europe. A useful added dimension to the discourse on civil society has been the topic of public sphere, which may be loosely defined as the area of societal activity that is relevant to the social and political order in general.[1] This addition links the sphere of autonomous social institutions and groups to the state in a more direct manner, and makes the topic of greater interest to the political sociology–inclined social historian. The idea of public sphere is also important in that it allows areas of social activity to be brought into the discussion, rather than just groups in the narrow sense.

These new approaches make the society itself the focus of study, though historians prefer to look at the political side of that society. Another approach that is striving to capture adjacent territory is the "new cultural history," which seeks to assign an enhanced place to the symbolic and cultural aspects of a society and see them as the constitutive elements of the social structure, rather than as unimportant derivatives of material conditions, as was customary a generation ago.[2]

The Middle East is unquestionably an important focus for such studies. On the one hand, the number of studies anticipating democratization of Middle Eastern regimes is growing, though limited for the time being to explaining the difficulties involved in this process.[3] I have also tried my hand at such explanations. In my *Social Origins of the Modern Middle East*[4] I argued that it was social relations rooted in agrarian practices that determined the rise of a landed magnate class in the Middle East since the mid-nineteenth century and its fall shortly after World War II. I also attributed the democratic developments in Turkey to the absence in that country of a nationally important landed ruling elite comparable to those that appeared in Egypt, Syria, and Iraq. While these arguments seem to me as cogent today as they were ten years ago, I admit that this explanation is only partial. Other sociocultural institutions and traditions must also be investigated and brought into the picture. Thus, in the study of the social origins of Western democracy no one can afford to neglect the role of chartered medieval towns in creating the preconditions for the emergence of modern Western democracy. Such considerations make comparable Islamic institutions of evident interest to the social historian. This chapter will seek out such institutions and spheres in the history of the Ottoman Empire, and will make an effort to look at them through the eyes of the new cultural history rather than of the traditional social historian.

STATE AND SOCIETY IN CLASSICAL ISLAM
AND THE OTTOMAN EMPIRE

I shall suggest here a new conceptualization of the role of the state in the Ottoman Empire vis-à-vis civil society. In some important ways this relationship between the state and the society constitutes a major break with traditional Islam, a break that has not hitherto been fully analyzed.

On the whole, the pre-Ottoman Islamic Middle East was characterized by alienation and deep animosity between the political authority and the society—or at least its prominent representatives, the `ulama'. This alienation was due to structural causes that are rather well known, so that a summary of the issue will suffice here.[5] The starting point is that the state had no independent basis in Islam. An independent basis was accorded only to the *umma*, the community of believers, which was supposed to live not by the commands of the ruler but by the *shari`a*, the sacred law of Islam. This law was to be known through the Qur'an and the deeds and sayings of the Prophet, as reported by his Companions. The ruler had no role in this theoretical framework, though the situation was complicated by the fact that the first four rulers, or caliphs, were also Companions, who certainly did exert an effort to gain a say in fixing the contours of the community.[6] The religious nature of these rulers was accentuated by the fact that it was they who won for Islam the main body of its empire, thus proving the veracity of the Islamic message in the world. But soon afterward the conquests came to a halt, the rulers lost any direct connection to the Prophet, and on top of this, the law started to acquire professional characteristics, to be mastered only through arduous study. The `ulama' on the whole won the day as far as the definition of the community was concerned, though the rulers often ignored this law in real life.

The rift created in this way was disastrously widened when the position of sultan came into being. While the sultan was the real ruler, it was the caliph who held a semblance of legitimacy, though it was realized by all that he was no more than a puppet. On the other hand the sultans wielded naked power, without any semblance of purpose or ideology.

These political developments were reflected in the political theory. The rift between the `ulama' and the ruler created a strong sense of uneasiness on the part of the former in their relation to the latter, which reflected negatively on the legitimacy they were willing to accord him. Hence derives the scathing criticism of the rulers and of all those willing to serve under them as qadis or in any other capacity. Government employees were considered by many jurists to be corrupt to the point of being unfit to give testimony in court. On the other hand, the disintegration of the caliphate created a state of political instability and frequent changes of government everywhere. Strife and civil wars increased as the moral caliber of the rulers deteriorated. It was under these circumstances that the final stage of medieval Islamic political theory came into being, whereby the Muslim was called upon to realize that moral worth was no longer to be expected of any government, that rulership belonged to whoever managed to seize it by force, and that to prevent civil war it was best to obey any such ruler.

The Ottoman Empire presents us with a new political reality, one that can be summarized as: 1) The historical caliphate disappears, and there is no question that the Ottoman sultan is the successor of the caliph. 2) On the other hand, the rift at the top between an actual and nominal ruler has ceased to exist. The sultan is the real and nominal ruler, even at the nadir of the empire in the seventeenth and eighteenth centuries. 3) There is political stability as never before in Islam, particularly since the late fifteenth century: there is no change of dynasty; no instance of power usurped by force; no known plot to effect such a usurpation; not one real break in the orderly succession of rulers. All this is unprecedented in Islam, and extremely rare in world history. 4) With the rift between `ulama' and ruler completely gone, the Ottoman state is on the whole highly legitimate. There are no known ideological attacks on its validity, whether by `ulama' or by other intellectuals; no governor of any province is known ever to have entertained formal separation from the empire; no rebellion ever broke out that was directed against the state per se (the Christians in the Balkans are a case apart).[7] In fact, as remarkable as the low level of legitimation of the late classical Islamic state is the high level of legitimacy of the Ottoman state, even in its latter days. It certainly does not leave much room for the myth that "Islam cannot tolerate the state"; the far-reaching legitimation enjoyed by the Ottoman sultans is undoubtedly one of the most puzzling enigmas of Ottoman history. The explanation is to be sought, I believe, in the special role played by the empire in the history of Islam. 5) The Ottoman Empire never saw itself, or depicted itself to others, as just another state, certainly not as just another Turkish state (dawla turkiyya).[8] On the contrary, it was somewhat akin to a reenactment of the polity of the rightly guided caliphs, inasmuch as Islam never again, after its initial success, spread its message geographically in such tremendous strides as under the Ottomans. It is unlikely that the symbolism of the similarity between the first caliphs and the first Ottoman sultans was lost on Muslims everywhere, or on the dynasty itself. Moreover, even in relative decline, the Ottoman Empire stood as the only bulwark against the infidels. In other words, the Ottoman Empire was unique in Islam in being throughout its history the cutting edge between the *dar al-Islam* and the *dar al-harb*. This role was naturally an extremely potent factor in its legitimation. For the Ottomans, naked rulership, rulership for its own sake, would be repellent. Small wonder that from early on the Ottoman sultans considered themselves as caliphs, avoiding the subtle question of Qurayshi descent.[9] Small wonder, too, that sultans such as Selim I (r. 1512–1520) and Suleyman the Lawgiver (r. 1520–1566) had the audacity to see themseves as *mahdis*, or messiahs, saviors of Islam.[10] We have here a new model: the non-caliphal, religiously relevant state.

Strong leverages of legitimation, and a sort of semi-permanent state of emergency, certainly allowed the Ottomans to create a relatively strong and centralized state. But two factors worked against this. One was the technological limitation on the ability to control extended areas in the sixteenth century; the other was that a strong ideological-Islamic core (and commitment) necessarily meant something also in terms of internal organization. The outcome was a series of important social institutions that gave substance to the Ottoman public sphere and to civil society.

OTTOMAN LAW AS PUBLIC SPHERE

Looking at processes going on in the Ottoman public sphere, particularly in the seventeenth and eighteenth centuries, there are two important areas of interface between the public and the government that I propose to deal with—law and *waqf*. I propose first to analyze the structure of Ottoman law as it existed in the central area of the empire in the seventeenth and eighteenth centuries.[11] I shall then trace the trajectory traversed by this law from marginal significance in the fifteenth century to centrality in the later period; and lastly, I shall try to trace the social force, or forces, that brought about this change.

Ottoman law in the seventeenth and eighteenth centuries can be analyzed under three headings: the nature of law actually enforced; the tribunal where the law was applied; and the procedure by which this tribunal enforced the law. A useful theoretical basis for this analysis is Max Weber's scheme of the basic forms of law: Sultanistic law is seen as unstable law, dependent on the whim of the ruler at any given moment, utterly despotic in nature. Patrimonial law is defined as law that is the will of the ruler, though enacted in the form of stable and predictable law.[12] Even more famous, and just as pertinent, is Weber's ideal type of *qadi* justice, which was seen as informal adjudication based on generalized ethical-political considerations, not on systematic reasoning and the application of a body of law.[13] It goes without saying that Weber's model for Sultanic law was the Ottoman legal system, and that *qadi* justice was based on Islamic countries, among them the Ottoman Empire. I shall argue here that Weber was factually mistaken, although that does not detract from the brilliance of his models.

The picture that emerges from the actual documentation is that Ottoman law was neither sultanic nor patrimonial, but more reminiscent of Weber's model of bureaucracy—characterized by objective rules, predictability, etc. The law that was enforced in Ottoman courts during this period was on the whole the *shari`a*, Islamic law.[14] This was especially so in areas of the law concerned with personal status, family, marriage, divorce, and inheritance. It is usually agreed that in the Islamic Middle East these areas were always taken care of by the *shari`a*. But surprisingly, areas of the law connected with economic life were also covered by the *shari`a*, with some local variations that may be deemed minor in nature. Bankruptcies, sureties, unpaid debts, partnerships, etc., were handled by the *shari`a*, despite the widespread consensus, formerly prevailing, that these areas of the *shari`a* were never part of living law in Muslim countries. Even more surprising, the main body of what may be loosely (and incorrectly) defined as the penal parts of the *shari`a* were in fact being enforced. The Ottoman state may well be the first state in Islamic history where this was the case.

The import of this finding for the topic at hand is that the main areas of the law enforced in Ottoman courts had nothing to do with the sultan—at least in the sense that he was not the source of legitimation of this law. At most, the sultan might help make the law effective in his state, but he was by no means considered above it, much less its source. Also of crucial importance is that what we have here is stable law—law liable to change over time but certainly not erratically, from day to day.

An important area of Ottoman law in this period was guild law, an institution not existing in classical Islam and therefore not forming part of the *shari`a*.[15] Today there is a widening consensus that guilds were nongovernmental institutions invented by the populace and thrust on the Ottoman state, which was forced to ratify and endorse them, at least as long as they did not directly contradict state interests.[16] Short of full-fledged charters, Ottoman guilds resemble medieval European guilds to a surprising degree.[17] Most guilds had a basic deed of agreement between the members, referred to in the documents as `ahd, mithaq, ittifaq, all conveying the idea of a pact, where guild regulations were set forth. These rules are always said to have been drafted by the members voluntarily and unanimously. There is no suggestion that they were imposed by the state. Many of these pacts even included clauses authorizing the collective to punish offenders. When a point of guild law was discussed in court, it was always a respectable member of the community who was called upon to state the law in the matter. Analytically, guild law was and remained

an unwritten law (although written documents were extensively used to ver-
ify its content), but it was nevertheless stable and well structured, extremely
important in the life of ordinary people living in the Ottoman city. And
although it was often enforced by a state court, its legitimacy came from below,
from artisans and merchants. The state was called upon to enforce these
agreements because, as was endlessly reiterated, they expressed old relationships and old privileges. Sometimes privileges (such as nominations to head a
guild) were awarded by the state under the false pretense that they were based
on guild members' agreement. When such cases were brought before the qadi,
he had no hesitation in declaring the sultanic order baseless and void, and in
all the cases I have seen, the central government fully concurred. The "old"
had stronger legitimacy than the word of the sultan, so long as public order
and war against the infidel were not involved. The guild constitutes a remarkable example of Ottoman law that was both well structured and not imposed
from above by the state. As an institution, it is a major case disproving the
claim, associated again mainly with Max Weber, that there were no corporate
communities in Islam, and a major proof that some real autonomies did exist
in the Ottoman Islamic city.[18]

Another area of Ottoman law that should be mentioned here is land law,
which on the whole might be deemed to constitute an Ottoman invention,
and as such, a sort of imposition from above. But it has to be borne in mind
that in actuality, Ottoman land law was far from an Ottoman state invention.
Formally it was an imposition, but in real life every province had its own pre-
Ottoman land law, which was confirmed after the occupation and simply went
on being applied. It is possible that as time went by, a convergence took place.
In any event, in the first Ottoman century wide differences existed in the
nature of the land law from one region to another, attesting that even here
the Ottomans were not driven by any "totalitarian" intentions.[19]

A second issue concerning the working of the Ottoman legal system in
the seventeenth and eighteenth centuries is the nature of the tribunal that
enforced this law.[20] While in earlier Islamic states the ruler had various personal tribunals invented and nominated by himself,[21] under the Ottomans
the qadi, the Muslim judge, officiated as the sole authority in all legal matters.
There is no trace of other state tribunals, and it is interesting that even old
Islamic tribunals such as the mazalim and the muhtasib disappeared from the
scene, the mazalim altogether[22] and the muhtasib as the performer of a judicial
function. There are some hints that provincial governors sometimes performed ad hoc judicial functions, but rarely, and only as a usurpation of
authority. The importance of this point in discussion of the public sphere lies,
again, in that the qadi, though nominated by the sultan, is an old Islamic
institution, whose legitimation did not derive from the ruler but from much
deeper cultural sources—sources that the sultan could exploit but could not
disregard or belittle. In fact, the Ottomans not only granted the qadi a monop-

oly over the judicial function, they also used him as the chief administrator of the Ottoman city. Almost every order addressed to the provinces that did not deal with military matters was addressed to *qadis*. The beauty of the arrangement from the point of view of the central government was that because of the technical-legal nature of the *qadis'* education, they usually did not develop political ambitions within the city itself (they reserved such ambition for their career in the `ilmi* way). For the Ottomans the outcome within the city was certainly efficacious, but it entailed a price—*qadis* and potential *qadis* had to be handled with great care and reverence. Hence, *qadis* enjoyed a wide measure of autonomy. Orders addressed to them never contained detailed instructions as to how to carry out their duties. They were instructed only to take care that justice was not obstructed or violated. Some of the tasks with which *qadis* were entrusted are truly awesome. An example is the distribution among the population of Bursa, for the year 1087/1676–1677, of a certain extraordinary tax. What transpires is that only the overall sum was set by Istanbul. Its actual distribution had to be worked out locally, among members of twenty-four central guilds, twelve *hans*, eleven collective residences (*odaha*), and fifty-five villages, obviously involving a major bargaining process. The court records of Bursa overflow with documents relating to this process. Important, and in my view highly symbolic is that the document presenting the final distribution in the *qadi* records shows it as having been reached *ba ittifaq-i cumhur*—that is, "by agreement of the public."[23] A tacit social contract surfaces here, something I shall return to later on. But the point is that somebody had to preside over the political process involved, and this was certainly the *qadi*, aided by other members of the *ilmiye*—no doubt, a key social group in the Ottoman city.

A third aspect of Ottoman law in the seventeenth and eighteenth centuries is the procedure used. An interesting discussion in the anthropological and sociological literature is this: Did the *qadi* actually enforce and apply the substantive law he was supposed to apply, or did a political and social bargaining process take place ending up in a compromise no more than marginally connected to the law. While the latter may apply in the case of Morocco[24] it certainly does not seem valid in our case. It is evident from the sources that we are much nearer to the pole of substantive law than to free-floating bargaining. Although we do not have transcripts of the deliberations but only after-the-fact summaries, it is important that the *qadi* puts the entire proceeding into the Islamic legal mold and treats it as a legal issue rather than as a subject of compromise. Sometimes compromise did interrupt the court proceeding, but it is indicative that it was never the *qadi* who effected the deal but always people from the outside. The importance of this point for the topic at hand is that a free-floating process of bargaining might easily mask sultanic elements of adjudication. Such a situation would also undermine the conclusion that Ottoman law was well structured and stable.

I want now to outline the historical process whereby Ottoman law developed from the fourteenth or fifteenth century to the eighteenth.[25] It is apparent from the sources that in the fifteenth century predominance of the *qadi* and the *shari`a* is absent. For example, the *qadi*, as in earlier Islamic states, did not deal with criminal matters but merely heard such cases and then transferred the matter to some other authority, the nature of which is not made clear in the sources. It must be assumed that this other authority was the provincial governor, simply because there seem to be no other candidates for the job.[26]

It is interesting of course to speculate what caused the rise of the *qadi*. My hunch is that as the evolution of the Ottoman Empire as a bureaucratic state went much farther than that of former Islamic states, it needed more highly articulated legal institutions than were formerly extant within Islam. It was no doubt in this way that the institution of Şeyhülislam developed as the head of the religious institution, and it was in this way, too, that the institution of *ifta'*, legal consultation, became part of the state bureaucracy, for the first time in the history of Islam. By the same token, a more highly structured judicial institution was needed, and the Islamic judge was readily available. It is also possible that the Ottomans elevated the *qadi* as part of their undoubted (though as yet insufficiently proven) concern to create a regime of checks and balances within their administration. The *qadi* was certainly a highly effective check on the power of the provincial governor.

That the *qadis* rose in status does not automatically mean that the *shari`a* rose with them. It certainly is not self-evident that the *shari`a* was strengthened from above, as one might expect in the context of the relations between state, law, and society. The fact is that at the same time that the role of the *shari`a* would seem to have been expanding the Ottomans enacted the criminal *qanuns*, so it would appear that they expected the *qanun* to serve as the state law for at least some time. But this never happened. I found that the penal *qanun* was never really applied. Heyd claims that in some cases *qanun* penalties were demanded but admits he did not see any evidence for this in practice except in rare cases.[27] Recent studies and collections of fifteenth-century documents support this conclusion: not a single case of *qanun* penalty has been discovered.[28] It seems reasonable to suppose, then, that the *shari`a* rose because the *qadis* and the `*ulama'* in general pushed it forward, and the Ottoman government did not see the issue as important enough to engage in an all-out conflict over it. It is my belief that this whole process of the rise of the *shari`a* was an expression of the deepening Islamic lifestyle that had probably been under way since the advent of Islam.

Some parts of this process clearly represent politics of law involving elements of the civil society that deserve a closer look. A major example is interest, a well-known anathema to traditional Islamic law. Somewhat enigmatically, the prohibition on interest was relaxed in the Turkish-speaking area of the empire at a very early period, sometime in the early fifteenth century; interest was accepted as legal, provided that the yearly increment was not called *riba* but *muamele, nama,* or *rabh*—all neutral terms conveying the meaning of profit. The new habit originated especially in the context of the cash *waqfs* that began to appear in the burgeoning empire in the fifteenth century. Legally these neutral concepts were considered valid tricks, though they were shockingly transparent. In any event, for the people of the time the legally problematic issue was that since *waqf* assets were supposed to be eternal and the value of money was notoriously unstable, cash money was not considered an appropriate object of endowment. It is here that early Ottoman jurists took the liberty of introducing a change and relaxation in Islamic law. The reasoning used by these jurists and other intellectuals of the time shows quite clearly that the innovation was accepted through pressure from below. Summarizing the position of Ebu Suud Efendi, the Ottoman Şeyhülislam, Mandaville says: "What appears is an appeal to continued popular usage (*ta`amul and ta`aruf*), to the welfare of the people (*istihsan*), and to both throughout with a tone of 'Let's be practical,' an appeal to common sense."[29] What these fine words meant in real terms is made clearer in the detailed letter of a Sufi shaykh to the sultan, specifying that the cash *waqf* was the basis of the economic existence of the entire institution. Without cash *waqfs* Friday mosques would be deserted. More generally, says this shaykh, the law should be especially responsive to the people's feeling: "God's legislation has no other purpose than to ease the way of His servants through the exigencies of the time. . . . One uses inadmissibility at times because it is better for the people of that time, at other times one does the opposite."[30] He further cites an opinion that says: "Be guided by whatever is more harmonious with how the people are living, what is kinder, better for them."[31] There is no doubt that the government was fully aware that tampering with the cash *waqfs* would cause severe social disruption; so despite the severe juridical controversy surrounding them in the sixteenth century, they continued to flourish until the end of the empire.[32] This entire issue goes a long way to show that popular feeling probably played a certain role in the rise of the *shari`a*, and the exact form this rise took.

The exact opposite occurred in Syria.[33] When the Ottomans came in 1516, they brought legal interest charging to a country unacquainted with developments in fifteenth-century Anatolia. The Syrian `*ulama*' were outraged by the innovation and protested it to provincial governors, even to the sultan himself. When interest cases came before the courts in Syria it was specifically pointed out that the interest charged was on the sufferance of the sultan—in other words, that the court had nothing to do with it. More important, says Rafeq, the objection of the population and `*ulama*' of Syria to the liberalization of interest accounts for the fact that the employment of interest was quite rare, and that cash *waqfs* did not appear in Syria. Rafeq's study is important in showing that popular as well as `*ulama*' feeling played a role in the form the law was taking. It also shows that groups within the civil society were fully aware that what they thought about the law was meaningful, and that the central government was morally and politically obliged to take their view into consideration. Two other examples in the study are mentioned in this context: taxes on marriage contracts and the law imposing fines on villagers quitting their villages. In both cases the Syrian `ulama' were publicly and vehemently critical of the Ottoman government. Another important point in Rafeq's study is that groups within the civil society were not afraid to speak out and criticize the Ottoman sultan over central state issues, and interestingly enough, nothing happened to them.

It might be claimed at this point that the `ulama' did not really constitute an element of the civil society, but rather were part of the Ottoman government. I do not accept this suggestion. In my view, the state in the Ottoman Empire is the sultan. Any other starting point necessarily leads to a theoretical and methodological impasse. It is to be borne in mind, for example, that two parallel `ulama' networks existed in the empire: one was an internal, Istanbul-based, *madrasa* system that led to the higher *qadi*-ships and thence to the office of Şeyhülislam; the other was a provincial, low *madrasa*, and low `ulama' setup that led nowhere, recruited only local people, and had a very dubious formal standing, if any at all. The Syrian `ulama' cited by Rafeq certainly did not see themselves as forming part of the Ottoman state, and this they explicitly declared. In fact under the Ottomans there are some remnants of the classical-Islamic pattern of complete dissociation between the state and the `ulama'. A remarkable seventeenth-century Palestinian example is Khayr al-Din al-Ramli, a *mufti* who held no official position yet issued a large number of *fatwas* to people who asked his opinion on all kinds of legal matters.[34] Moreover, his opinions attained fame, which in the course of time made him one of the most important intellectuals in the entire Middle East.[35] All along he remained completely unconnected with the state, though he fully acknowledged the legitimacy of the Ottoman dynasty, whom he saw as the legitimate upholders of Islam "in the present time." Nevertheless, an important aspect of his legal activity is scathing criticism of various legal policies of the Ottoman state, such as tax farming—which in his view was tantamount to gambling and hence illegal enrichment[36]—and the prohibition on peasants leaving their villages without paying a fine to the fief holder.[37]

It might be contended that since al-Ramli only gave private written opinions, he did not have to fear the government. But this view seems to me unconvincing. Bearing in mind that he was already famous in his lifetime, it stands to reason that his *fatwas* would be well known over substantial areas of the Middle East. Yet, he himself did not seem to be under any threat or danger, and in fact no evil ever befell him. Were the Ottomans unaware of his criticism? Unlikely, in my view. Their restraint must be interpreted as an unwillingness to penetrate too deeply into the fabric of the civil society they governed.

It is questionable whether even the higher `ulama' are to be viewed as forming an integral part of the state. In the eighteenth century this group formed a sort of `ulama' aristocracy, which held a monopoly over high ilmiye posts in the face of resistance from all quarters.[38] In this connection it should be recalled that one of the more important phases in the rise of English democracy was the split between the English monarchy and the aristocracy. Analytically, it is hard to see the English aristocracy as less part of the central government than the Ottoman high `ulama'.

THE WAQF INSTITUTION AS PUBLIC SPHERE

The waqf[39] is clearly one of the most important public institutions in the Ottoman city, as in Islam in general. From very early on, people from all walks of life bequeathed all types of property to diverse beneficiaries, familial or charitable, for motives ranging from a deeply religious desire to perform charitable acts to a narrow, selfish wish to disinherit one's daughters. Sociologically, it makes sense to talk about big waqfs and small waqfs; but whatever their size, they constituted important elements of the public sphere and of social organization that gave substance to civil society in the Ottoman Empire. So pervasive was the waqf institution in Ottoman society that one is almost tempted to view it as a key institution in the way the cockfight was seen by Geertz to be a key institution in Balinese society.[40] As such, it represents a theoretical problem to traditional social historians, who have tended to view society as an arena of purely selfish interests, with every action of the individual motivated by selfish, material interest. I believe the waqf institution was a major casualty of such an approach, a situation that can no longer be maintained.

Some of the big waqfs in an Ottoman town look more like a branch of the central government than an autonomous public sphere, but in reality the situation was much more complicated. Founded by the sultan himself, usually after the conquest of the place or upon ascending to the throne, every substantial Ottoman city had several such waqfs. Each contained, on the one hand, several villages (sometimes as many as twenty-five) and, on the other, several revenue-consuming institutions, such as the Friday mosque, poor kitchen, Qur'an school, madrasa, etc.[41] It must be significant that sultans opted to provide basic services in the form of personal bestowal rather than through a faceless bureaucracy, and it seems that the explanation must be sought in the symbolic link between the ruler and the ruled. The fact that these services also included food rations in the imaret (soup kitchen) is all the more symbolic here. By the Islamic law of waqf, all these institutions were knit together in one institution by a founding deed that was designed to ensure the perpetuity of the waqf. Once established, the waqf could not be annulled nor its funds diverted to any purposes other than those set out in the founding deed. These institutions provided the main services in the Ottoman city, and the main civic activity was obviously focused around them. True, they retained a strong connection to the central government, which nominated the managers. Nevertheless, these *waqfs* provided room for intensive civic activity, since the discretion of the managers was severely restricted by the founding deed and by considerations of Islamic equity and decorum. If the manager failed to provide food measuring up to the traditional standard in the *waqf*'s kitchen, he immediately found himself sued in court by a group of respectable citizens, invariably headed by `ulama', usually teachers in *madrasas*, the real public opinion leaders in a city such as Bursa. Every now and then *waqf* properties needed repairs, often of major proportions. To guard against accusations of corruption, managers—at least in seventeenth-century Bursa—carried out renovations only with the prior detailed authorization of the court, based on inspection of the site by a special committee in which `ulama' always took part. Thus, although the manager was nominated by the central government, the local community, headed by the `ulama', exercised a supervisory function every step of the way. The *qadi* records overflow with cases where citizens brought cases involving the *waqf* and not one ever suggested that it was not their business to do so. My understanding of this situation is that local communities saw themselves as having the de facto right to ensure that the affairs of the sultanic *waqfs* were run in the interests of the city's inhabitants, and even by them.

Another important group of *waqfs* were those established by members of the Ottoman elite on their own initiative.[42] In fact, most of the big *waqfs* not founded by the sultans themselves were apparently founded by *askeris*, members of the ruling institution. It was widely believed in the past that such *waqfs* were not real charitable *waqfs*, as they tended to present themselves, but rather constituted a stratagem by the elite to divert state funds and privatize them. The main suggestion was that a substantial part of the revenues was earmarked for the family, including the practically unlimited cut of the manager, always a family member.[43] This view no longer seems tenable, at least on a statistical basis. In early Ottoman Edirne *waqfs* by *askeris* were patently charitable, seemingly no tricks involved.[44] Likewise, in Istanbul *waqfs* of the sixteenth century the private elements can be separated from the public ones, with no less than 80 percent of the revenue of *waqfs* established by *askeris* earmarked for public purposes.[45] It is thus simply not true that *waqfs* by *askeris* were designed to divert public funds. So how are they to be explained? Edward Thompson provides a possible clue in his explanation of the eighteenth-century English moral economy, as does Natalie Davis of the rites of violence in sixteenth-century France;[46] that both were designed to strengthen communal bonds. I suggest that something similar is to be observed in the Ottoman *waqf* institution. Members of the bureaucratic elite established charitable institutions to foster bonds of social connection based on sharing with the lower classes, to enhance feelings of community and ultimately legitimacy. While such an approach of government to the civil society is not particularly surprising or even noteworthy, for a regime as supposedly despotic as that of the Ottomans such an approach seems to me quite remarkable.

Small *waqfs* were also an important element of the public sphere, many of them being after all charitable by nature. A survey of small *waqfs* conducted in Bursa in 1077/1666–1667 may serve as an example.[47] It contained 374 separate *waqfs*, all purely charitable, many of them defined as an amalgamation of several small *waqfs*. The entire list may in fact represent up to two thousand separate endowments. For a city of some thirty thousand residents this is a huge number (the implied comparison is with a modern Western city of the same size, but that of course is a problematic comparison). Some are defined as mosque *waqf*, since of course every city neighborhood had a mosque and all were by definition maintained by *waqfs*. Most or all quarters also had what was called *waqf-avariz*—that is, *waqf* donated for the purpose of paying the *avariz* tax of the quarter, a tax levied on real estate and the main regular tax paid by the urban population in the Ottoman Empire during this period.[48] The fact that these *waqfs* were specifically established for the benefit of a group of people defined by a residential quarter is to my mind an indication that the quarter was considered a corporative group—by the populace, if not by the government. Similarly, many *waqfs* in sixteenth-century Istanbul not only were for the benefit of a quarter, but even nominated the entire body of the quarter's residents as collective inspectors, thus underpinning an obviously existing meaningful community in that city.[49] Moreover, unlike the Haramyn administration in Algiers,[50] in Bursa these *waqfs* were administered individually by managers, the great majority of whom were `ulama'; the *qadi* exercised only a general supervisory function, this survey being itself an example of that supervision. Thus, we have here a large network of *waqfs* providing various services for the public and run by the public itself, with a minimum of intervention on the part of the central (or local) government. Assuming that all substantial towns in the Ottoman Empire had such extensive networks, it is obvious that small charitable *waqfs* constitute a major example of the autonomous working of civil society and the public sphere in the Ottoman Empire.

THE HISTORIOGRAPHIC DEBATE ABOUT OTTOMAN CIVIL SOCIETY

The existence of a public sphere and civil society in the Ottoman Empire is still debated among scholars. Sherif Mardin, in a study on Islam and civil society,[51] sets the West against the East in an all-embracing dichotomy. Western civil society is seen as a dream and a postulate, which consisted in "the idea that social relations are both sustained and energized by autonomous, secular collectives with legal personality operating within a frame of rationalized self referential law."[52] Since nothing of this was found in Islam, there was thought to be no trace of an autonomous civil society. The problem with this analysis is first of all that Mardin seems to idealize developments in the West. Yet civil society and secular and self-referential law were not born the mature concepts they are today; they developed only gradually, for the most part as ad hoc practical compromises between competing forces—as in the case of the monarch versus the aristocracy in England. It was a centuries-long battle between these two forces, and later a real fear of the power of the proletariat, that produced the English compromise, not a rosy liberal dream.[53] And just as Mardin's picture of the West is idealized, so his view of the Ottoman Empire seems to be exaggeratedly negative.

Recent studies have done much, however, to dispel such old theories, according to which the Ottoman Empire was a state of unbridled Oriental despotism; the sultan had total power and the entire state was his personal oikos, to use the Weberian term for personal estate. Gilles Veinstein, who studied the sultanic orders of Suleyman the Magnificent (r. 1520–1566) noted the gap between the first part of the decrees and the second, more substantial, part.[54] In the first part, the sultan presents himself as a magnificent ruler, the like of whom the world has never seen, in terms of both strength and virtue. Clearly implied is that it is unthinkable that anyone implicated in an order will not do his utmost to carry it out to the full. But a careful reading leads to a different conclusion. Orders were very often not carried out and had to be repeated again and again. There is no telling how many of these orders were in fact never implemented. The author rightly concludes that the sultan's ability to turn his words into actions was much more limited than he would have cared to admit.

Surprisingly, an earlier study by Sherif Mardin provides another basis for the realization that there were serious cracks in the wall of Ottoman despotism.[55] Here Mardin claims that a notion of implied social contract between the ruler and the ruled was embedded in the Ottoman political formula. This contract, which in his view was Islamic in nature, connected with the idea of hisba—that is, the obligation on the ruler to do what is right and forbid what is wrong—a well-known code in the classical Islamic outlook on life, at least as expressed by the `ulama'. Mardin adds that a component of this theory is that if the ruler does not perform this duty, the obligation passes to the community. He further claims that this implied contract is expressed in the revolts of soldiers and elements of the lower social classes that one encounters in the chronicles of the empire. But the truth is that these revolts do not usually invoke Islamic forms of legitimation; more often than not they make reference to violations of the old and accepted ways. For example, the reason for the killing of Şeyhülislam Feyzullah Efendi in 1703 was presented by the rebels as his violation of the traditional code of behavior expected of an Ottoman Şeyhülislam—that is, nonintervention in state politics.[56] Hence, while I fully accept Mardin's suggestion of the existence of an Ottoman social contract as the fundamental basis of state-society relations, the basis of this theory probably goes deeper: Barrington Moore saw such a contract as a universal component of the relations between rulers and ruled in all or most polities,[57] and this seems more appropriate for what we see in the Ottoman Empire.

That the sultan was not considered an unpredictable despot can also be gauged from a look at the Vienna Şikayet Defteri, a book containing some 2,500 complaints, all relating to the year 1675, sent by citizens from all over the empire to the sultan, about wrongs committed mainly by officials.[58] This book is but one of an entire series of such books, preserved in the Ottoman archives, attesting that the genre of complaint writing was extremely popular with the subjects of the Ottoman sultan. While this indicates that there were wrongs to be complained about, it is even more important that there existed channels to reach the highest possible authority in order to complain, and hope for the redress of wrongs. How many wrongs were actually righted we do not know, but that so many thousands of citizens in the empire each year tried this course indicates that they continued to see the sultan as a source of justice, over and above local power holders. Also important: the complaint was not thrown away but carefully written down, along with an order to the resident qadi to look into it and do what is right and just. That the flow of complaints did not dry up over the years must be interpreted to mean that at least a certain percentage of the complaints were resolved. Above all, nowhere in the entire body of complaints in the Vienna Şikayet Defteri is there any instance of the sultan defending an officeholder or giving his backing to suspected wrongdoing. The language of the orders impeccably follows Ottoman and Islamic law. Against the theory that the sultan was restricted by nothing[59] stands the theory that the sultan was severely restricted by the concept of adalet, justice. Judging by the public record, the second concept seems stronger.[60]

Another study highly pertinent to our discussion is a recent article by Halil Inalcik, which explicitly takes off from Max Weber's concepts of sultanism and patrimonialism, only to claim that while the official Ottoman discourse depicted the sultan as unfettered by any law or authority, reality was much more complicated. The masses possessed means to influence the sultan—for example, by deserting villages—and the government was not beyond heeding such possibilities.[61] The study also draws attention to an important though little studied Ottoman institution—the meşveret, a large-scale ad hoc consultative body of dignitaries that the sultans used to convene at times of serious international emergencies. Though these bodies had no official grounding, the right to express opinions on such occasions was free, and there is no doubt that an emergent consensus in such assemblies had a bearing on the sultan's subsequent decisions.[62]

However, it is a study by Suraiya Faroqhi that bears most directly on the topic at hand.[63] It is in fact a conscious effort to look for autonomous sociopolitical institutions in Ottoman society, and the outcome of the search is that autonomous elements were certainly not lacking. The janissaries and `ulama' before the nineteenth century constituted semiautonomous forces; the provincial notables (a`yan) of the town of Ankara in the late sixteenth century got together to carry through a substantial civic project—the construction of a city wall; the a`yan of the little town of Çorom convened and launched a complaint to the central government on town matters. These and a plethora of other examples show that cities and towns saw themselves as meaningful collectives, possessing a certain amount of authority and legitimate political power. In the face of this rich documentation, the old idea that the individual was only a member of the umma seems oddly simplistic, an ideological construct at best, that if not false in itself, overlooks other social and psychological levels of existence.

To conclude, there is ample evidence that Ottoman society featured several institutions that worked on the basis of autonomous powers and initiatives. A prime example is the case of the guilds, which developed voluntaristic regulations that only later were confirmed by the government. Such is also the case of socially central institutions such as the waqf and even of a politically central institution such as the law in general. Furthermore, towns and quarters emerge as collectives possessing meaning and value in the eyes of their members and even in the eyes of the government. The guild was the paradigmatic institution, expressing the entire gamut of the relations between the Ottoman government and the populace. By a tacit, symbolic, social contract, the government refrained from countering, undermining, or disregarding customs, privileges, and rules of conduct favored by the citizens, as long as these did not directly contradict the security of the state or Islamic moral conduct in general.

NOTES

1. See Somers 1995; Calhoun 1993.
2. Hunt 1989; Somers 1995, 127–29.
3. See Norton 1995; Deegan 1994.
4. Gerber 1987.
5. See Siegman 1964; Crone and Hinds 1986;Lambton 1981; Lindholm 1996.
6. This is the specific topic in Crone and Hinds 1986.
7. This is particularly true from about the mid-sixteenth century on. See Fleischer 1992.
8. See Haarman 1988, who correctly emphasizes the big difference between the role of "Turkish" states versus that of the Ottoman state in Islam.
9. See Imber 1992.
10. See Fleischer 1992.
11. See Gerber 1994.
12. Weber 1964, 347.
13. Weber 1969, 213, 229, 264, 317, 351.
14. Gerber 1994, chapters 1 and 2.

15. Gerber 1988, chapter 3; Gerber 1994, chapter 4.

16. Ze'evi 1996, 154ff.

17. The next paragraph is based entirely on Gerber 1994, chapter 4.

18. See Eickelman 1964 for a good example of the literature using the supposed lack of guilds in Islam as a springboard for the argument that it is pointless to seek autonomous institutions under Islam.

19. See Gerber 1987, chapter 2.

20. Gerber 1994, chapter 2.

21. Ibid., 60–61.

22. It is true that the imperial divan also functioned as a court, but this took place only on rare occasions.

23. Bursa Sicilli (hereafter BS), B103/316, 91b, 1087/1676–1677. There are many such lists in the *qadi* court records of seventeenth-century Bursa, and all take care to note that public agreement was involved in their preparation. Obviously, people in Bursa at the time considered this highly important, and it is of course also noteworthy that there was a stock phrase to relate to that "public." For other examples of such lists see B112/326, 83b, Safar 1090/1679; B83/284, 88b, 1085/1674–1675.

24. See Rosen 1989.

25. Gerber 1994, chapter 2.

26. Inalcik 1980–1981; Jennings 1986; Ongan 1974.

27. Says Heyd: "In most criminal cases recorded in the court registers of the fifteenth and sixteenth centuries . . . no penalty is mentioned at all. Often it is not even stated whether the cadi found the defendant guilty." See Heyd 1973, 254.

28. Jennings 1986; Ongan 1974; Inalcik 1980–1981.

29. Mandaville 1979, 298.

30. Ibid., 302-3.

31. Ibid., 303.

32. See Çizakça 1995.

33. See Rafeq 1994.

34. Al-Ramli (d. 1081/1670). 1893–1894.

35. For a biography of al-Ramli see Gerber 1999, 19–20.

36. Al-Ramli 1893–1894, vol. 2, 178.

37. Ibid., vol. 2, 184–85.

38. Zilfi 1983.

39. The bibliography on the *waqf* institution is rapidly proliferating. As a token only see Marcus 1989, passim; Roded 1989; Schwarz and Kurio 1983; Winkelhane and Schwarz 1985; Gerber 1988; Hoexter 1998b.

40. See Geertz 1979.

41. Gerber 1988, chapter 8.

42. Barkan and Ayverdi 1970; Gerber 1988; Marcus 1989.

43. Gibb and Bowen 1957, 169.

44. Gerber 1983.

45. Barkan and Ayverdi 1970.

46. See Desan 1989.

47. BS, B135/350, 1077/1666–1667.

48. See also Çizakça 1995.

49. Barkan and Ayverdi 1970, passim.

50. Hoexter 1998a.

51. Mardin 1995.

52. Ibid., 278.

53. Skocpol 1973.

54. See Veinstein 1992.

55. Mardin 1988.

56. Zilfi 1988, 198–99.

57. Moore 1978.

58. Gerber, 1994, chapter 5.

59. Inalcik 1993, though it should be noted that the theory is raised only to be rejected.

60. Important information on complaint activity via the *mühimme defterleri* is also presented in Faroqhi 1986.

61.. Inalcik 1993, 16.

62. Ibid., 12–13; also Aksan 1993.

63. Faroqhi 1986.

CHAPTER FIVE

THE QĀḌĪ'S ROLE IN THE ISLAMIZATION[1] OF SEDENTARY TRIBAL SOCIETY

AHARON LAYISH

INTRODUCTION

The discourse pertaining to such terms as *civil society* and *public sphere* is closely connected with the history of Western society and state.[2] This point should be borne in mind when attempting to translate these terms into the reality of Muslim society and state. In theory, there is no separation of state and "church" in Islam.[3] Although theocracy is not the commonest political system in modern Islam,[4] significant remnants of this religio-political system have survived in some contemporary Muslim countries. For instance, the 1980 Egyptian Constitution maintains that the *sharīʿa* (the non-codified Islamic law) is the main source of legislation (Article 2).[5] Muslim countries have adopted Western conceptions of political system, including the separation of powers—a principle totally alien to Islamic classical theory. However, it seems that the process of internalizing this principle has not so far been completed. Moreover, since the early 1970s there has been an increasing tendency toward the Islamization of the legal system in such countries as Libya, Iran, the Sudan, and Pakistan by means of statutory legislation and court decisions making the validity of statutory provisions conditional on their conformity to the *sharīʿa*.[6]

Taylor distinguishes three modes of civil society in the West: the first exists in societies where there are free associations, not under tutelage of state power; the second (with a wider sense) exists where society as a whole can structure itself and coordinate its actions through such associations, which are free of state tutelage; and the third (which is an alternative or supplement to the second) exists where the ensemble of associations can significantly determine or inflect the course of state policy.[7]

The premodern Muslim society seems to fit in with the first (the narrowest) mode of civil society. Prior to the integration of the *ʿulamāʾ* (sing. *ʿālim*;

scholars of religious sciences) in the state establishment one could trace in the Muslim society substantial elements of civil society. Levtzion analyzes the ʿulamāʾ's role as intermediaries between the rulers and their subjects to the extent that the ʿulamāʾ enter the definition of "free association, not under tutelage of state power": on the one hand, they bestowed legitimacy using their religious prestige to secure the obedience of the masses to the ruler's authority; on the other hand, they acted as representatives of the masses communicating to rulers the popular grievances. The ʿulamāʾ's attitude toward the political authorities was ambivalent: they recognized the need for a strong government to defend Islam from external and domestic threats; but as an independent (also in economic respects) class or association they considered almost every government by definition as oppressive and declined to cooperate with it or accept governmental nominations so as to avoid being corrupted. As guardians of the sharīʿa and the public morals it was their duty, they believed, to guide the political rulers, from outside, on how to apply the sharīʿa properly.[8] In this respect one may compare the role of the uninstitutionalized ʿulamāʾ to that of the intellectuals in Western civil society.

The process of integration of the ʿulamāʾ into the state establishment, which had started already in the Middle Ages, has been completed in the twentieth century. The muftī (a specialist in sharīʿa who gives authoritative legal opinions), perhaps the most important agency for the development of the sharīʿa and the preservation of its vitality, the qāḍī (the judge of a sharīʿa court), in charge of the application of the sharīʿa in day-to-day reality, and other religious functionaries have been incorporated into the civil service with a view to implementing the government's policy.[9] It goes without saying that the loss of independence from the political authority diminishes the ʿulamāʾ's ability to fulfill their traditional role as intermediaries and guardians of the sharīʿa and the public morals. In this respect contemporary Muslim society has lost a vital element of civil society, though the function of the ʿulamāʾ may have been taken over by secular intellectuals and other associations.

THE FUNCTION OF THE SHARĪʿA
IN SEDENTARY TRIBAL SOCIETY

THE QĀḌĪ'S AUTONOMY

This chapter is concerned with the role of the qāḍīs, an essential part of the ʿulamāʾ, in contemporary Muslim society. To what extent is the sharīʿa court a "public sphere" in the sense that the qāḍī is capable of formulating norms of social, ethical, and legal behavior independently—that is, outside the control of the political authority—and of imposing them on Muslim society? An attempt will be made below to assess the sharʿī qāḍī's autonomy and his impact on tribal society in the process of sedentarization in modern Libya (broadly speaking from the early 1930s to the early 1970s) and the Judean Desert (from the last quarter of the nineteenth century to the early 1970s) on the basis of legal documents collected from the *sharī'a* courts of Ajdābiya and Kufra in Libya and of Bethlehem, and tribal arbitrators in the Jerusalem-Bethlehem region.[10] The case pertaining to denial of paternity, which appears at the end of this chapter is meant to provide an illustrative notion of the *qāḍī*'s scope of autonomy, which is significant in the context of public sphere.

On the face of it the question seems to be irrelevant since the *qāḍī* is part of the state apparatus. He is a delegate of authority invested with the power of jurisdiction (*qaḍā'*). He is nominated either by the caliph himself (who, in theory, retains the power to exercise justice in person) or by his intermediate representatives (*wazīr*, governor of a province, etc.).[11] In other words, the ruler appoints the *qāḍī*, pays his salary, and dismisses him from office when he deems it necessary. One might be tempted to conclude that this pattern of delegation intrinsically does not allow the *qāḍī* a wide measure of autonomy.

Moreover, among the *'ulamā'* and *fuqahā'* (sing.: *faqīh*; jurists, experts in *fiqh*, the science of the *sharī'a*, the sacred law of Islam) it is the *muftī*, rather than the *qāḍī*, who best represents the class of (religious) intellectuals of premodern Muslim society. This assertion refers first and foremost to the original concept of the *muftī* dating back to the 'Abbāsids (750–945), before he became integrated into the the political establishment.[12] Even today there are—alongside nominated *muftīs*— independent *muftīs* whose status is a function of their learned reputation.[13] Indeed, *muftīs*, not *qāḍīs*, were the creators and exponents of the *sharī'a*, which is a set not only of legal norms but also of ethical values. The *sharī'a* is a "jurists' law"—that is, a system of law that developed outside an official legislature and the control of the executive authority. All the efforts of rulers—during the formative period of the *sharī'a*—to institutionalize the independent *fuqahā'* in order to shape the legal norm to suit political purposes were in vain. The *sharī'a* did not undergo a formal process of codification until the late nineteenth century. The first codification was the *Mejelle*, the Ottoman Civil Code (1869–1876). From the strict *shar'ī* point of view, codification itself implies the transformation of the *sharī'a* from a jurists' law to statutory law, with all the attendant consequences: departure from the religious-legal literature; disruption of the *shar'ī* legal methodology of sources of law (*uṣūl al-fiqh*); and collapse of the legal professional class of the *fuqahā'* and *muftīs*, the authorized exponents of the *sharī'a*.[14]

On the other hand, the judicial practice of the *qāḍīs* was never regarded as a formal source of law. The historical contribution of *qāḍīs* to Islamic law took place during the Umayyad Empire (661–750), prior to the emergence of the class of *muftīs*. By using unrestricted personal reasoning or discretion (*ra'y*) and religious ethical norms derived from the Qur'ān, the *qāḍīs* succeeded in assimilating elements of foreign legal systems that gradually penetrated into legal practice. In this respect they laid the foundations for the creation of the *sharīʿa;* but case law—that is, law settled by precedent[15]—was never recognized by Islamic legal theory as a source of law. Islamic law developed as an expression of a religious ideal in contrast to practice.[16] A sophisticated legal methodology was created later by the *muftīs.* The "judicial practice" (*ʿamal*) that emerged in Morocco beginning in the late fifteenth century seems to be a single instance of a "realist" form of Islamic jurisprudence that was intended to bring custom within the orbit of Mālikī law. Its significance from the point of view of legal theory is, however, disputed by scholars.[17]

Although the *qāḍī* is subject to the ruler who appoints him to the office and can dismiss him at will, he nevertheless enjoys a measure of autonomy with regard to the application of the non-codified *sharīʿa* in matters that are within the *sharīʿa* court's jurisdiction. The *qāḍī* is subject to the ruler only administratively; otherwise—that is, as far as the substantive law applicable in court is concerned—he is subject to the *sharīʿa* alone.[18] From the point of view of the *qāḍī,* codification implies subordination to legal norms shaped by earthly legislature outside the control of the *fuqahāʾ.* Thus, with regard to the *sharīʿa* courts of Ajdābiya and Kufra from the early 1930s to the early 1970s, the *qāḍī* was totally independent in this respect. The first codification of the law of personal status in Libya took place in 1972 (but unfortunately, its application is not reflected in the decisions available to me).[19] In case of doubt in any substantive or procedual matter the *qāḍī* might—though this happens quite rarely—consult any Mālikī *muftī* or a legal treatise, according to his free choice.[20] The ruler had no standing in this matter. Moreover, the ruler was concerned in the first place with the maintenance of public order (including cases of homicide or bodily injury, which are in fact within the domain of Islamic private rather than public law) and, as might be expected, matters of personal status were not usually of great concern, unless a certain legal norm disturbed public order.[21] On the other hand, the law applicable in the *sharīʿa* court of Bethlehem, under whose jurisdiction the Bedouin of the Judean Desert fall, underwent codification. The *sharīʿa* applying to matters of personal status was replaced by the Ottoman Family Rights Law of 1917 and by the Jordanian family laws of 1951 and 1976, successively.[22] The *qāḍī's* autonomy in this court, as far as the material law is concerned, is less than that of the Libyan *qāḍī* in the period under review.

SEDENTARY TRIBAL SOCIETY, CUSTOM, AND *SHARĪʿA*

The population of Cyrenaica and the Judean Desert, which is the object of this study, is different with respect to social, economic, and political conditions, and school of law and material law applicable in the *sharīʿa* courts. Moreover, substantial differences exist even within Cyrenaica itself between the regions of Ajdābiya and Kufra. In spite of these differences, Cyrenaica and the Judean Desert share one fundamental feature: in both cases tribal societies in the process of sedentarization are being brought within the orbit of the *sharī'a*.[23]

Ajdābiya, a district center in the cultivable plain near the Mediterranean coast, has always been an important center, owing to its location at a strategic junction of roads leading to Tripoli in the west, Benghazi, Alexandria, and Cairo in the east, and Kufra and Khartoum in the south. The town was the seat of the Sanūsī government during the short period of indirect rule under the Italians. The people in this area are part of the Sa'ādī confederation of tribes, the principal tribes being the Maghāriba and Majābira. In the town of Ajdābiya, however, they are outnumbered by members of other tribes and clans. Kufra, far in the south, consists of oases, and is also located on trade routes. Kufra was the administrative center for the Sanūsiyya and a command headquarters during the resistance to French expansion. The Zuwayya tribe is the largest population group and the dominant one; but there are other tribes, black-skinned and white-skinned, immigrant laborers from Chad and the Sudan; *Ikhwān* ("brothers"—that is, descendants of officials and servants of *zāwiyas* of the Sanūsī order who remained in Kufra after the abolition of the order); and emancipated slaves integrated into the Zuwayya genealogy. The tribes in these two regions are in different stages of sedentarization.[24]

The Bedouin in the Judean Desert are a group of tribes in the Jerusalem-Bethlehem region: al-Sawāḥira east of Jerusalem, al-'Ubaydiyya east of Bayt Sāḥūr, the al-Ta'āmira tribes extending from Bayt Sāḥūr in the north to Bayt Fajjār in the south, and al-Rashā'ida southeast of Taqū'a. The settlement of these Bedouin, which began in the 1920s and was almost complete by the 1970s, was accelerated by proximity to Jerusalem and Bethlehem and by domestic security policy. Al-Ta'āmira tribes have established settlements of their own in existing Judean villages and in the suburbs of Bethlehem. About half of these Bedouin no longer live within a tribal framework.[25]

As is known, normative Islam, with its system of beliefs, institutions, and laws, plays no central part in the shaping of a nomadic society.[26] Folk religion, including saint worship and intercession, still predominates. Moreover, in Cyrenaica vestiges remain of the Sanūsiyya, an instance of Ṣūfī order, adapted to the institutional and normative system of a tribal society—although the Sanūsī establishment started to disintegrate after the Italian invasion in 1911.[27] Custom survived even when its followers had nominally adopted Islam. Western and Muslim scholars have observed that although Bedouin in various parts of the Muslim world consider themselves to be Muslims, their knowledge of Islamic doctrine, worship, and ethics is modest (this applies also to the Cyrenaican Bedouin even after the Sanūsī revivalist movement had become established in their midst). Thus, they are negligent in the carrying out of such religious obligations as peforming public prayer in the mosque on Fridays, and customary law has the upper hand in its encounter with Islamic law. Their acceptance of Islamic law is partial and slow. Although the Islamization of the

Bedouin has been going on for centuries it has not yet been completed in every respect.[28] As might be expected, the Bedouin are not fully aware of this process. They identify themselves as Muslims. They believe in Allāh and resort to him in various circumstances.[29] They regard tribal law as part of their Islamic heritage, although some of the customs are inconsistent with normative Islam.[30] The fact that the Bedouin identify their daily practice with the *sharī'a* in every respect is naturally of great significance. The outside observer, however, cannot and should not stop at this point but rather must make a clear distinction, devoid of value judgment, between orthodox *sharī'a* and tribal custom.[31] There is ample evidence to the effect that the Libyan *qāḍīs* themselves are fully aware of the distinction between *sharī'a*, custom *('āda)* and statutory law *(qānūn)*. The *wakīl qāḍī* (the *qāḍī's* deputy) of Bethlehem, Shaykh Muḥammad Saʿīd Jamāl al-Rifāʿī, maintains that "custom *(ʿurf, ʿāda)* is binding law *(ḥukm mulzim)*, provided that it does not conflict with an explicit provision *(naṣṣ)* of the Qurʾān and the *sunna*."[32]

The sedentarization of the Bedouin in modern times brings them under the control of the central government, one aspect of which is the *sharī'a* court. Under Italian rule the Bedouin of Cyrenaica applied to the *sharī'a* courts only to a limited extent, preferring to settle their affairs according to tribal custom.[33] In the early 1970s their recourse to the *sharī'a* courts increased although they did not cease to apply concurrently to the tribal courts.

Researchers have suggested several explantations for the Bedouin's application to the *sharī'a* courts:[34]

> 1. Sedentarization, which brings the Bedouin closer to normative Islam and hence increases their respect for the *qāḍī's* moral and religious authority and his function as the nominal head of the school of law *(madhhab)*.
> 2. The spread of religious education and modern means of communication.
> 3. Geographical proximity to urban, religious, administrative, and economic centers.
> 4. The imposition—on the initiative of the central government—of *sharʿī* jurisdiction on the Bedouin along with the abolition of statutory tribal jurisdiction (in the case of Jordan),[35] with a view to strengthening the Muslim establishment as a means to consolidate the government's position in tribal society. From the point of view of the central government, it is easier to rule through its control of institutionalized normative Islam rather than trying to control popular religion and customs that vary from one place to another and are dominated by indigenous leaders competing among themselves for power.
> 5. Administrative exigencies in a modern state. Thus, for example, confirmation of marriage by a *qāḍī* or a *sharʿī* solemnizer is required to ensure that no impediments to marriage exist between the parties that may render the marriage irregular *(fāsid)* or null and void *(bāṭil)*. Registration of changes in marital status by the *sharī'a* court is also required to secure social allowances and education and medical care for children, and a *sharʿī* order of succession is required to effect property rights and transactions in the land registers.

6. Equality of all parties, regardless of their tribe, origin, color, or legal position in the *sharīʿa* court. (There is evidence of the rights of manumitted slaves being protected there).[36] True, the position of women and cognates under the *sharīʿa* is not equal to that of men and agnates, respectively. However, their position under the *sharīʿa* is much better than under tribal customary law. Indeed, some evidence suggests that the *sharīʿa* court is preferred especially by people whose position in traditional society is weak and who therefore cannot realize their rights under the tribal customary system. Thus, the *sharīʿa* court is applied to by divorced women who have been denied their financial rights or by heirs deprived of their share in the estate under customary law. The applicants expect the *sharīʿa* court to determine their rights under the *sharīʿa*.[37]

7. The executive power of the *sharīʿa* court provides legal security for the realization of legal and financial rights between the parties.

Although there can be no doubt that application by sedentary Bedouin to the *sharīʿa* court reflects to some extent a genuine religious transformation,[38] administrative exigencies and practical considerations are no doubt the main causes of this phenomenon. In any case, once the process of sedentarization starts, normative Islam gradually becomes a more binding lifestyle as regards worship, religious duties, and law in those domains with respect to which the sedentary Bedouin apply to the *sharʿī* judicial system and the exponents of the *sharīʿa*—namely, in matters of personal status and succession.

THE *QĀDĪ*, CUSTOM, AND *SHARĪʿA*

From the *sijills* of the *sharīʿa* courts and the documents collected from tribal arbitrators, one may conclude that the more the Bedouin become sedentarized the closer they are brought within normative Islam.[39] The complex of relations between *sharīʿa* and tribal custom may be divided into two main categories. In one custom reigns supreme, outside the control of the *sharīʿa*, with only minor concessions to the *sharīʿa*. Included in this category are "gift" (*ʿaṭāʾ*) marriages[40] that do not meet the *sharʿī* requirements for contractual validity (offer and acceptance, etc.) and other residual traces of customary marriage according to which a woman is not a party to the marriage contract, such as the marrying off of a girl by her guardian (*walī*) against her will (*wilāyat ijbār*), contrary to the Ḥanafī doctrine with respect to a girl who has reached maturity. Also in this category is exchange marriage (*tabādul zawjāt, shighār*)—that is, the mutual waiver of the payment of dower for the two brides, each of them representing the dower of the other;[41] customary legal maxims couched in rhyme pertaining to deferred dower payable upon divorce or death of one of the spouses;[42] *khulʿ* ("divestiture," divorce by agreement, by which the wife redeems herself from the marriage for a consideration), in which a promissory note (*quṣṣa*) in the amount of the dower is drawn up and made payable to the divorcing husband upon the marriage of the divorced wife to another man.[43]

Other cases in this category are divorce by means of the archaic *ẓihār* oath, which renders the wife a blood relative within the forbidden degrees for marriage[44] and homicide and bodily injury regulated by pure customary law.[45]

The other category prominently displays the impact of the *sharī'a* in areas in which it wields assimilative power over custom. In this category, the *qāḍīs* play a decisive role in bringing a Bedouin population within the orbit of the *sharī'a*. Unlike the independent *muftī*, the *qāḍī* is directly and constantly confronted by the Bedouin; his ability to display a tolerant attitude toward custom, to compromise with it while adopting and absorbing it into the *sharī'a*, may create a favorable climate in which a custom-bound population will apply to a *shar'ī* judicial authority. On the other hand, a *qāḍī's* uncompromising effort to enforce the *sharī'a* in letter and spirit, regardless of the modest Islamic knowledge of those applying to the court, may turn the Bedouin population away from its jurisdiction. It has been observed in various regions of the Islamic world that nomads accept the *shar'ī qāḍīs'* decisions only insofar as such decisions agree with the customary norm.[46]

How do the *qāḍīs* react to the confrontation between the *sharī'a*, which they are expected to apply, and tribal customary law dominant among the Bedouin? Do they uncompromisingly impose the *sharī'a* on the Bedouin, thus risking the latter's withdrawal from the *sharī'a* court? Do they submit to tribal custom, thus abusing their role as exponents of the *sharī'a*? Or do they seek a golden path between the two and meet custom half way, knowing this to be the only way to bring the Bedouin closer to the *sharī'a*? Naturally, much depends on the education and professional training of the *qāḍī*, his religious and social backgound, and his personal motivation. Unfortunately, I have no such information regarding the Libyan *qāḍīs*.[47] There is no indication in their decisions that they were influenced or inspired by the legal methodology of the Grand Sanūsī. Although the Sanūsī belonged to the Mālikī school, he felt free to deviate from it with respect to some issues. Moreover, under the influence of Ibn Taymiyya he did not regard himself as bound by *taqlīd*, the established body of law, of the Mālikī school, and claimed for himself some freedom to exercise personal *ijtihād* (reasoning).[48] The *qāḍīs* of Bethlehem, who are bound by the Ḥanafī school of law, seem to have a formal and solid education in Islamic law, both codified and uncodified.

Several tendencies can be distinguished in the judicial practice: the *qāḍīs'* reconciliation with custom (as, with regard to customary *khul'*, reinstatement of the divorced wife unrestrictedly regardless of the waiting period and the quota of three divorces; the circumvention of the *shar'ī* rules of inheritance; and customary "*Jāhilī*" will) and enforcement of the *sharī'a* while rejecting custom completely (as with regard to the legal consequences of divorce).[49] In Libya, *dār 'adl*, a tribal arbitrator who has been incorporated in the *sharī'a* court to the extent that he is treated by the *qāḍī* as a *shar'ī* notary (*'adl*) of the court, is a unique example of the symbiosis of custom and *sharī'a* to which the *qāḍī* makes a vital contribution. This institution, which provides a mecha-nism for handling marital disputes, falls within the gray zone between custom and *sharī'a*.[50] The *qāḍī*s of Bethlehem give retroactive effect to customary marriages of Bedouin not performed by a *shar'ī ma'dhūn* (solemnizer) and accept the testimony of Bedouin shaykhs certifying that the marriage was per-formed by a valid (*ṣaḥīḥ*) *shar'ī* union "in accordance with the custom of 'Arab al-Sawāḥira." This phenomenon has also been observed among some of the Israeli *qāḍī*s.[51] Shaykh 'Abd al-Qādir 'Abd al-Muḥsin 'Ābidīn, the *qāḍī* of the *Sharī'a* Court of Bethlehem, would say: "Since reconciliation is stronger than the *qāḍī* (*al-ṣulḥ yuqawwī al-qāḍī*), because it is based on agreement between the parties, it effects the *qāḍī*'s decision." Moreover, he would attest that an arrangement by mutual agreement (*bi'l-tarāḍī*) was frequently achieved with the help of tribal notables (*wujūh al-'ashā'ir*), and that when a *qāḍī* was unable to solve a particular problem, he would refer the parties to an arbitrator. Among the Bedouin of the Judean Desert it has been observed that the par-ties appoint arbitrators to prepare the ground (*tamhīdan*) for the settlement of financial matters between them and then rush to the *sharī'a* court to obtain *shar'ī* legitimation for the proposed settlement. There is ample evidence for the close cooperation between the customary arbitrator and the *shar'ī qāḍī*.[52] Customary substantive and procedural law still plays an important role in the Judean Desert.[53]

The *qāḍī*s' tendency to reconcile with custom may bring about deviations from orthodox *sharī'a*, as in the case of a *khul'* agreement (endorsed by court) in which it is stipulated that the divorced wife is prohibited from marrying someone before her ex-husband has been compensated by the dower of the future husband.[54]

The Mālikī school, like other Sunnī schools of law, does not recognize custom (*'āda*, *'urf*) as a formal source of law. Yet custom has a solid basis in the Mālikī corpus of law due to the fact that the Medinese practices (*'amal*) were incorporated into that school and granted the status of Prophetic *sunna*. In other words, custom has been absorbed into the oral traditions; hence its sta-tus as a formal source of law has ceased to be relevant.[55] This may explain why the Mālikī school applicable in Libya is more inclined than any other school to compromise with custom. The eclecticism of the Mālikī school found, since the fifteenth century, sophisticated expression in the judicial practice (*'amal*) of the *sharī'a* courts in North Africa, which in the view of some observers became a source of law in its own right.[56]

The Libyan documents do not point to a sophisticated, systematic approach by the *qāḍī*s aimed at absorbing custom by the *sharī'a*. Moreover, there is no significant evidence in our documents of the *qāḍī*s' recourse to religious-legal literature,[57] which may imply unwillingness on their part to invoke the *fuqahā'*, who are charged with the task of adapting the *sharī'a* to changing social conditions by means of expert legal opinions (*fatwās*). On the other hand, some evidence in Libya suggests that the *qāḍī* is occasionally approached in his capacity not as a judicial authority but rather as a *muftī* competent to issue a legal opinion *(jawāb)* in matters pertaining to divorce, succession, validity of a conversion into foreign currency, and the apportionment of tax burden among the parties to a camel-hiring contract.[58] When acting in his capacity as a *muftī* the *qāḍī* functions by virtue not of his nomination by the ruler but rather of his reputation as an independent *faqīh*.

The *qāḍīs'* decisions in Libya are generally characterized by a formalistic approach.[59] Occasionally, however, while imposing the religious-legal consequences derived from any given act, they may reproach a party to a dispute who has violated a religious-legal norm. In one case, in which a husband divorced his wife by five repudiations at one session, the *qāḍī* ruled that the first three exhausted the husband's *sharʿī* quota and the rest made a mockery of the Qurʾānic verses.[60] This style of the *qāḍī* was meant to strengthen awareness of the *sharīʿa* in a custom-bound population applying to the *sharīʿa* court out of practical considerations.

As mentioned earlier, an agreement between the parties is "stronger than the *qāḍī*." However, in the absence of such an agreement, the *qāḍīs* of Bethlehem, charged with adjudicating matters of personal status and succession of the Judean Desert Bedouin, reject custom altogether and apply the *sharīʿa* in its codified version under Jordanian family law, even when they know this will involve intolerable hardship.[61] It is interesting to note in this connection that some of the Israeli *sharʿī qāḍīs* dissolved marital unions on the ground that they had been concluded according to tribal custom rather than the Ottoman Family Rights Law of 1917 (which was adopted in Palestine in 1919) and ordered the parties to conclude *sharʿī* marriages.[62] Deviation from statutory provisions of the family law would create grounds for appeal to the Sharīʿa Court of Appeal. The scope of judicial discretion available to the *qāḍīs* of Bethlehem that could be used to bridge the gap between *sharīʿa* and custom was by the nature of things restricted to cases where there was no need to hand down a decision based on statutory provisions—that is, cases that were settled by mutual consent of the parties. Among the Bedouin of the Judean Desert, some evidence points to a kind of sophistication designed to facilitate the adoption of the *sharīʿa* by means of Shāfiʿī *fatwās*—that is, outside the control of the *sharīʿa* court. This applies, for example, to cases of reinstatement of a triply divorced wife. Under the Ḥanafī doctrine, which is dominant in the Sharīʿa Court of Betlehem, the intent *(niyya)* of the husband to divorce his wife is irrelevant, and the triply divorced wife is therefore not legally permitted to her ex-husband unless an intermediate marriage to a third party has taken place. Under the Shāfiʿī doctrine, on the other hand, lack of intent to divorce the wife is taken into account *(muʿtabara)* and thus may spare the inconvenience involved in an intermediate marriage.[63] The Libyan *qāḍīs* use their discretion to invoke the principle of *maṣlaḥa* (public interest) to bridge the gap between *sharī'a* and custom. In the twentieth century, the ability of the *sharī'a* court to bring the Bedouin within the orbit of normative Islam has declined due not only to the codification of the *sharī'a* but also to the competition of civil courts and the process of secularization.[64]

As noted earlier, in classical theory, the *qāḍī* is a delegate, either direct or indirect, of the caliph. The findings accumulated from the *sijills* of the *sharī'a* courts suggest, however, that the *qāḍīs* regard themselves rather as representatives of the Muslim community at large by virtue of their commission to apply the *sharī'a*. Their moral integrity and inner conviction of fulfilling a public mission is in the best tradition of the *muḥtasib*, the Islamic inspector of the market, anchored in the religious command: "to promote good and discourage evil" (*al-amr bi'l-ma'rūf wa'l-nahy 'an al-munkar*). In other words, the *qāḍī* regards himself as responsible for enforcing Islamic morals and behavior in the Muslim community. Such a function is incumbent on any individual who seeks to gain religious merit by his zeal for the *sharī'a*, due to the limited role of the public authority in Muslim society (thus, there is no office of public prosecution in Islam).[65] It is interesting to note in this connection that in a land dispute settled in a Sudanese court by mutual consent of the parties and made effective by judicial decision (*ḥukm riḍā'ī*), the court was inspired by the Qur'ānic commandment "to promote good and discourage evil." Later, one of the parties changed his mind, but the judicial decision was sustained by the court of appeal on the grounds that "the statutory law (*qānūn*) and the *sharī'a* authorize [the *qāḍī*] to combine the office of the judge with the function of the *muḥtasib* (*al-jam' bayna waẓīfatay al-qaḍā' wa'l-ḥisba*)."[66]

DENIAL OF PATERNITY—A DECISION HANDED DOWN BY THE SHARĪ'A COURT OF AJDĀBIYA

SUMMARY

The case discussed below[67] is meant to illustrate the *qāḍī*'s scope of autonomy to the extent of deviating from the strict *shar'ī* norm and adopting local customs and institutions. In doing so the *qāḍī* was inspired solely by the welfare of all the parties concerned. Yet he used his judicial discretion and religious authority to resolve the dispute within the bounderies of the *sharī'a* court, thus bringing the sedentary Bedouin closer to normative Islam.

After a series of disputes between the spouses that resulted in the wife leaving her husband's house and moving to her father's house as "an angry woman," the court instructed the spouses to stay with a certain tribal notary (*dār 'adl*) so that the latter might report to the court about their behavior. After some time it became apparent that the woman was pregnant. Her husband denied paternity of the child. The woman at first acknowledged that she was pregnant by a stranger. Later, however, she claimed that her husband had intimidated her into making this acknowledgment. She explained that while she had been "an angry woman" in her father's house, before moving to the *dār ʿadl*, her husband had continued to visit her in secret and have sexual relations with her at will; moreover, he had acknowledged having caused her pregnancy, and later on, while under the protection of the *ʿadl*, they had lived together in complete harmony until her father-in-law showed up and incited her husband against her.

The *ʿadl* confirmed in court that the couple's mutual relations had been normal until her father-in-law appeared on the scene, after which the husband denied his part in the pregnancy. After the wife had acknowledged that she was pregnant by a stranger, the *ʿadl* summoned her and, pointing at a saint's tomb, enjoined her to tell the truth. Recourse to the sanction of the holy man's tomb had its effect: the woman withdrew her first acknowledgment and attributed her pregnancy to her husband. The latter, however, persisted in denying paternity.

The *qāḍī* rejected the husband's denial, apparently on the grounds that the *liʿān* procedure had not taken place. According to this procedure, in cases of unproven charges of adultery against the wife it is possible to dissolve the marriage through a process of mutual imprecation; while paternity is denied, the parties are not subject to the Qurʾānic sanctions prescribed for adultery (*zinā*) and unproven charges of adultery (*qadhf*). The *qāḍī* ascribed paternity to the husband and enjoined him to return the wife to his house, to treat her well, restore her dower, her trousseau, and her jewelry, and pay her maintenance retroactively for the period during which he had neglected to do so.

LEGAL BACKGROUND[68]

Denial of paternity, as in the case under review, is tantamount to an accusation of adultery (*zinā*). The offense can be established either by the wife's acknowledgment (four acknowledgments are required) or by the testimony of four eyewitnesses to the act of sexual intercourse. Once the offense has been established, the wife is liable to Qurʾānic punishment (*ḥadd*)—that is, death by stoning (*rajm*)—provided she is *muḥsana*—that is, that the marriage has been consummated. If, however, the husband fails to establish the offense, he is liable to the Qurʾānic punishment for unfounded accusation of adultery (*qadhf*), eighty lashes and removal of the right to testify until he repents.[69]

If the husband cannot prove his allegation but nevertheless continues to deny paternity, he is expected to initiate the procedure of *liʿān*. According to this procedure, which is based on the Qurʾān (24: 4, 6–9) and the *ḥadīth*, the husband must swear four oaths (by analogy to four witnesses required to establish adultery) in which he invokes the name of God to the effect that he is telling the truth, and a fifth oath to the effect that if he lies he will be liable to God's imprecation. If he fails to swear these oaths after having accused his wife of adultery, he will be liable for the *ḥadd*-punishment for *qadhf*. The wife must swear four oaths in which she invokes the name of God to the effect that her husband is lying and that she is innocent, and a fifth oath to the effect that if her husband is telling the truth she will be liable to God's anger. If she fails to swear these oaths she will be liable to the *ḥadd*-punishment for *zinā*. If the husband keeps silent while pregnancy becomes apparent, he is liable to the Qur'ānic *ḥadd* and may not resort to the *li'ān* procedure. The *ḥadd* applies also in the event that he retracts from his denial of paternity.

For the *li'ān* procedure to be effected, the marriage must be valid or presumed (*ḥukman*) to be valid. If the marriage is irregular (*fāsid*) the woman is regarded as a stranger. If both the husband and wife adhere to the *li'ān* procedure, then they are exempt from the Qur'ānic punishments—lashes and stoning, respectively (*li'ān* averts [*yadra'u*] the *ḥadd*); they are not allowed to have sexual relations with each other (*istimtā'*) even before the marriage is dissolved by court. According to the Mālikī school the marriage is dissolved (*furqa*) by the act of mutual imprecation (*mulā'ana*), and the *qāḍī*'s decision is required only to make dissolution effective (*munaffadh*). *Li'ān* is regarded as judicial dissolution (*faskh*) rather than (as under Abū Ḥanifa's doctrine) irrevocable (*bā'in*) unilateral repudiation (*ṭalāq*); in fact, it is tantamount to eternal (*mu'abbad*) dissolution, which creates a permanent prohibition for marriage, as in the case of prohibition on grounds of fosterage (*raḍā'*).

Li'ān precludes the husband's paternity of the child (the child is related only to his mother), and there exist no mutual rights of inheritance (but the child and his mother inherit each other) or maintenance. If the procedure of *li'ān* takes place before consummation, the wife is entitled to half of her dower. Nevertheless, some of the legal effects of paternity are left intact as a precaution in case paternity between the husband and child is established in the future: no option of retaliation (*qiṣāṣ*) exists if one of them causes the death of the other; they and their relatives are prohibited from marrying each other on grounds of affinity (*muṣāhara*). And finally, the child who is the object of the denial is not regarded as a child of unknown paternity and therefore may not be claimed for the purpose of paternity by a stranger.

THE *QĀḌĪ'S* DECISION

In this case, the *qāḍī* rejected the husband's denial of paternity and ruled that paternity should be attributed (*ilḥāq*) to him (court's decision, line 33). There is a clear indication to the effect that the *qāḍī* was aware of the *li'ān* procedure, and one wonders why he did not mention it explicitly. After having established the validity (*thubūt*) of the marriage between the spouses, their intimate association (*mu'āshara*), and their legal marital relations (*khulṭa*), the *qāḍī* drew attention to the fact that the husband had not invoked the procedure especially laid down in the *sharīʿa* for the denial of paternity (*nafy al-ḥaml*) (lines 31–32). There can be no doubt that he was referring to *liʿān*.

As noted, denial of paternity is tantamount to an accusation of adultery, and if it is not proven either by four acknowledgments or by eyewitnesses—as in the present case—a ground is created for the *ḥadd* punishment for *qadhf*—that is, eighty lashes. Yet the *qāḍī* totally ignored the Qurʾānic sanction without attempting to explain his omission. One possible explanation is that the *sharīʿa* court in contemporary Libya has no jurisdiction over matters pertaining to *sharʿī* penal sanctions (*ḥudūd*).[70] However, this does not provide a fully satisfactory explanation. Paternity and its denial are matters of personal status within the sole jurisdiction of the *sharīʿa* court,[71] although this court may not effect the attendant penal sanction if the husband cannot prove his accusation. One would expect the *qāḍī* to draw attention to the *sharʿī* legal norm involved, or at least to make some value judgment regarding the fact that the husband has violated the Qurʾānic prohibition of *qadhf*. Nothing of the kind is to be found in the judgment.

A more satisfactory explanation is that the *qāḍī* was motivated by the interests of the wife and, even more so, the yet-to-be-born child. He was fully convinced that the wife was pregnant by her husband and hence there was no reason, in his mind, to dissolve the marriage. As a result, he decided to concentrate on rehabilitation of the marriage in spite of the husband's continued denial of paternity. It goes without saying that the *liʿān* procedure was not helpful to this end. Moreover, an accusation of adultery, even if unproven, may cause severe damage to the reputation of the wife in addition to the dissolution of the marriage. Similarly, denial of paternity may affect the child's right to receive maintenance from his father and to inherit from his estate. Instead, the *qāḍī* enjoined the husband to take his wife back to the conjugal dwelling, restore all her financial rights and personal effects, and pay her maintenance retroactively. One should bear in mind that maintenance includes *maskan sharʿī*—that is, legal conjugal dwelling "in the neighborhood of virtuous persons" (*bi-jiwār qawm ṣāliḥīn*)[72] rather than in a desolate dwelling (line 1)—which may have been the initial cause of the dispute between the spouses. If this explanation is correct, we have to do here with a clear instance of applying the principle of *maṣlaḥa*, public interest, in judicial practice.

The *qāḍī* here does not regard himself as being bound by the *sharʿī* norms pertaining to the denial of paternity. In fact, he seems to be guided purely by pragmatic considerations. He has no inhibitions whatsoever about resorting to a tribal notary (*dār ʿadl*) for handling this particular marital dispute. As explained elsewhere, *dār ʿadl* is a tribal customary institution that became incorporated in the *sharīʿa* court. The *sharʿī qāḍī* makes a decisive contribution to this end in his efforts to bring tribal society within the orbit of normative Islam.[73] The *ʿadl*, on his part, enlists the sanction of a holy man's tomb[74] to cause the wife to withdraw her first acknowledgment according to which she was pregnant by a stranger. The *qāḍī* does not seem to be disturbed by this procedure while assessing the accumulating evidence for rejecting the husband's denial of paternity. Indeed, the court's decision demonstrates the consolidated status of tribal custom and popular religion in the daily life of a tribal society in the process of sedentarization.

The case under review illustrates the extent of the *qāḍī*'s judicial discretion to accommodate the *sharī'a* to social reality. In theory, he is bound by the *sharī'a* in its Mālikī version. In practice, he uses his own discretion to bridge the gap between idealistic *sharī'a* and custom. Unless a violation of public order is anticipated as a result of the *qāḍī*'s decision, no intervention on the part of the ruler is expected. Such an intervention is unlikely in matters of personal status. Hence, one may conclude that the *sharī'a* court fulfills a vital role in the public sphere in the sense that the *qāḍī* is capable of formulating norms of social, ethical, and legal behavior independently—that is, outside the control of the political authority.

APPENDIX

THE COURT'S DECISION AND ITS TRANSLATION

THE ARABIC TEXT

[١] [...]¹ تنفق طيب في حصيدة الزرع السابقة للتاريخ حيث استودعها بالبيت وغصبها [٢]وعندما اظهرت لوالدها عدم رغبتها في القيام بنفقة الحصادة لم يوافقها [٣]على ذلك فامرت المحكمة السيد ابريك المذكور بان يرجع بالمراة لبيته الخاص [٤]وبارجاع النظر في خصوصها الى رجوع والدها من الكفرة. ثم وجه السؤال الى الزوج [٥] فاجاب نافيا للحمل ومعترفا بانه واخاه عبد الرازق قد سلبا منها الكساء [٦]والفوطة والسوار. ثم بتاريخ ١١ فبراير ١٩٤٨ الموافق ٣٠ ربيع اول ١٣٦٧ [٧]احضرت المحكمة الزوجين والسيد ابريك المذكور وسئلا بهل لكما اقوال [٨] خلاف ما ذكرتماه سابقاً² اجابت الزوجة بان تقريرها الاول باطل [٩] وذلك من ضغط زوجها عليها وتخويفها لها والحقيقة ان حملها لزوجها [١٠]لا شك عندها في ذلك وان زوجها دائماً يتصل بها وهي مغتاضة [مغتاظة] ببيت [١١]ابيها ولم ينقطع عن مخالطته لها كلما سنحت له فرصة بعد حضورها [١٢]الاول وتقريرها السابق اي منذ مدة قريبة قد زارها ليلاً بالبيت[١٣]الذي تنام فيه وخالطها وان زوجها كان يعلم بحملها ومعترفاً به وكانت [١٤] معاشرته لها حسنة الى ان زاره والده واجتمع به طويلاً فتغيرت [١٥] سيرته معها فسئل السيد ابريك المرقوم في ما يعلمه بين الزوجين المذكورين [١٦] اجاب بقوله بعد مراجعتهما بجواري بايام قد عزمت على الذهاب [١٧] الى اجدابية فسالتهما منفردين عن حالة معاشرتهما حيث ربما نمر³ [١٨]بالحكمة الشرعية لاجل الاخبار فكان جوابهما يدل على انهما متفقين مع [١٩] بعضهما اتفاقاً حسناً ولكن بعد رجوعي من [١١] اجدابية قد وجدتهما بالعكس [٢٠]وعلمت بقدوم والد الزوج الى المنتجع في غيابي وبعد ذلك اتاني [٢١] الزوج معلناً ان زوجته تبين بها حمل نسبته لغيره. وقال السيد [٢٢] ابريك ايضاً فاحضرت الزوجة ببيتي واشرت لها على ضريح سيدي جبريل [٢٣]ووعظتها بان لا تقول الا الحق فلم تبدي جواباً وانسحبت من بيتي وبعد [٢٤]ثلاثة ايام اتاني الزوج واخبرني باعتراف زوجته فذهبت معه الى البيت [٢٥]وقررت اعترافها السابق فجاوب عن ذلك الزوج مصراً على ما قرره سابقاً [٢٦] وانكر زيارة والده له وهو بجوار السيد ابريك وعلى نفي الحمل بقوله [٢٧] عندما ذهبت زوجتي من بيتي بالعام الماضي كانت حائضاً وبعد ذلك [٢٨]لم نتصل بها الا في جيرتنا للسيد ابريك ثم في يوم ١٢ فبراير الجاري حضر [٢٩] الوكيلان المرقوماني وسئلا هل لديهما خلاف ما ذكر فاجابا بالنفي [٣٠]فامر السيد ابريك بتسليم حاميتها < حمايتها> الى ابيها وامر هذا باستلامها

[٣١] وبناء على ما ذكر في المحاضر السابقة ونظراً لثبوت الزوجية والمعاشرة [٣٢]والخلطة وان الشريعة حددت لنفي الحمل تحديداً لم يثبت في هذه [٣٣]المحاضر لذلك قرر فضيلة القاضي الحاق الحمل بالزوج والزم الزوج بترجيع [٣٤] ما سلب من زوجته من صداقها وكسوتها وحليها وهو الكساء⁴ والفوطة والسوار [٣٥] المذكورات والزامه ايضاً بنفقة اهمالها التي صار تقديرها [٣٦] باجنيهين ونصف عن خمسة اشهر الى فبراير ١٩٤٨ وبترجيع زوجته [٣٧]وبحسن معاشرتها وحكم بذلك وامر بتسجيله والاشهاد عليه⁵ بتاريخ ١٦ فبراير ١٩٤٨.

---

¹ Regrettably, the beginning of this document is not available for inclusion here. However, on the basis of a preceding document, it is possible to conclude that the matter was decided by Shaykh Rāfi' 'Abd al-Raḥmān al-Qāḍī, the Qāḍī of the Sharī'a Court of Ajdābiya. See Layish and Davis 1988, 89, no. 115 (taken from the sijill of Sharī'a Court of Ajdābiya, p. 188, no. 185 of 12 February 1948).

² The words ذكرتماه سابقاً have been corrected in the document and appear in the margin of the document.

³ The grammatical form of the imperfect verb with n- in the first person singular reflects spoken usage in the Maghrib. For further details see Blanc 1974, 206 and 209.

⁴ This word was copied twice in the original, the second time at the beginning of line 35. A note to this effect (مكرر) is mentioned in the margin of the document, which implies that the repetition is cancelled.

[۳۸]شـ_____ود الـ_____ح_____ال٬

[۳۹]الامر كما ذكر فيه|

[٤٠]قاضي اجدابية

(القاضي عبد الرحمن رافع[٤١]

---

5 Some words were omitted from line 37 in its original version. This line has here been reconstructed on the basis of corrections in the margin of the document.

6 The conclusion to this document is not available to me. See fn. 1 above.

TRANSLATION[75]

[1] [. . .][76] [the wife had claimed in court that she] was supporting herself (tun-fiq) on gleanings from the harvest of a field from the [season] that preceded the date,[77] due to the fact that [her husband] had lodged her in a desolate dwelling (istawḥadahā)[78] and unlawfully seized [her belongings] (ghaṣabahā).[79] [2] When she revealed to her father her unwillingness to support herself (nafaqa) on the harvest, he did not agree with her [3] on this point.[80] Then, the court instructed the aforementioned sayyid Ibrīk to return the wife [from the conjugal dwelling] to his own private home[81] [4] and to reexamine the case on her father's return from Kufra. Afterwards, the [qāḍī] addressed a question to the husband [5] who responded by denying (nāfiyan) the pregnancy [paternity] (ḥaml),[82] and acknowledging that he and his brother ʿAbd al-Rāziq had taken away from her by force (salaba) [her] garment, [6] her apron, and [her] bracelet. Subsequently, on 11 February 1948, which corresponds to the 30th of Rabīʿ Awwal 1367, [7] the court summoned the two spouses and the aforementioned sayyid Ibrīk, and both [spouses] were asked: "Do you want to make statements (aqwāl) [8] that contradict what you have previously said [in court]?"[83] To this, the wife answered that her first statement (taqrīr) was null and void (bāṭil) [9] because it had been given under pressure (ḍaghṭ) and intimidation from her husband, and that in reality, she had been made pregnant by her husband. [10] She had no doubt concerning that fact because her husband continued to maintain contact with her during the period when she was "an angry woman" (mughtāḍa) [mughtāẓa][84] in her father's [11] house, and he did not cease having sexual relations (mukhālaṭa) with her whenever the occasion allowed; indeed, even after her first appearance [12] [in court] and her recent preceding statement, he visited her at night in the room [13] in which she slept and had sexual relations with her (khālaṭahā). [She also said that] her husband knew about her pregnancy and acknowledged it [14] and that he had lived in harmonious intimacy (muʿāshara) with her [after having moved to the dār ʿadl] until his father visited him and they had a long meeting; whereupon [15] his behavior toward her changed.[85]

The aforementioned sayyid Ibrīk was asked [to state] what he knew [concerning the relations] between the aforementioned couple. [16] He answered, saying: "A few days after they resumed their conjugal relations (murājaʿatihimā) under my protection (jiwār),[86] I decided to go [17] to Ajdābiya, and I asked each of them separately concerning their initimate association (muʿāsharati-himā), since there was a possibility that I might pass by [18] the Sharīʿa Court in order to report information (ikhbār) [concerning the spouses under his protection]. Their answers indicated that there was complete harmony between them. [19] However, on my return from Ajdābiyya I found the two of them in an opposite frame of mind, [20] and I was informed that in my absence the husband's father had come to the pasturage. Subsequently, the husband came to me [21] to inform me of his wife's pregnancy, which she attributed to someone else." *Sayyid* [22] Ibrīk also said: "I brought the wife to my home and, pointing to the tomb (*ḍarīḥ*) of Sīdī Jibrīl, [23] I exhorted her to say nothing but the truth.[87] However, she left my house without saying a word. [24] Three days later, her husband came to me and informed me that his wife acknowledged (*i'tirāf*) [that her pregnancy was by him]. I accompanied him home [25] and the wife confirmed what she had previously acknowledged [that she was pregnant by her husband]. To this her husband responded by insisting on what he had previously declared [viz., that the pregnancy was not by him]." [26] He [viz., the husband] denied [in court] that his father had come to visit him while under *sayyid* Ibrīk's protection (*jiwār*). [He persisted in his] denial (*nafy*) of the pregnancy [paternity] saying: [27] "When my wife left my home last year [and moved to her father's house as "an angry woman"] she was menstruating (*ḥā'iḍ*). After that [28] I had no contact with her until [we placed ourselves] under *sayyid* Ibrīk's protection (*jīra*)."[88]

Afterwards, on the 12th of the month of February of the current [year], [29] the two aforementioned proxies (*wakīlān*)[89] appeared [in court], and they were asked if they had [anything to say] that contradicted what had been stated. They answered negatively. [30] *Sayyid* Ibrīk was ordered to transfer (*taslīm*) her protection (*ḥāmiyatihā*) <*ḥimāyatihā*>[90] to her father and the latter was ordered to accept (*istilām*) it [viz., the protection].[91]

[31] On the basis of what had been said in the preceding depositions (*maḥāḍir*) and with due regard to the certification (*thubūt*) of the marriage contract, the spouses' intimate association (*mu'āshara*),[32] their sexual intercourse (*khulṭa*), [and also with due regard to the fact that] the *sharī'a* established a procedure (*ḥaddadat . . . taḥdīdan*) for the denial of pregnancy [paternity] (*nafy al-ḥaml*)—no proof of which had been produced [showing that this procedure had been carried out][92] in these [33] dispositions—[on the basis of all these,] his honour the Qāḍī ruled that the pregnancy should be attributed (*ilḥāq*) to the husband,[93] and he obliged him to restore [34] to his wife everything he had taken by force: her dower, her clothing and her jewelry which are her garments, her apron, and her bracelet which have been mentioned. [35] He likewise obligated him to provide [arrears] maintenance from the time that he had neglected to pay it (*nafaqat ihmālihā*). This was valued [36] at two and a half pounds for a period of five months until February 1948. [He also obliged him] to take his wife back [37] and to treat her well. He duly handed down [the verdict], instructed that it be entered, and required [the witnesses] to testify (*ishhād*) to it on 16 February 1948.

[38] Witnesses to the proceedings (*shuhūd al-ḥāl*).

[39] The matter being as indicated above

[40] the Qāḍī of Ajdābiya

[41] Rāfi' 'Abd al-Raḥmān al-Qāḍī

NOTES

My colleagues Miriam Hoexter, David Powers, Frank Stewart, and Knut Vikør read an earlier version of this essay and made useful comments for which I am most grateful.

1. "Islamization" in this essay denotes the process of bringing tribal society closer to normative Islam, not conversion. Cf. Levtzion 1979a, 19, 21; 1981, 78.

2. See e.g. Taylor 1990; Calhoun 1992; Cohen and Arato 1992. I am indebted to Professor S. N. Eisenstadt for these references.

3. Mayer 1987, 130–39.

4. Layish 1984b; 1987.

5. Some Egyptian judges in civil courts, by invoking Article 2, refused to apply statutory provisions contradictory to the *sharīʿa*. See Layish and Shaham *EI²*b.

6. Mayer 1987, 150–66.

7. Taylor 1990, 98.

8. Levtzion 1979b.

9. Layish 1989, 5.

10. The Libyan legal documents were placed at my disposal by Professor John Davis of Oxford University. The legal documents from the Judean Desert were collected with the assistance of my colleague, the late Dr. Avshalom Shmueli of Tel Aviv University. I am profoundly grateful to both of them. The findings and conclusions below are drawn freely from my previous research conducted on the basis of these material sources with a view to presenting them within an integrative thesis on *sharīʿa* and custom in tribal societies and within the context of public sphere.

11. The most authoritative source on the history and organization of the office of the *qāḍī* is Tyan 1960. See esp. 100ff. For a short survey see Tyan *EI²*. Cf. Levtzion 1979b, *passim*.

12. Masud, Messick, and Powers 1996b.

13. Layish 1996.

14. For details see Layish and Shaham *EI²*b.

15. Cf. Black 1990, 216.

16. Schacht 1964, 19–22; Coulson 1964, 28–35; Layish 1984a, 54. For a different view see Crone 1987, 15–16.

17. Milliot 1953, 156–69, 167–78; Berque *EI²*; Coulson 1964, 143ff.; Schacht 1964, 61–62; Serrano [Ruano] 1996; Layish 1984a, 55.

18. The *qāḍī*'s autonomy is greater than that of the civil judge, who is bound by statutory legislation and by precedents of the supreme court.

19. For further details see Layish 1991, 14–15; 1998, 19–20.

20. The Islamic legal treatises most commenly cited in the courts' record were written by Ibn ʿĀṣim (d. 829/1426) 1958, ʿIllaysh (d. 1299/1881–1882) n.d., and al-Ṣāwī (d. 1241/1825–1826) 1806. Cf. Powers 1994.

21. The Italians sought to retain a certain measure of normative supervision over the decisions of the *qāḍī*s in matters that were contrary to public policy. The "sleeping embryo" *(ḥaml nāʾim)* is a case in point. For details see Layish 1991, 5–6; 1998, 57 doc. 38.

22. Anderson 1976, 41; Layish and Shaham *EI²*a; Layish *EI²*c, *EI²*b, *EI²*a.

23. Cf. Levtzion 1981, 80.

24. The assessment regarding sedentarization is disputed by J. Davis. See Davis 1998, 11. Cf. Layish 1991, 15–18 and the sources indicated there.

25. For further details see Layish and Shmueli 1979, 29.

26. Cf. Gellner 1969, 8ff., 135–36; 1984, 23–24, 30; Levtzion 1979a, 20; 1981, 79; Shaham 1993, 192–93 and the source indicated in n. 3.

27. Davis 1987, 110 n. 15.

28. Cf. Levtzion 1979a, 7, 19–20; 1981, 78.

29. For details see Layish and Shmueli 1979, 41–42.

30. For details see Layish 1991, 170–71; Gellner 1969, 47; 1981, 100; 1984, 38; Evans-Pritchard 1949, 62; Colucci 1927, 24; Milliot 1953, 157, 166; Layish and Shmueli 1979, 31; al-ʿAbbādī 1988, 163, 179–83, 198–99, 406–7, based on Oweidi 1982, 121, 134–37, 149, 321–22 and Coulson 1964, 135–36; Laoust 1939, 519ff.; 1965, 323, 324; Smith 1963, 48ff.; Goldziher 1981, 238ff.; Baer 1964, 132 and the sources indicated there; 1969, 13, 14; Henninger 1959, 125ff. and the sources indicated there (I am indebted to Professor M. J. Kister for this last reference).

31. Cf. Gellner 1969, 68, 105ff., 129ff., 135; Rosen 1995, 194–97, 201, 206; Davis 1998, 12.

32. For Libya see Layish 1991, 175–76, 185–91. For Bethleham see Layish 1984a, 41–42.

33. Cf. Gellner 1969, 105ff.; Lewis 1984, 153.

34. For details see Davis 1987, 223–25, 228; Layish 1991, 127, 182–83; 1984a, 39–40 and the sources indicated there. Cf. Levtzion 1979a, 21; 1979b; 1981, 79.

35. The statutes pertaining to the establishment of tribal courts, including the Tribal Court of Appeal of 1936, were abolished in 1976. Jordanian law still applies in the West Bank. See al-ʿAbbādī 1988, 114ff., 445. In Israel, the tribal courts in the Negev, which had been established during the British Mandate, were abolished though their judicial basis has been left intact. I have found no indication in Libyan *sharīʿa* courts of the existence of statutory tribal courts, but there is ample evidence that matters were settled out of *sharīʿa* courts in accordance with tribal law, most probably by tribal arbitrators on a voluntary basis and with the mutual consent of the parties, as is the case in the Judean Desert. Tribal arbitrators (with no formal status) in the Judean Desert deal with issues pertaining to matters of personal status and succession (in competition with the *sharīʿa* courts), penal matters (homicide and bodily injury), property, obligations, and contracts (in competiton with the civil courts).

36. See Layish 1998, 78–79 doc. 62.

37. Cf. Shahar 1997, 24–25. Cf. Kressel 1992, 94–95, 166, 184.

38. There is evidence that already in the nomadic period Bedouin of the Judean Desert would visit the al-Aqṣā Mosque, the Dome of the Rock, and the markets of the old city of Jerusalem on Fridays. Layish 1980–1982, 220; 1996, 276 and the source indicated in n. 25. On the performance of religious obligations among the Bedouin of central Sinai see Stewart 1988, 7, 17, 44, 53n., 194; 1987, 53; Lewis 1984, 152–53. I have found no evidence in the *sijills* (court records) to the effect that the Bedouin resort to the *sharīʿa* court is inspired by their desire to belong to the Islamic body politic; such a possibility, however, cannot be ruled out.

39. Cf. Levtzion 1981, 78.

40. For details see Layish 1995b; Cf. Nāṭūr 1991; Lewis 1984, 145–46, 152–54.

41. Layish and Shmueli 1979, 35–37. Cf. Kressel 1992, 226, 230 (waiver of *sharʿī* inheritance rights).

42. Layish 1998, 29–30 docs. 5–6.

43. Ibid., 45–46 docs. 25–27. Customary *khulʿ* has also been observed among Israeli Muslims. See Layish and Shmueli 1979, 37–38.

44. See Layish 1998, 38 doc. 15.

45. Ibid., 72–73 docs. 55-56; Layish 1980–1982, 211.

46. For additional details see Layish 1991, 185–86 and the sources indicated there; 1980–1982, 218, 221; Cf. 1975, 334; 1974, 407ff.; al-ʿAbbādī 1988, 123–25; Oweidi [al-ʿAbbādī] 1982, 88–89.

47. For the name index of the *qāḍī*s and the *nāʾib*s (deputy *qāḍī*s) see Layish 1998, 103.

48. On the legal methodology of the Grand Sanūsī with special reference to *ijtihād* and *ijtihād fiʾl-madhhab* see Vikør 1994; 1995. See also Layish 1991, 204 and the sources indicated there.

49. For more details see Layish 1991, 172ff.; Layish and Shmueli 1979, 37ff.

50. For details see Layish 1995a.

51. Layish 1984a, 42; 1974, 398–99, 402–3.

52. I was present at a meeting in court between the *qāḍī* and a tribal arbitrator, who discussed ways of settling a family dispute that was to have been heard in court. For details see Layish and Shmueli 1979, 44; Layish 1984a, 41.

53. Layish 1980–1982, 211–12.

54. For details see Layish 1991, 186–99.

55. Libson 1997, 133–37.

56. See also p. 86 above and the references in n. 17. Cf. Layish 1991, p. 206. Ibn ʿĀṣim 1958 (see n. 20 above) incorporated in his *al-ʿĀṣimiyya* or *Tuḥfat al-ḥukkām* (see bibliography) the Andalusian judicial practice (*ʿamal*). The Libyan documents contain some evidence of the impact of the Mālikī judicial practice on day-to-day reality. See Layish 1998, e.g., 80 doc. 65 (*musāqāt*), 82 doc. 69 (*shahādat al-lafīf*).

57. Layish 1998, 24 doc. 1, 49 doc. 31, 67 doc. 50; 1991, 145–46.

58. Layish and Davis 1988, 122 doc. no. 156, 123 doc. no. 157; Layish 1998, 84 docs. 71–72.

59. Layish 1991, 206–7.

60. Layish 1998, 55 doc. 36.

61. Layish 1984a, 41ff.

62. See Layish 1974, 399.

63. For further details see Layish 1996.

64. Layish 1984a, 55-56; 1980–1982, 221 and the references indicated there. Cf. Shaham 1993; Shahar 1997.

65. See Schacht 1964, 52, 207; Cahen and Talbi *EI²*. Cf. Layish 1984b, 35–37. Similarly, conversion to Islam can take place by the mere recitation of the *shahāda* (Muslim creed) in the presence of witnesses without resorting to any public agency (Anderson 1970, 235, 374). It is significant to mention in this connection that the concept of public law is not developed in Islam. Thus homicide and bodily injury fall within the domain of torts—that is, private law to which the state is not a party (Schacht 1964, 75; Anderson 1951a, 811–28).

66. *al-Ṣaḥāfa*, 5 August 1984, 2.

67. Layish 1998, 60 doc. 41 (taken from the *sijill* of Sharīʿa Court of Ajdābiya, 189–91 no. [186/7], 16 February 1948).

68. Unless stated otherwise, this survey is based on Shalabī 1973, 597–605; Ibn ʿĀṣim 1958, 76–79 lines 502–17, 246 line 1694; al-Ṣāwī 1806, vol. 1, 456–61; Mālik (d. 179/796) 1989, 228–30; ʿIllaysh n.d., vol. 2, 76.

69. Peters 1996.

70. Layish 1991, 4ff.

71. Cf. Powers 1994; Shaham 1997, 158–59.

72. See below, n. 78.

73. See Layish 1995a, 198ff.

74. On the saint's role as an agent of Islamization in tribal society see Gellner 1969, 9ff. 135; 1984, 38; Morsy 1984, 48; Levtzion 1979a, 16ff.

75. Lines are not numbered in the original text. Numbers in [ ] brackets have been introduced in both the Arabic printed text and the English translation in order to facilitate comparison between the two. Omitted words in the facsimile production have been reconstructed and inserted in { } brackets. In cases in which a particular word appears to have been written incorrectly, thereby yielding a meaning incompatible with the context, a corrected version has been suggested in < > brackets. My student Muḥammad Ṭāṭūr read the document and made some useful suggestions for which I am most grateful.

76. The missing beginning of the document seems to include some details on the dispute between the spouses, a reference to a previous court meeting in which the wife acknowledged that she was pregnant by a stranger, the qāḍī's appointment of Ibrīk as a notary (dār ʿadl) to examine the issue, and the qāḍī's instruction that the spouses stay with this notary. See below, lines 7–8, 11–12, 15ff.

77. The reference is probably to the date on which she proclaimed herself "an angry woman" and moved to her father's house. See below, line 10.

78. Instead of lodging her "in the neighborhood of virtuous persons" (bi-jiwār qawm ṣāliḥīn) or "in the midst of virtuous trustworthy neighbours" (wasṭ jīrān ṣāliḥīn maʾmūnīn) within the meaning of "legal conjugal dwelling" (maskan sharʿī). See Layish 1995a, 205–6 and Shalabī 1973, 436, respectively. "Virtuous neighbors" are needed so that the wife does not feel lonely (lā tastawḥish) and lose her sanity. See Meron 1971, 210–11. Another possible translation of istawḥadahā: "sought to isolate her" or "sought to be alone with her."

79. See Ibn ʿĀṣim 1958, 218, lines 1498ff. Cf. lines 5–6 below. ghaṣabahā means also "raped her," but this connotation does not fit the present context.

80. In other words, the woman expressed her desire to leave the conjugal dwelling but her father discouraged her from doing so.

81. It appears that the couple had already stayed in the same dār ʿadl, whose function is to observe the couple's behavior and submit his report to the court. See Layish 1995a. Cf. dār amīn in Fierro 1985, 86ff.

82. As we shall see later, this is a case of a pregnancy begun while the woman was "angry" living in her father's house before moving to dār ʿadl.

83. This seems to refer to the wife's first admission that she was pregnant by a stranger.

84. The status of "an angry woman" seems to be common practice in Cyrenaica. See, e.g., Sharīʿa Court of Ajdābiya, 176 no.172 of 30 October 1947 (mughāḍaba); 27 no. 52 (date not available); Mohsen 1975, 114. Cf. Layish 1975, 98 n. 66 and the references indicated there.

85. Due to the fact that the intimate relations between the spouses (while the wife was living in her father's house) were kept secret, the father may have convinced his son that the wife's pregnancy would be attributed to a stranger and that it was appropriate for his son, to safeguard family reputation and honor, to deny paternity. Had it not been for the status of "the angry woman" the presumption would have been that "paternity belongs to lawful wedlock" (*al-walad li'l-firāsh*). See Coulson 1971, 23; Peters 1980, 126–27, 145.

86. For details on *jiwār* see Layish 1995a, 206–8.

87. The Bedouin believe that holy men and their tombs are sources of *baraka*, divine blessing. The *ʿadl* here enlists the sanction of the local Ṣūfī saint's tomb as a means of deterring the wife from lying about her pregnancy; the expedient proved successful. Cf. Layish 1998, 71 doc. 54 (Sīdī ʿAbd al-Salām al-Asmar); Layish 1995a, 204 and the references indicated there; Davis 1987, 146–47; Mohsen 1975, 57–59 (according to the customary law [*darāʾib*] of Awlād ʿAlī in the Western Desert, if the defendant refuses to take an oath at the saint's tomb he loses his case in favor of the claimant); al-Sūrī 1984, 395–96; Gellner 1969, 9ff.; 1984, 28; Evans-Pritchard 1949, 8–9, 65, 82–83, 117; Levtzion 1979a, 17–18; Hart 1996, 360; Morsy 1984, 49; Ginat 1987, 84, 120.

88. Cf. *jiwār*, lines 16, 28 above; al-Quṣūṣ 1972, 57; Layish 1995a, 207–8.

89. Their identity may have been mentioned in the missing beginning of the document.

90. Cf. al-Quṣūṣ 1972, 57.

91. The *ʿadl's* function ends after he has reported to the *qāḍī* concerning the essence of the dispute between the spouses and their respective responsibilities vis-à-vis the dispute. The wife returns to her father's house before the *qāḍī's* verdict is effected.

92. It appears that the *qāḍī* here is referring to the procedure of *liʿān*.

93. Cf. Sharīʿa Court of Kufra, no. 23 of 14 April 1933 (the *Qāḍī* attributed the pregnancy of a divorced woman to her ex-husband on the basis of the testimony of witnesses); no. 28 of 18 July 1933 (a woman claimed to have been raped by a stranger; the *Qāḍī* refused to attribute her pregnancy to this stranger because she had failed to notify someone of the rape immediately after its occurrence).

CHAPTER SIX

THE DYNAMICS OF SUFI BROTHERHOODS

NEHEMIA LEVTZION

SHARI`A AND MYSTICISM IN THE PUBLIC SPHERE

Islamic religious law is the totality of God's commands that regulate the life of every Muslim in all its aspects. Islamic law is the most typical manifestation of the Islamic way of life, the core and kernel of Islam itself. Theology has never been able to achieve a comparable importance in Islam; only mysticism was strong enough to challenge the ascendancy of the Law over the minds of the Muslim, and often proved victorious.[1]

The shari`a, a God-ordained law, is entrenched in a deep-rooted public sentiment and forms the basis for the Muslim social order. Sanction of the religious law contributed to the formation of a Muslim public opinion that accorded the shari`a and the `ulama' near monopoly of legal and moral legitimization, and endowed the qadi with a degree of autonomy vis-à-vis the rulers. The shari`a was developed as an autonomous legal system by fuqaha' (jurists), who asserted their position as the sole interpreters of the Prophet's heritage.

Since their formation in the eighth and ninth centuries, the various legal schools not only represented different interpretations of the law but were also solidarity groups. Only the Hanbali school of law retained these characteristics over a long period; the other schools of law ceased to function as mobilizing social movements after the twelfth century, and this role was taken over by Sufi brotherhoods and related organizations.

Islamic orthodoxy emphasizes the distance between God and man, as comparable to that between a slave and his master: like a slave, a man can please God only by strictly observing his commands. Sufi mystics developed alternative ways of approaching God, through spiritual and physical exercises. Sufis therefore do not have to observe the precepts of the religious law, as do others.

Islamic mysticism began as a marginal esoteric movement, considered heretic by the jurists. The rupture between jurists and mystics reached a dramatic peak with the execution in 922 of al-Hallaj, who claimed to have reached a complete union with God. But in the tenth and eleventh centuries more Sufis accepted the Islamic law as binding. Sufism became integrated into the mainstream of Islam, and before long religious leaders (`ulama') were simultaneously Sufi shaykhs and legal scholars.

THE ORGANIZATION AND STRUCTURE
OF EARLY SUFI BROTHERHOODS

Small communities of a master and his disciples *(murids)* replaced the loose master-disciple relationship of early Sufism. These entities continued to be known as *tariqa* (plural: *turuq*), but the literal meaning of "a devotional path" gave way to such terms as *brotherhood* or *order*.

Before the eighteenth century, however, brotherhoods did not have a central organization and were not actually self-supporting social organizations.[2] The loosely structured Sufi brotherhoods nevertheless became active in the public sphere, by allying themselves with more structured social organizations. In the countryside they became embedded in tribal or territorial units, which charismatic shaykhs were able to manipulate. In urban societies the brotherhoods were linked to voluntary organizations, like the *futuwwa*, the urban movement of young men. Later, in the Ottoman Empire, the Sufis were allied with the *akhi* association of young men and the trade guilds, as well as with *ghazis* (warriors on the frontiers of Islam) and the Janissaries.

For most Muslims the connection to Sufi brotherhoods was through the cult of saints *(awliya')*, which from the twelfth century on became central to the religious experience of Muslims. It was through the shaykh and the tomb, rather than through the `alim and the mosque, that Islam reached the common people. One was born and socialized around the shaykh's tomb and the *baraka* (divine blessing) that emanated from it, and each village, town ward, and tribe had its saint's tomb. Visitations to saints' tombs were the highlights of religious life, particularly for women, who went to the saint's tomb on Fridays, when the men went to the mosque for the Friday prayer.[3] By giving confidence to individuals, through the power of their protective amulets, the saints helped to maintain social stability.[4]

Sufis were deeply concerned with the life of the community. Shaykhs voiced the people's grievances and condemned tyranny and oppression. They played a part in conciliation and arbitration, and their houses were sanctuaries.[5]

Individual Sufis and brotherhoods oscillated between individualistic denunciatory piety and community-oriented legalistic world affirmation. Pious withdrawal from the world was characteristic of the more popular and less orthodox brotherhoods. The more legally *shari`a*-oriented brotherhoods were "this world" oriented. A positive attitude to "this world" also provided the framework within which political engagement became licit and spiritually acceptable.[6]

SUFIS AND THE STATE

Most `ulama' depended on the state, either because they held appointed positions or because they were associated with institutions supported by the state. On the other hand, Sufi shaykhs were not economically dependent on the rulers, because they received gifts and contributions from the people.

Not being dependant on the state, Sufis operated beyond the frontiers of dar al-Islam. From the tenth century on Sufi shaykhs lived among the infidel Turkish nomads of the steppes and were instrumental in converting them to Islam. Following the Mongol conquest and the destruction of the Muslim state, only the Sufi shaykhs of all men of religion continued to provide leadership to the Muslim communities. They also associated themselves with the Mongol rulers, and by the end of the thirteenth century had converted them to Islam.

The institutionalization of Sufism advanced when rulers began to endow hospices (khanqahs) for Sufis. The khanqah organized Sufism under the control of the state, aiming to foster the type of Sufism that conformed with the teachings of the shari`a.[7]

Besides the state-supported khanqahs there were completely independent, modest personal lodges (zawiya or ribat) of shaykhs. The zawiya served both as the residence of the shaykh and as a meeting place for members of the tariqa. The shaykh was buried in his zawiya, which then became a place of pilgrimage, with an annual festival.

Sufi lodges at strategic positions helped the expansion of Muslim commercial networks within and outside of dar al-Islam. In the fifteenth and sixteenth centuries a number of tekkes (lodges) were established on major roads in the Balkans to serve as inns. These inns accommodated poor scholars, military personnel, and wayfarers and received financial support from the central administration.[8]

Muslim rulers sought the favor of saints, built lodges and mausoleums for them, and made public pilgrimages to their tombs. Sufis justified royal patronage by their duty to guide the rulers.[9] Some sultans became murids of shaykhs, which implied a spiritual submission to the latter. When the shaykh `Izz al-Din b. `Abd al-Salam died, the Mamluk sultan Baybars (1260–1277) said: "Only now has my authority been consolidated,"[10] so powerful was the influence of the Sufi shaykh over the Sultan. From the Sufi viewpoint, the rulers hold power only through the grace (baraka) of the saint; indeed, powerful saints might be influential in making and unmaking kings.[11]

Association with the court brought deviant Sufi brotherhoods closer to orthodoxy in practice and in doctrine.[12] Compared to the problematic relations of the Chishti Sufis with the political authorities in India, the leaders of the Suhrawardiyya were always enthusiastically involved with Muslim rulers and accumulated great wealth and landed interests.[13]

When Christians invaded *dar al-Islam*, Sufis rallied rulers with the spirit of *jihad*. This was the case of one `Abdallah al-Yunini *(Asad al-Sham)* who joined Salah al-Din's campaigns, and of Ahmad al-Badawi, who called for *jihad* at the time of the Crusade of Louis X. In fifteenth-century Morocco al-Jazuli and his followers joined the *jihad* against the Portuguese. In the first half of the fourteenth century Sufis accompanied the Muslim armies in their advance southward into the Indian subcontinent.[14] Wandering dervishes, the *babas* from Central Asia, were the spiritual guides of the Turkish *ghazis* in the thirteenth and fourteenth centuries. Sufi shaykhs consecrated the *ghazis* as warriors in the cause of Islam.[15]

The Ottoman sultans tolerated socially deviant dervishes, who often also exhibited Shi`i-oriented beliefs and practices; but this attitude changed at the beginning of the sixteenth century, when the Ottomans were threatened by the Shi`i propaganda of the Safawids. Political pressure on suspected dervishes then increased, and dervish groups sought respectability by joining the ranks of the Bektashiyya brotherhood, which itself became more orthodox at that time, at least outwardly.[16]

The Janissaries became formally associated with the Bektashis at the end of the sixteenth century. The supreme Bektashi shaykh was appointed "colonel" of a Janissary unit, and eight Bektashi dervishes were assigned to Janissary units as chaplains. In formal parades the Bektashi shaykh marched in front of the *agha* of the Janissaries. The Janissaries adopted the uniform of the Bektashiyya and participated in their ceremonies. They were called "the children of Haji Bektash."[17]

Khalwati shaykhs were invited to Istanbul in the sixteenth century to join the fight against the heretics, particularly on the western frontier of the Balkans. Close relations between Khalwati shaykhs and Ottoman sultans continued until the middle of the seventeenth century, and for almost two centuries the Khalwatiyya had the largest number of *tekke*s and affiliates in the Ottoman capital.[18]

THE CONVERSION OF CHARISMA TO ECONOMIC AND POLITICAL POWER

In the seventeenth century the Ottoman central authority weakened in Anatolia, and people turned to religion in search of stability. In such circumstances Sufi shaykhs became influential by converting their charisma to economic and political power. But the Ottoman state never became weak enough to permit the rise of Sufi shaykhs to such powerful positions as in certain parts of Morocco.[19]

In the segmentary political and social system of Morocco, where the central authority is too far away to be effective, holy men who live near the tomb of a saintly ancestor provide the continuity and the stable framework for that political system. Their moral authority helps to guarantee political, legal, and ecological arrangements reached through their arbitration. The saints also play an important role by anchoring the local society in the wider system of Islam. For the local tribesmen, they represent the religion of the central tradition, and guarantee the tribesmen's incorporation into it.[20]

The situation in Sind seems to have been somewhat similar to that in Morocco. Since temporal authority was a distant force with which they had little contact, local tribes in Sind tended to follow Sufi pirs, whose power base was in the countryside. Pirs of important shrines possessed substantial land holdings and political power, and wielded great influence over the lives of the people. Like the saints of the Atlas in Morocco, pirs in Sind acted as "professional neutrals" to balance opposing interests. Indeed, the social order was based on the bond between pir and murid, because individuals felt more secure under the patronage of a powerful pir. It is significant, however, that both in Morocco and in Sind, individual shaykhs, not brotherhoods, wielded real power.

One of the most powerful individuals was the Naqshabandi shaykh ʿUbaydallah Ahrar (1404–1490) in Samarqand, who converted the charisma of a Sufi shaykh to economic and political power. He exploited the decline of the authority of the Timurid sultans and gained almost absolute influence over the sultan Abu Saʿid (1451–1468), who was his murid. Ahrar also accumulated considerable land holdings, as a result of peasants selling their holdings to him in order to become his disciples and enter under his protection (himaya). Ahrar protected them from taxation, as well as other excessive and arbitrary burdens deemed contrary to Islamic principles, by threatening emirs with his spiritual powers. In typical Naqshabandi fashion, Ahrar reconciled his worldly engagements with a state of mind of being mentally disengaged from worldly matters. Wealth in the context of his spiritual world symbolized a favor bestowed by God.[21]

INITIATION AND DHIKR

Sufi congregations in hospices and around tombs attracted the common people. They sought access to the baraka of the shaykh, and to participate in the collective sessions of the dhikr. Such affiliates needed only the simplest form of initiation and a basic mystical training. They took the oath of allegiance (bayʿa) and accepted the shaykh as teacher and leader, but continued their normal life. As the circle of devotees grew, Sufi brotherhoods became devotional movements where lay affiliates found relief from worldly anxieties.[22]

The most important part of Sufi liturgy is the dhikr (literally: the act of remembering). It is a litany tirelessly repeated, consisting of formulae containing the names of Allah. There are two modes of dhikr: the silent dhikr, known as khafi (hidden) or qalbi (by the heart) and the vocal dhikr, known as jahri (public) or lisani (by the tongue). The two modes are equally legitimate, and both have authoritative traditions;[23] but the silent dhikr was thought to be more respectable and was practiced by those who were more advanced along the spiritual path. The vocal *dhikr*, considered more popular and practiced in a collective ceremony, helped to induce a mystical experience in the ordinary man relatively quickly, through rhythmical exercises.

The silent *dhikr* was typical of the more orthodox *shari`a*-oriented brotherhoods. Mustafa al-Bakri (1688–1749), who inspired the reform of the Khalwatiyya in Egypt, adopted the vocal *dhikr* and presided over vocal *dhikr* ceremonies in Jerusalem, where participants would faint from excitement and exhaustion. His disciple al-Hifni conducted ceremonies of vocal *dhikr* in Cairo. These ceremonies became so popular he had to repeat them for days and nights to admit the many thousands who wanted to attend.[24]

One may speculate as to why Mustafa al-Bakri, whose reform of the Khalwatiyya was toward greater orthodoxy, changed to the more popular form of *dhikr*. The reason was probably that the vocal *dhikr* offered greater scope for the participation of common people in the rituals and helped to popularize the *tariqa* and win adherents. This move might be better appreciated in the wider context of the structural, organizational, and ritual changes that Sufi brotherhoods experienced in the eighteenth century.

STRUCTURAL, ORGANIZATIONAL, AND RITUAL CHANGES IN THE EIGHTEENTH CENTURY

In the eighteenth century, brotherhoods transformed from old patterns of decentralized diffusive affiliation into larger-scale organizations, more coherent and centralized. Led by charismatic shaykhs, the reformed Sufi brotherhoods cut across regional, ethnic, and political boundaries to mobilize wider popular support,[25] and they incorporated local saintly lineages. Local shaykhs, who had controlled the spiritual life of the common people, became regional representatives, *muqaddams* and *khalifas* in hierarchically structured organizations.[26]

Before the eighteenth century, Sufi shaykhs obtained initiation into several *turuq*, and often shifted their principal allegiance from one *tariqa* to another.[27] But Mustafa al-Bakri insisted that his own disciples be affiliated exclusively to the Khalwatiyya and ordered them to break their former allegiance to other *turuq* and shaykhs.[28] Exclusivity gave greater cohesion to the *tariqa*, and added to the commitment of its adherents. The Tijaniyya, an offshoot of the Khalwatiyya, adopted the concept of exclusive affiliation with even greater zeal. The Tijaniyya, in its turn, influenced rival *turuq* in the Maghrib and in West Africa, in particular the Qadiriyya, which also became more assertive and cohesive.[29]

The restructured Sufi brotherhoods reached out to the common people and mobilized popular support, thus contributing to the penetration of a more meaningful religious experience into the lower levels of Muslim society and spreading from the urban to the rural population.

In the countryside of West Africa, the growth of Islam from the seventeenth century brought about a new rural religious leadership. Unlike the urban scholars, who had been spokesmen of the merchants, the new leadership articulated the grievances of the peasants. They criticized the rulers and contributed to the radicalization of Islam, thus preparing the ground for the great reformist movements, better known as the *jihads*.[30]

MYSTICAL VERSE IN VERNACULAR LANGUAGES

Looking for common features of Sufi movements across the Muslim world I have observed that written Islamic literatures in the vernacular languages appeared simultaneously all over the Muslim world in the seventeenth and eighteenth centuries, and that the predominant literary genre in all the vernacular literatures was the mystical verse. This development is explained by the expansion of Islam to the countryside, where the knowledge of Islam could be disseminated to the illiterate peasants and herdsmen only in the vernacular languages.

The need to write down oral mystical poetry in folk idioms arose also with the growth in scale of the brotherhoods, whose leaders sought to communicate with affiliates living in remote communities. Poems in the vernaculars, which had earlier been transmitted and recited orally, were committed to writing in the Arabic script, and copies of the written texts were sent out to the literate representatives of the shaykh in different localities, who then recited these texts to an illiterate audience.

In India, Sufis turned to the regional idioms—Urdu, Sindhi, and Punjabi—for preaching and teaching because the sacred languages—Arabic and Persian—were inaccessible to the masses.[31] The discourse of the elite continued in Arabic and Persian, the classical languages of Islam, whereas the vernacular literature was important in building bridges to the common people.[32]

Muslim literature in China, written mostly in Chinese characters, developed from the middle of the seventeenth century. As elsewhere, mystical works were important. This literature was composed in an easy style, inclining toward the spoken language because it addressed the masses.[33]

The preaching of Imam Mansur in 1785 in the Caucasus is said to have been in simple language and directed to the peasants.[34] In the sixteenth and seventeenth centuries, a period of literary decline in Egypt, works of theology and law were written in bombastic style, but Sufi texts were composed in the simple down-to-earth language of the people.[35] Sufis all over the world then began to adapt their idiom and style to achieve efficient communication with the people they sought to mobilize.

The efficiency of preaching and exhortation in the vernacular to mobilize popular support is described in the case of `Uthman dan Fodio, the leader of the *jihad* in what is today Northern Nigeria: "Then we rose up with the

Shaykh, helping him in his mission work for religion. He traveled for that purpose to the east and west, calling people to the religion of God by his preaching and his poems (qasidas) in a non-Arabic language (`ajami)."³⁶ When `Uthman dan Fodio saw that his community was ready for the jihad, "he began to incite them to arms . . . and he set this in verse in his non-Arabic Qadiri poem (qasida `ajamiyya Qadiriyya)." This mystical verse had a hypnotic effect on devotees on the eve of the jihad.³⁷

SUFI BROTHERHOODS IN THE PUBLIC SPHERE

Mysticism, an inward and individualistic mode of worship, is unlikely to create a social space. After the tenth century the esoteric form of piety, elitist in nature, gradually became the most popular mode of devotion in Islam, mainly through the contribution of brotherhoods. It was the brotherhoods that brought Sufism from the private to the public sphere, to play an important sociopolitical role in the communal and religious life of the Muslims for a period lasting seven centuries.

Before the seventeenth century most of the brotherhoods had been loosely organized and localized, and had not been self-supporting social organizations. Brotherhoods reached all social strata through the cult of saints. The baraka (grace) of the saints imbued individuals with confidence and helped maintain social stability. Commercial fairs and religious festivals took place around saints' tombs. Moreover, Sufism offered a social space of religious experience to women, who had hardly enjoyed any place in formal religious life.

The political authorities sought to control the activities of the Sufis by the endowment of hospices (khanqahs), which organized Sufism under the control of the state and fostered shari`a-abiding Sufism. Some Sufi brotherhoods avoided the courtly scene and cultivated the ideal of ascetic poverty. But other brotherhoods were closely associated with rulers and accumulated great wealth. Even socially deviant dervishes were attracted to the rulers' courts, where they were pressured to conform to the shari`a. According to the Sufi vision of authority, rulers were entrusted with a temporary lease of power through the baraka of a saint. Muslim rulers thus sought the favor of saints, and sometimes became disciples of Sufi shaykhs.

Sufis, unlike other `ulama', could function also outside the Muslim state, and Sufi lodges helped the expansion of Islam beyond the frontiers of dar al-Islam. Where the central authority was weak, people sought security with Sufi shaykhs, who transformed their charisma into economic and political power, gaining possession of substantial land holdings and wielding great influence over the lives of the people. Wealth represented a blessing bestowed by God, and such shaykhs managed to reconcile the possession of worldly assets with mental disengagement from this world.

Sufi brotherhoods being esoteric organizations, induction into them needed an initiation ceremony, not only for those wishing to become *murids* but also for those who only sought access to the blessing of the shaykh. A collective *dhikr* evolved to induce a mystical experience for the ordinary man in a relatively short space of time. With a much larger circle of devotees, brotherhoods became more a devotional than a mystical movement.

Sufi brotherhoods thus fulfilled multiple roles in Muslim societies; they provided moral guidance to voluntary associations, opened opportunities for release from the hardships of everyday existence, gave confidence to individuals, and helped sustain social stability. They also maintained lines of communications between the common people and the authorities.

Before the eighteenth century these brotherhoods had been localized and had influenced only their immediate communities. But in the eighteenth century Sufism experienced a radical change, when brotherhoods transformed from old patterns of decentralized, diffusive affiliations to larger-scale organizations, more centralized and coherent.

Changes in rituals emphasized the hierarchical and centralized nature of the reformed *tariqa* and the expanded role of the shaykh. Brotherhoods offered larger scope for the participation of the common people in their ceremonies, facilitating the recruitment of new adherents.

A new Muslim leadership emerged that articulated the grievances of the masses, criticized the rulers, and contributed to the radicalization of Islam. The discourse of the public sphere in Muslim societies addressed social and political issues, and in order to reach the illiterate it was written in the vernacular languages. In this way, written Islamic literatures in the vernacular languages developed simultaneously all over the Muslim world in the seventeenth and eighteenth centuries, with mystical verse as the predominant genre.

Reformed brotherhoods gave rise to movements of renewal and reform in the eighteenth century. One may be tempted to speculate that these reformed premodern movements could have led Muslim societies into the modern period with a sense of revival. But this process was truncated when leaders of these movements redirected their major efforts from internal reform to defending *dar al-Islam* against the invading European powers. Ultimately they were all crushed by the overwhelming military power of the Europeans.

NOTES

1. Schacht 1974, 393.
2. Karamustafa 1994, 88–89; Levtzion 1997.
3. Trimingham 1971, 232.
4. Ibid., 220–21, 234; Karamustafa 1994, 87–89.
5. Trimingham 1971, 27, 230, 237–38.

6. Algar 1976, 44; 1990, 152.

7. Fernandes 1988, vol. 1, 24.

8. Faroqhi 1976, 73-75; 1981, 99–101, 113; Norris 1993, 101–2, 109.

9. Eaton 1993, 94.

10. Quoted in Abu Zahra, 1953, 143.

11. Eaton 1993, 31, 83.

12. Eaton 1978, 45–48, 50–53; Ernst, 1993, 47.

13. Ansari 1992, 5, 30.

14. Eaton 1978, 284.

15. Trimingham 1971, 83; Faroqhi 1993, 197; Zarcone 1993, 71.

16. Ocak 1993, 249–51; Trimingham 1971, 83; Faroqhi 1981, 92; Karamustafa 1993, 243; 1994, 83–84, 94–95.

17. Birge 1937; Zarcone 1993, 71; Goodwin 1994, 148–52.

18. Trimingham 1971, 75; Zarcone 1993, 80; Clayer 1994, 65–67, 70.

19. Faroqhi 1993, 197, 205–6.

20. Gellner 1969, 41ff; 1981, 114–30.

21. What is offered here is a preliminary analysis of the role of Ahrar as a charismatic shaykh, based on Paul 1991; DeWeese 1993; Gross 1988; 1990.

22. Trimingham 1971, 27–28, 186, 199–200; Eaton 1978, xxxi.

23. See Gardet *EI²*.

24. al-Jabarti (d. 1240/1825–1826) 1879–1880, vol. 1, 300; Weigert 1989, 109–11.

25. For a more detailed analysis see Levtzion 1997 and Levtzion and Voll 1987.

26. Clancey-Smith 1994, 41–45; Karrar 1992, x, 20; Algar 1990; Abu-Manneh 1990, 295; Hofheinz 1990, 28–29; Grandin 1990, 645.

27. Eaton 1978, xxxi–xxxii, 207; Winter 1982, 92, 97.

28. al-Jabarti, 1879–80, vol. 1, 295; vol. 2, 61; Weigert 1989.

29. Abun-Nasr 1965, 15–57; Martin 1969; Brenner 1988.

30. Levtzion 1987, 23–26.

31. Schimmel 1975, 131, 135, 163; Shackle 1993, 163, 265, 285–88; Roy 1984, 58; Eaton 1978, 91. It is significant that in the independent state of Bijapur, where, being far from the Mughal court, the influence of Persian culture was weaker, literature in Dakhni developed from the fifteenth century, more than two centuries before the appearance of Urdu literature.

32. Schimmel 1973, 48–50; 1976, xi, 11.

33. Aubin 1990, 496–97.

34. Bennigsen 1964, 195.

35. Winter 1982, 27.

36. Ibn Fudi (d. 1245/1829) 1963, 85.

37. Ibid., 51; see also Hiskett 1975.

CHAPTER SEVEN

THE WAQF AND THE PUBLIC SPHERE

MIRIAM HOEXTER

Much of the discussion on whether Middle Eastern states have the necessary ingredients for the development of democracy has centered on the questions of civil society and the nature of relations between the state and society. The "Oriental despotism" thesis, long in vogue in the literature, saw these two questions as inseparable: the despotism that characterized the Oriental state precluded the existence of any autonomous organization or civil society; or as Turner put it, "The concept [of civil society] has been used as the basis of the notion that the Orient is, so to speak, all state and no society."[1] The absence of a civil society thus constituted the principal theoretical postulate of the "Oriental despotism" case, which, according to Turner, was "a reflection of basic political anxieties about the state of political freedom in the West."[2] By now, the existence of a plethora of civic associations in the Middle East, though not structured on the Western model, seems to be widely recognized.[3] However, emphasizing the despotic nature of rulers, their lack of legitimacy, and their lack of concern for the welfare of the public, the predominating picture in the literature concerning the relations between state and society is that of a more or less total separation and estrangement of the two.[4]

I propose to challenge this rather unsatisfying picture by looking at the relations between rulers and society from the broader perspective suggested by the concept of the public sphere. The importance of this concept—defined as a zone of autonomous social activity between the family and the ruling authorities—lies largely in that it goes beyond appeals to the formal institutions of the Western civil society model, to address the entire realm of societal and cultural life that has relevance to the social and political order.[5] It thus broadens the scope of discussion to include aspects that have hitherto been largely neglected, such as informal ties, the moral-ethical values that form a society's image of the good order, and the symbols that reflect the common values and social ideals of the particular society.[6] I shall look at the relations between society and its rulers through a particular prism—that of the Islamic endowment institution, the *waqf*.

Hodgson, in his discussion of the *shari`a* as a civic force, lists the *waqf* foundations, along with the *shari`a* laws and the Sufi (mystic) orders, as the three religiously sanctioned integrative institutions holding together all Islamic groupings in the town.[7] Within this framework the *waqf* fulfilled a particular role: it became the vehicle for financing Islam as a society,[8] or, as I prefer to formulate it: the *waqf* served as a major means through which the Islamic idea of the social order proper for the *umma* (the community of believers) was implemented. Throughout the premodern Islamic world, endowments (*waqfs*) were made by rulers as well as by all strata of the Muslim population. They provided for the financing and maintenance of a host of public services and did so through an institution that, across the centuries, had retained its basic characteristic as an institution whose rules were an integral part of the *shari`a*—the sacred law.[9] The *waqf* is thus an ideal prism through which to examine both the moral values underlying the Islamic perception of the public sphere and the ways they were put into practice.

This chapter is divided into two parts. In the first I shall discuss some doctrinal points that I believe are relevant to the perception of the public sphere characteristic of the Islamic cultural area and their reflection in the *waqf*. In the second part, I shall examine the impact of the *waqf* on the formation of the public sphere and the nature of the discourse it generated.

THE *WAQF* AND THE PERCEPTION OF THE PUBLIC SPHERE

UMMA AND *SHARI`A*

The central importance accorded in Islamic political discourse to the community of believers (the *umma*) is perhaps the most significant difference between the way Islamic culture and Western culture view the nature of the public sphere and the relationship between the rulers and society.

The interests of the community of believers and the norms that should guide the lives of individuals and the community were the main concerns of Muhammad. After his death, public life was, to a large extent, posited as the collective responsibility of the *umma*. The Qur'an and Muhammad's *sunna* (practices established by the example of the Prophet's life) provided the norms of public life and served as guidelines for the community as to how to discharge its responsibilities.[10] The *umma* inherited the task of spiritual guidance of the community after Muhammad, and its consensus (*ijma`*) on the legitimacy of the ruler as well as on details concerning the development of social and cultural norms was considered infallible.[11]

With the elaboration of the *shari`a*—the sacred law, or the rules and regulations governing the lives of Muslims, derived in principal from the Qur'an and *hadith*[12]—the role of interpreters and custodians of Muhammad's legacy of the norms and ideals of good order proper to the community of believers passed, in the main, to the shari`a specialists—the fuqaha', or, more generally, the `ulama'. However, the umma—in its original meaning of the entire community of believers as well as in its more restricted meaning of the community of believers living under one of the legitimate Islamic rulers—never lost its central position as the moral community. Moreover, the umma retained its right and ability to influence the public sphere, although this did not necessarily imply participation in daily policymaking.

Umma and shari`a were thus the center of gravity around which all activity in the public sphere revolved. Their central position in the premodern Islamic world created a situation radically different from the one prevalent in Western civilization: it placed the umma as the most significant group in the public sphere, and above the ruler. The shari`a embodied the norms of public order, and its preservation was the main moral obligation of both the community and the ruler.

Some implications of these basic tenets of the Islamic view of the public sphere and their reflection in the endowment institution will be discussed in the sections that follow.

THE INDIVIDUAL AND THE PUBLIC SPHERE

Creation of a waqf has always been the act of an individual. The endowment itself as well as all the details embodied in the endowment deed were determined by the individual endower, who alone was promised a reward for his good deed in the hereafter.[13] Endowments by rulers and their entourages are perhaps the best example, emphasizing the individual responsibility of the endower. When endowing an asset, a ruler never did so as a representative of the realm. His act of endowment, like that by anyone else, was the act of a private individual. An endowment by the realm, the political system as a body or institution, let alone an endowment by any other body or group, is simply unknown to Islam and unacceptable according to the terms of the law of waqf. Thus, an endowment of arable land, which in the Ottoman Empire belonged to the state, was preceded by a procedure of temlik—a procedure whereby ownership of the land to be endowed was passed to the person, usually a member of the ruler's family or entourage, who intended to create a waqf.[14]

While the act of creating an endowment was that of a private individual, the beneficiaries of the endowment were always located in the public sphere, whether in the first stage (the endowment would then be described as a waqf khayri) or in the last stage of the devolution of beneficiaries, after the extinction of the primary and intermediary private beneficiaries (the endowment would then be described as a waqf ahli). By endowing his property the individual participated in the formation of the public sphere, thus expressing his sense of belonging to the community of believers and his identification with its values.

The *waqf*, then, reflects the basic Islamic notion concerning the relation between the individual and the community: in contrast to West European culture, where the distinction between private and public acts was very pronounced, what Hodgson termed "the unitary contractualism of Islamdom" "denied any special status to public acts at all . . . to the point where it ruled out all corporate status and reduced all acts to the acts of personally responsible individuals." [15] The public sphere in Islam was thus conceived of not as an antithesis to the private individual but as an integral or synthetic component of his life as a Muslim. [16]

THE CONCEPTION OF CHARITY

Endowing one's asset has always been considered a *sadaqa*—an act of charity recommended by the *shari`a* that entitled the founder of the endowment to recompense in the world beyond. In fact, the term *waqf*, by which the Islamic endowment institution is known, is an abbreviation of the original *sadaqa mawqufa*. [17] The basic idea of the endowment as a continuous or eternal charity is reflected in the definition that appears in virtually every *waqf* manual: *al-waqf sadaqa jariya fi sabil Allah ta`ala*—the *waqf* is a continuous charity for the sake of God and his religion. [18]

The institutionalization of the *waqf* called for a definition of a charity and thus a legitimate beneficiary of endowments. A valid purpose for the benefit of which one could endow the produce of one's property was defined as *qurba*—that is, anything likely to bring the founder nearer to God. [19] Obviously this was a very broad definition, reminiscent of what Hodgson called "occasionalism," which he considered one of the hallmarks of the Islamicate social order (as against Occidental "legitimism"), symbolized by the arabesque and representing "an elaborate surface formalism, adaptable to any substance." [20] This broad definition allowed for the inclusion, as beneficiaries of an endowment, of family members, freed slaves, the poor in general, or the poor belonging to a specific social group, even a group of animals, side by side with mosques, *madrasas*, Sufi orders, the water supply system, bridges, etc. This broad definition ensued from the most basic conception of Islam, which, from its inception, never conceived of itself as a religion regulating only the sphere of worship but as a political community guided by and devoted to Allah in all spheres of human activity. [21] According to this conception a contribution toward the welfare of the community, just as care for one's own family, was considered an act likely to bring a person closer to Allah.

The idea of charity, then, was defined in Islam in a much broader and more flexible manner than in other cultures. [22] The definition of *qurba* does not differentiate between private and public well-being; each is assigned equal value and importance in furthering the interests of the community of believers.

THE UMMA, THE RULING AUTHORITIES, AND THE `ULAMA'

The way *waqf* foundations—conglomerations of large numbers of endowments serving a public purpose—were handled reflected the basic Islamic perception of rights, responsibilities, and competencies in the public sphere. An acquaintance with its major characteristics is therefore indispensable to an understanding of the subject.

Sunni doctrine distinguishes between two spheres of claims or rights: those of men, known as *huquq al-`ibad*, and those of God, termed *huquq Allah*. The first covers claims of private individuals in their dealings with one another and was always recognized as belonging in the sphere of jurisdiction of the `ulama'—the specialists in *shari`a* law. *Huquq Allah*, the claims of God, are traditionally identified with the general interests of the community of believers (the *umma*).[23]

The point to be borne in mind concerning this distinction is that claims or rights accrued to only two categories: the individual and the *umma*.[24] Insistence on the rights of private individuals and on the primacy of the *umma*—not the state or the ruler—in the public sphere was thus at the very root of Islamic political thought.

However, the *umma*—the entire community of believers as well as the local Muslim community in a specific region or town—was an uninstitutionalized reference group. A kind of latent competition ensued between the `ulama' and the rulers as to who was entitled to represent the interests of the *umma* and stand up for the community's rights. The modus vivendi in this competition may be summarized as follows: From quite an early stage in Islamic history,[25] the `ulama', not the rulers, were recognized as the bearers and interpreters of the norms and basic values of the proper Islamic social order. The rulers, on their part, were made responsible for the implementation of these norms, the protection and promotion of the general interests of the community of the faithful. They were to attend to these responsibilities in fulfillment of their obligation to ensure the rule of the *shari`a* in the territories under their control—an obligation that alone legitimized their rule. They did so under the watchful eyes of the `ulama', and in cooperation with some of them. It is important to remember that the `ulama' very rarely acted as a concerted group. They were hardly a group in the sociological meaning of the term. Usually it was the expertise in the *shari`a* of the individual `alim, not his membership in a specific group, that gave him the authority and the backing of the *umma* to speak up in defense of Islamic norms and social values against rulers who deviated from these norms.

As early as the classical period, rulers were granted extra-*shar`i* authority to take political and administrative considerations into account in their pursuance of the interests of the Islamic community. However, one important reservation was attached to the ruler's discretion: his actions could in no way be in blatant contradiction of the substantive principles of the shari'a.[26] Rules and regulations promulgated by rulers in this capacity were considered ad hoc measures. They were binding in the territory under the particular ruler's con-trol but usually did not assume normative character. Since they were not con-sidered an integral part of the shari'a, they are almost totally absent from the legal literature (fatwas, furu').

How did this modus vivendi work in practice? Endowments serving gen-eral public and charitable purposes belonged in the realm of huquq Allah.[27] The modus vivendi therefore applied in their case. In pursuance of their extra-shar'i prerogatives, rulers asssumed direct or indirect responsibility for the administration of many of the largest and richest public foundations. Also, in a number of cases they allowed for the diversion of some of the income of these rich foundations to purposes other than those designated by the founders of the endowments. Sometimes this deviation from the strict letter of waqf law led to outright abuse of endowed property; but this was not the rule. Usually, the money diverted from its original purpose helped rationalize the manage-ment of foundations in general, by providing the means necessary for costly periodic restoration work in major mosques, expenses that could not have been met solely from the annual income of these mosques. In other cases, sums were spent on distributing charity to the needy or on furthering other general interests of the Islamic community.[28] Although a deviation from the strict letter of waqf laws, spending money to meet these needs was very much in line with waqf ideology and has never, as far as I know, met with objections or criticism from the 'ulama'.

In all other matters the rich foundations controlled by the ruling author-ities remained within the jurisdiction of the 'ulama'. The assets making up their patrimonies never lost their waqf status, which meant that all these properties were non-negotiable in principle and subject to the laws of waqf. The interpretation of these laws and their implementation remained in the hands of the specialists—the 'ulama'—not the ruler. Instances of rulers who blatantly violated waqf property or manipulated waqf rules in cooperation with some qadis are recorded in the literature.[29] The fact is, however, that the supreme authority of waqf laws has never in premodern times been questioned outright or even tampered with. The above modus vivendi was thus main-tained for centuries in principle and to a very large extent also in practice.

The picture that emerges from the above discussion is that of rulers responsible for the organization and daily functioning of the public sphere but devoid of authority to determine the basic values governing many of its aspects. The norms, the ideals of good order, and the basic rules expressing them were laid down in the shari'a and left to the interpretation of the 'ulama'. The legitimization of the ruler depended on his observation of these rules, and the umma, usually through the intermediacy of the specialists, had the right and the obligation to supervise the manner in which he fulfilled his obligation. In other words, the community of believers had built-in claims on its rulers concerning the nature of the public sphere. If the protection against arbitrary acts by rulers was the main purpose of the chartered rights granted in Western civilization to various corporative organizations, the commitment of the Islamic ruler to uphold the *shari`a* had a much broader significance. It implied an obligation on the part of the ruler to make sure that the public sphere in the territory under his control was construed in conformity with the basic moral norms and values of Islam, and that the law was administered according to the specific rules of the *shari`a*. The ruler's adherence to these norms and rules was the touchstone of his relations with the community under his control.

THE DYNAMICS OF CHANGE

In terms of the above-mentioned modus vivendi the `*ulama*' were entrusted with the mission of preserving and protecting the Islamic norms embedded in the *waqf* institution and embodied in the detailed and intricate laws of the *waqf*. This, however, did not mean that these laws remained unchanged throughout the centuries. Research in the past few years has largly dealt the coup de grâce to the notion that dominated the literature for a long time—to the effect that Islamic law was unchanging and immutable. This notion is certainly unacceptable concerning the Islamic endowment institution, with its obvious practical economic and social implications and with a record of survival over many centuries and throughout a vast cultural area.

Some of the basic questions relevant to any discussion of the dynamics of change in the domain of Islamic law concern the nature of change, the mechanisms used, and the people responsible for its introduction. The subject certainly deserves more detailed study.[30] Only a few points can be raised here. I shall concentrate on the role played in the process of change by the rulers on the one hand and custom (`*urf*, *ta`aruf*, *ta`amul*) on the other. I believe that these two aspects of the dynamics of Islamic law have particular relevance to our understanding of the nature of the discourse between rulers, `*ulama*', and the general public.

The need to take into consideration social and economic realities was the principal incentive for the introduction of change in laws in general and in those regulating the *waqf* in particular. Generally speaking, this was done by allowing a flexible interpretation of operative details while taking great care to preserve the basic principles or norms underlying the law.

Actual change, adopted and approved by the *shari`a* court—with or without prior consultation with a *mufti*[31]—usually preceded its legal formulation and adoption as a rule binding on all adherents of the school of law. The latter was a lengthy process, during which `*ulama*' from all over the Islamic world expressed their learned opinion on the subject until, at a point that is difficult to determine, a change was accepted as "the preferred view" (al-rajih) or "the sounder view" (al-asahh al-mukhtar) of a particular school of law.[32] The participation of rulers in these scholarly discussions seems to have been extremely rare.[33] I have not come across a single case in which the ruler actually initiated a change in a basic waqf law. However, intervention by a ruler was sometimes called for in order to clinch an issue that had given rise to a lengthy and indeterminate debate among the `ulama'. It was thus that in 951/1544–1545, following a long debate of the issue by the specialists, the Ottoman sultan Sulayman I Kanuni (r. 1520–1566), at the obvious instigation of the chief mufti, issued an order limiting substantially the scope of exchange transactions in endowed properties.[34]

The history of cash endowments is another, better-known case in point, combining custom, a learned debate by the `ulama', and a decision by the ruler. Cash endowments appeared in the Ottoman Empire as early as the first decades of the fifteenth century.[35] Although the endowment of cash money is problematic in many ways from the point of view of the shari`a, it became a custom or, as Mandaville put it, "it seems to have been an indigenous product of the flexible Ottoman judiciary."[36] When, in the course of the first half of the sixteenth century, cash waqfs became the dominant mode of endowment, they gave rise to a vehement debate among the `ulama', which soon spread to broader circles of the Ottoman public. The debate was settled by an imperial order, issued to all qadis of the empire, to approve endowments of cash. Some points in this story are relevant to our discussion. First, it helps us gauge correctly the role of the ruler in this process. The sultan was not actually involved in the learned debate and did not express his opinion on the points of law. His decision in the form of an imperial decree to the qadis of the empire was needed in order to clinch a lengthy discussion, put an end to the confusion it caused, and ensure uniformity of adjudication on the issue in the territories under his rule.[37] Second, the case of cash endowments demonstrates the great influence of custom and public opinion on the process of change. In his decision, the sultan was certainly influenced by his chief mufti—the famous Ebu Suud (d. 1574)—who, in addition to a fatwa he issued, composed a long treatise on the subject, which Mandaville summarizes as "an appeal to continued popular usage (ta`amul, ta`aruf), to the welfare of the people (istihsan), and to both throughout with a tone of 'Let's be practical,' an appeal to common sense."[38] However, one may assume that the voice of the people carried no less weight with the sultan. This was typically expressed by a scholar who did not belong to the official `ulama' hierarchy. Bali Baba was a representative of a settler family in Sofya, where he built a Sufi (mystic) lodge, became the leader of the Halveti Order, and was known for his scholarship and sanctity. He wrote a letter to the sultan describing the confusion resulting from the conflicting views on the subject of cash endowments and supplicating him to issue an order that would cut throught the doubts. Dwelling on the actual consequences the annulment of thousands of cash *waqfs* would have on the practice of religion, on welfare, on education, and on other vital interests of the community of believers, he explained, quoting famous `ulama', that "God's legislation has no other purpose than to ease the way of His servants through the exigencies of the times. Some rules of the sharia are overturned by changes through time, out of necessity and to ease difficulties." On these grounds Baba Bali pleaded with the sultan to decide for the admissibility of cash endowments "because it better suited the conditions of the people of our time."[39] Long-established custom and the interests of the community thus carried the day and brought about what obviously was a substantive change in the law of *waqf*.

Change in a particular stipulation of the law was not necessarily applicable in the entire Islamic cultural area. The `ulama' distinguish between two types of custom: general custom, applicable in all parts of the Islamic world, and local custom, applicable only in a specific region.[40] Indeed, many changes in *waqf* laws had a distinctive local coloring.[41] Thus, we know of a large number of long-term or permanent leases of endowed properties within the same school of law. These arrangements differ in detail from one another, have different names in different regions of the Islamic world, and represent local custom.[42] We know little of how such customs came into being. There can be little doubt, however, that their purpose was to provide solutions to existing local problems and their conflict with stipulations of the law. It seems reasonable to assume that the local population actually affected by the situation induced many of these changes. It is hard to determine whether the local community merely exerted informal pressure or actually petitioned for a specific change. It certainly expected its leaders—`ulama' and/or rulers—to come up with solutions in response to its changing needs. Whatever the case might have been, the local solution was the product of a joint endeavor by the local population demanding a change, some `ulama' formulating the change, and the local ruling authorities endorsing the new ruling.

The need to introduce changes in the law thus often gave rise to a discourse in which the `ulama' played an important role but which involved both the community and the rulers. This discourse was based on the recognized need for a change. No less important, for all participants in this discourse the only conceivable change was such as would conform to the rules of the *shari`a* and be approved by its protectors—that is, one that remained within the framework of the Islamic norms and values that all of them shared.

THE IMPACT OF THE WAQF ON THE PUBLIC SPHERE

The second part of the discussion will focus on three main subjects: the impact of endowments on the formation of the urban public space; their contribution to the crystallization of autonomous groups within the *umma*; and the nature of discourse between the rulers, the `ulama'*, and the community generated by endowments.[43]

THE URBAN PUBLIC SPACE

The *waqf*'s contribution to the shaping of the urban public space can hardly be overestimated. A major part of the public environment in towns actually came into being as a result of endowments. This was true for new cities as well as for those parts of existing towns that developed under Islamic rule. Mosques, *madrasas*, *zawiyas*, caravanserais, as well as the town's water supply systems, etc., were built as endowments. No less important, the building of a mosque or *madrasa* was often accompanied by the construction of large parts of the town's economic infrastructure, particularly shops and sometimes even whole markets, which were part of the endowment and whose rentals were intended to finance the salaries of the mosque's or *madrasa*'s staff, the daily functioning of the institution, and the cost of maintenance, repairs, etc. In other cases already existing immovables of all sorts (usually located in the neighborhood of the mosque) were acquired by the founder of the mosque and endowed for these purposes.[44] Indeed, one can hardly imagine the public space of any large town in the Islamic cultural area without these contributions based on endowments.

THE CRYSTALLIZATION OF AUTONOMOUS GROUPS

The *waqf* also served as a vehicle for the crystallization of various autonomous groups in the space between the private individual and the ruling authority. The broad definition of charity, enabling the endower to select a particular public segment of his choice as beneficiary of his endowment, made this possible. On many occasions endowers selected as public beneficiaries of their endowments not a general Islamic purpose but a more limited one to which they felt personally attached, such as a specific school of law, a *zawiya*, a Sufi order, a professional guild, the inhabitants of a particular neighborhood, the *ashraf* (descendants of the Prophet), groups of common origin such as the Andalusians in Algiers, etc. The *waqf* thereby withdrew from the ruler's influence properties that served to finance the independent interests of various groups within the community. These endowments were usually administered by the head of the group: the guild's leader (*amin*), the leader in the town of the descendants of the Prophet (*naqib al-ashraf*), or a resident of a neighborhood chosen by its inhabitants. The income from the endowments served to finance charity within the group, help needy members with payment of their taxes, assist in organizing and financing social activities, maintain places of worship and meeting for the members of the group, such as neighborhood *zawiyas* or mosques.[45] In other words, the *waqf* served as a vehicle whereby a given common identity, based on common origin, profession, or residence, was enhanced and assumed the nature of an autonomous social group, keen on protecting and advancing the particular interests of its members and thus an influential factor in the public sphere.

In much the same way endowments served to enhance the social standing of notable families—the *a'yan*—who, through endowments, succeeded in drawing into the orbit of their influence a large number of clients, thus ensuring the longevity of the family's influence in the town. This was done by establishing *waqfs* for public purposes—for example, a mosque or a *zawiya*—and securing their administration for generations to come to a member of the family, who, by the terms of the endowment deed, was given the responsibility to appoint the personnel, decide their salaries, etc.[46] Similar aims were achieved by creating endowments known as *khayriyya khassa*. Particularly important in this category were endowments providing resources to finance the activities of the family's guest house. These guest houses served for social gatherings, especially the celebration of religious holidays, which were usually accompanied by preaching, prayers, and sometimes *dhikrs* (collective Sufi litanies). On these occasions food and even some clothes were handed out to large numbers of people, and the officiating preachers, teachers, etc., were each rewarded for their services, the endowment deed specifying the sums to be spent on each item.[47] Endowments of this nature were one of the important tools whereby local families secured themselves a power base independent of the ruling authorities, a leading position within the local community, and the necessary backing to stand up to the rulers in protection of the community's interests.

The *waqf* thus played an important role in turning the amorphous *umma* into a society composed of autonomous interest groups that, although they never acquired the status of legal entities, exercised much influence in the public sphere. The *waqf* also fostered the development of an autonomous leadership that could and often did speak up for the local population. Indeed, the distribution of endowments among the various public purposes in a given town reflected its social fabric and the special character of the local *umma*, as well as the relative social importance attached to neighborhoods, professional guilds, schools of laws, or groups of origin. Examination of endowments for various public purposes in a given town over time can reveal changes in the relative importance of disparate groups in the population. It can also help identify the local leading families and indicate changes in their social standing in the town.

THE RELATIONS BETWEEN RULERS, `ULAMA', AND COMMUNITY

I shall focus on three aspects of these relations: the bond between rulers and the community created by endowments made by rulers; the discourse generated by the proliferation of endowments; and the involvement of the `ulama' and the community in the administration of large public foundations.

Many of the largest public foundations all over the Islamic world were endowed by rulers, their immediate entourages, and senior members of the ruling elite. They served a variety of political and social purposes, including promotion of the colonization and Islamization of conquered territories and the establishment and maintenance of such public services as welfare, social, religious, educational, and general municipal services. They were often used as instruments of public policy and helped enhance the ruler's power and prestige.[48] As in the case of gift relationships in other civilizations, endowments by rulers also served to establish bonds between the ruling authority and the general population, based on appreciation and gratitude, and generating a measure of loyalty on the part of the beneficient population. Considering that the same purposes could have been attained by simple "gifts"—that is, by allocations out of the state's resources controlled by the rulers—the fact that in the cultural area we are concerned with these "gifts" were given in the form of individual *waqfs* had, I believe, a particular significance: They symbolized the adherence of the endowing ruler to the norms of good order inherent in the ideology of the Islamic endowment. Thus, while the solidarity the ruler strove to create by the "bread and circuses" évergétism was described by Veyne as a wish by the ruler "to offer symbolic proof that they [the rulers] were in the service of the ruled,"[49] the *waqfs* endowed by rulers in the Islamic cultural area established a much more significant bond of shared norms and moral values between rulers and their subjects. The irreversibility of the act of endowing one's property and the basic notion of the *waqf* as an eternal charity conferred upon this moral bond an element of permanence and continuity. Also, above and beyond a certain feeling of gratitude generated by the "bread and circuses" évergétism, the message of shared values, or the message of a shared "lifeworld" of Islam projected by rulers' endowments, generated a public opinion that approved of, even legitimized, the rule of the endowing ruler.

The proliferation of endowments brought about a situation where not only public buildings but also a large proportion of the real estate in towns and in many cases in the rural areas as well, acquired *waqf* status. This meant that the laws of the endowment institution determined major issues relevant to the urban economy—such as the nature and details of the leasing arrangements of principal parts of the urban properties. Moreover, important issues concerning the town's development—for example, the need to recycle properties in order to provide the space necessary to accommodate new economic enterprises, for the extension of the town's water system, for population increases, and the like—often necessitated transactions in endowed properties, which were subject to *waqf* rules. This implied that all these issues were determined independently of the rulers' wishes. They were handled by the `ulama', who alone were in charge of interpreting the law and determining how it would be implemented. Because of its impact on the town's economy and development, and its influence on the daily life of the local population, the *waqf* thus generated an ongoing discourse involving the local community, the `ulama', and the rulers. I have already alluded to the nature of this discourse and the role of each of the participants in bringing about important changes in waqf laws.[50] Details concerning the regular leases of endowed properties, the type of local long-term leases, as well as local policies geared to either limiting the scope of such leases, and also of exchange transactions, or allowing for their proliferation, were often determined to suit local social and economic circumstances and were the result of a similar discourse. It was thus that specific local circumstances in Ottoman Algiers brought about changes of policy concerning regular leases as well as long-term and exchange transactions of endowed property. Pressure from below, a dynamic approach of the `ulama' toward the interpretation of waqf laws, and the rulers' cooperation combined to bring about solutions whereby the letter of the law was made to coexist with the requirements of real life. Although these solutions allowed for a relaxation of some of the rules of the endowment institution, they did not clash head-on with its basic rules. Moreover, while accommodating the needs of the town and its inhabitants, special care was taken to protect the financial interests of the waqf.[51]

The administration of public foundations generated a lively discourse in the public sphere. Many of these foundations, which served the entire local population or catered to general Islamic purposes—for instance, the holy places of Islam—were made up, wholly or principally, of endowments by rulers and their entourages. In other cases their patrimony comprised a large number of private endowments that reached their final khayri stage after the demise of their primary and intermediary beneficiaries.[52] All such endowments whose khayri beneficiary was the same—e.g., the holy places of Islam—were lumped together and administered jointly. The ruling authorities had an obvious interest in these large agglomerations of properties, which produced a very considerable income. They therefore kept either direct or indirect control of their administration.[53] However, once endowed, the property no longer belonged to the founder, but, according to the prevailing view of the Hanafi school of law, to God. The ruling authorities thus controlled these public foundations, including those endowed by rulers, not as owners but in their capacity as guardians of the interests of the umma. As in other matters of public interest, the responsibility of rulers in the case of these foundations was considered part of their basic duties to ensure observation of the shari`a, the norms of social order proper to the community of believers, and the furthering of the general interests of the umma in the territories under their control.

Obviously, the local community had a vested interest in the way the rulers carried out their duties concerning the waqf. Some of its members— mainly `ulama' but also the many others who provided the various services a mosque or a madrasa required—were employed in the establishments maintained by waqfs and depended on them for their salaries. The poor and the needy for their part depended on public foundations that provided charity, clothes, and food. The religious and municipal services maintained by public foundations were of direct concern to the entire urban population. Last but not least, the general attitude displayed by the ruling authorities toward the public endowments they administered indicated to the local population the way the *waqfs* they themselves had established, or were likely to establish in the future, would be treated.

In concrete terms, the local community expected the rulers to make sure that the *waqf* status of endowed properties was honored—that is, to protect the properties from such arbitrary acts as confiscation or embezzlement by officeholders or abuse by those who wielded power; to ensure the regular distribution of public foundation income among the legal beneficiaries (e.g., salaries to the servants of the foundation, distribution of charity or food to the poor); and to see to it that *ahli* endowments arrived at their ultimate destination. Rulers were also expected to see to the periodic repair and renovation of major establishments maintained by endowments whose cost involved sums over and above the income produced by their patrimony. As a matter of course the ruler was expected to contribute his share to the community by making his own endowments and encouraging his household and entourage to do the same.

As special guardians of the *shari`a*, `*ulama'* had the important task of keeping a watchful eye on the way rulers discharged these duties. Indeed, there are many examples of initiatives taken by `*ulama'* and of their cooperation with the ruling authorities to introduce measures geared to protecting the interests of public foundations. Followup on the line of private beneficiaries of *ahli* endowments and ensuring that upon their extinction the endowed property entered the patrimony of the public foundation designated by the founder was certainly one of the thorniest problems facing many charitable foundations. It could hardly have been handled without the *qadis'* cooperation. One of the earliest reports mentioning this problem dates from the eighth century. Kindi (d. 350/961) tells us that in 118/736 the *qadi* of Cairo, Tawba b. Nimr realized that many endowments were being usurped and passed on as regular inheritances. Since the ultimate beneficiaries of these endowments were to be the poor and the destitute (not the heirs of the founder), the *qadi* decided to take these endowments under his wing so as to protect them from usurpers.[54] Measures designed to meet this difficulty were undertaken by various rulers before the nineteenth century. One example, reported in some detail in the sources, is that of the reforms carried out in Algiers toward the end of the seventeenth or beginning of the eighteenth century[55] and in Constantine in 1776.[56] The rulers, in concert with the local `*ulama'*, issued orders to prepare special registers that would include all public foundations supported by endowments. Alongside the name of each foundation were to be listed all endowment deeds made in its favor, particularly those in which the foundation appeared as ultimate beneficiary. The document produced as a result of these orders was known as "the *waqfiyya* of Algiers," and served as an efficient tool in enabling Algerian public foundations to carry out the necessary followup on *ahli* endowments. In addition to this immediate aim, the very initiative as well as the efforts involved in preparing the document served a broader aim: to signal to the local population that its rulers were intent on protecting endowed assets in general. Indeed, this initiative played an important role in the substantial rise in the rate of endowments in Ottoman Algiers in the ensuing period.[57]

Qadis in the Ottoman Empire were assigned specific duties concerning public foundations. They were ordered to keep an eye on the administrators of such foundations and to audit the financial statements the administrators appointed by Istanbul were obliged to prepare annually. Qadis were also required to assist in the preparatory work preceding major repair and maintenance work on *waqf* property, on which the Ottoman center decided from time to time.[58]

The local population was sometimes directly involved in the administration of public foundations. This was the case in Ottoman Algiers, where for a long time the administration of the largest of all public foundations in the town—the Waqf al-Haramayn—was entrusted to a governing body of four, including two representatives of the local population.[59] In other instances, the local population exercised a more informal supervision over the administration of public foundations. An example that reports in some detail the manner in which such an informal supervision was carried out in Jerusalem at the end of the eighteenth century is given by Peri. In a number of cases beneficiaries of the two largest public foundations in Jerusalem complained to the ruler of improper management; the complaints attest to the detailed acquaintance of the petitioners with the foundation's situation and their close watch over the administrators.[60] Given the stake members of the local population had in the proper working of public foundations, one is justified, I believe, in assuming that such informal supervision was not confined to Jerusalem but was in fact carried out in other places and periods as well.

In extreme cases of outright violation of public *waqfs* by rulers—involving the diversion of income from their charitable or educational purposes, or the withholding of salaries, stipends, and food rations from `ulama' and students—the local population, led by the `ulama', reacted with violent outbursts, riots, and outright revolt and instigation against the rulers.[61] As in the case of the "moral economy," these riots should not be seen as merely spasmodic outbursts motivated by economic plight. Thompson's interpretation of the food riots in eighteenth-century England as an expression of grievances operating within a popular consensus based on moral and social norms as to what were or were not legitimate economic practices,[62] applies in our case as well. The norms in our case were those of the *shari`a* in general and *waqf* laws in particular, which enjoyed a high measure of consensus among the population and thus helped mobilize large proportions of the Cairene population to side with those directly affected by the ruler's violation of these norms, which were considered an integral part of the ruler's "contract" with the community.

The endowment system also made it possible for the community to express its criticism by means of exit rather than voice.[63] The local population's rate of endowment for public institutions, and particularly for foundations catering to general Islamic concerns—such as the poor of the holy places of Islam—was an important criterion by which the prestige of the town and its rulers were judged by the general Islamic community. Refraining from creating new endowments or keeping their rate at a low level reflected unfavorably on the ruler's renown and thus provided the local community with an effective means of expressing its distrust of the ruler's performance of his duties toward the community and its general discontent with the ruling system. A fairly high level of endowments by the local population, on the other hand, implied general confidence of the public in the rulers' intentions and ability to protect their *waqfs* and abide by Islamic norms of proper public order.[64] The proportion of endowments by a local population over a period was thus an excellent indicator of the kind of relationship between a local community and its rulers and the existence or absence of discourse between them.

Thus, although the local *umma* was an uninstitutionalized body with no voting rights, it had a variety of informal but efficient ways to claim what it considered its rights.

CONCLUSION

Perhaps the most important difference between the Western civil society model and the public sphere in pre-nineteenth-century Islamic societies was the informality of the latter. While the discourse between ruler and society in the West was based on a formal relationship rooted in the well-defined rights of autonomous groups, the discourse in the public sphere in the Islamic cultural area was based on informal understandings rooted in the basic adherence of all to common moral values and social norms.

Study of the *waqf* reveals a very lively public sphere, involving rulers, governors, and senior officials, side by side with all strata of the Muslim community—rich and poor, male and female—all of them participating in the creation and improvement of the public space. Indeed, through the *waqf* all elements of society, including its rulers, were mobilized in the service of the *umma*—that is, in the service of implementing the Islamic conception of the public sphere, which focused on the community of believers and the norms appropriate to its social order.

The broad definition of charity—that is, of what constitutes a legitimate beneficiary of endowments—allowed for the use of *waqf* to sustain a great variety of recipients, from family members to a plethora of institutions serving the entire community. It also helped crystallize interest groups in the space between the household and the ruling authorities, thus creating arenas of the public sphere independent from the official sphere.

The rules governing the endowment institution, combined with the proliferation of endowments, their predominance in the public space and their social and economic importance, actually deprived rulers of the exclusive prerogative to decide on a large number of issues concerning the interests of the community, and triggered a continuous discourse with the community, and its representatives concerning the administration and policies of major issues in the public sphere. This discourse had its own dynamic, instigated by the practical economic and social implications of the *waqf* and determined by a joint effort of the community, the `ulama'`, and the rulers.

The *waqf* thus served as an important integrative institution holding together the society and its rulers. Rather than separation and estrangement, it established a strong bond of shared values, common cultural symbols, and common language between rulers and society. The participation of rulers in the creation of endowments symbolized the bond of values shared with the society under their rule and conferred a measure of legitimacy on the rulers. Moreover, the many public foundations created by rulers and their entourages obviously refute the thesis that rulers were careless of the public, its needs, and its well-being.

NOTES

1. Turner 1984, 39.

2. Ibid., 40. On the "Oriental despotism" thesis see also Springborg 1987, esp. 414–31; 1992, esp. 18–20.

3. Ibid.; For more recent summaries of this point, connecting it to the question of democracy, see Lindholm 1996, esp. 338–48; Sadowski 1997; Eickelman 1996, esp. x–xi.

4. E.g., Lambton 1981; Vatikiotis 1987; Lapidus 1996; Lindholm 1996 and further literature there. See also Sadowski 1997 for a criticism of the research on this topic.

5. Somers 1995, esp. 123–27; Calhoun 1993, esp. 269.

6. These have been particularly emphasized and developed by political anthropology and the new cultural history. See Hann and Dunn 1996; Hunt 1989.

7. Hodgson 1974, vol. 2, 119.

8. Ibid., vol. 2, 124.

9. As to the difficulty of rendering the term *shari`a* into English, see ibid., vol. 1, 334, n. 1. For a more detailed definition see below.

10. Mottahedeh 1980, 7.

11. See, e.g., Lambton *EI²* and bibliography there.

12. Calder *EI²*.

13. For the basic rules governing the *waqf* see Heffening *EI*.

14. See, e.g., Inalcik 1973, 148; Gerber 1983, 38–39.

15. Hodgson 1974, vol. 2, 346–47.

16. The same idea was reflected in the idea of the *hisba* – see Cahen and Talbi, *EI²*.

17. See Schacht 1953, 443–52; Heffening *EI*; Cahen 1961, 44–45, 56.

18. E.g., al-Kasani (d. 585/1189) 1910, vol. 4, 221. The idea, as well as the terms *sadaqa jariya* or *sadaqa mawqufa* appear in virtually every treatise on the *waqf*. See, e.g., al-Shaybani (al-Khassaf) (d. 261/875) 1904, *passim*.

19. On the notion of *qurba* see Anderson 1951b, 292–99.

20. Hodgson 1974, vol. 2, 345–46.

21. See Pruett 1984, whose article revolves around the idea that "for the Muslim, Islam is the command to submit to Allah in every aspect of his life," and a critique of the Orientalist who "has dismissed this fundamental consideration from his reading of Islam. That is to say, he fails to see the transcendent truth and good in the Muslim tradition and thinks of it as a cultural artifact only" (44).

22. See Baer 1981; Hoexter 1987. A comparison of the meaning of charity in Islam and in other cultures awaits serious study and is beyond the scope of this paper. For some beginnings in addressing this comparative aspect see, e.g., Jones 1980.

23. See, e.g., Johansen 1981, 298, quoting Kasani; Heyd 1973, 204–7, 209, quoting Mawardi; Inalcik *EI²*.

24. Sometimes a third category of rights, *haqq al-saltana* (the right of the state) is mentioned in the sources. It certainly did not grant the ruler or the state any intrinsic rights of their own. What it did was to grant the ruler the right to prescribe extra-*shar'i* punishments, in protection of the rights of society. As Heyd shows, in the object of punishment and its general thrust, *haqq al-saltana* was rather similar to *haqq Allah*, both being identified with the rights of the Islamic community and the public interest. See Heyd 1973, 204–7. For further details see below.

25. Crone and Hinds 1986, esp. 80–97, place the victory of the `ulama' and the rejection of caliphal guidance in spiritual matters in the `Abbasid period, and its formal acknowledgment in the period after the *mihna* in 234/848. See also Hurvitz, this volume.

26. On *siyasa shar'iyya* see Coulson 1964, 129–30,172; 1957, 51. The most comprehensive exposition of the doctrine is Heyd 1973, 198–207. For the dating of the process whereby *siyasa* was incorporated in the *shari'a* see Johansen 1979, 54–61; 1981, 302.

27. For the combination of *huquq Allah* and *huquq al-`ibad* in the *waqf* institution see Hoexter 1995. This paragraph is based on ibid.

28. On this subject see Hoexter 1998a, chapter 6.

29. See e.g. Hoexter 1997, esp. 322 and n. 10. Despite instances of corruption among them, the `ulama' as a reference group were never discredited to the point of actually losing their role as transmitters and interpreters of the norms of the proper social order.

30. On the mechanisms of change see, e.g., Johansen 1993b; Hallaq 1994; Gerber 1998.

31. On the role of the *muftis* see, e.g., Hallaq 1994; Powers 1990; Masud, Messick, and Powers 1996a. In some places, e.g., Ottoman Algiers, a formal institution— the *majlis `ilmi*, composed of the Hanafi and Maliki *qadis* and the *muftis* of the two

schools of law—was set up to deal with major or difficult points of law—see Hoexter 1984, 256–58.

32. On *tarjih* and *tashih* see Hallaq 1994, 51–53. See also n. 30, above.

33. This, as well as the basic division of responsibilities between rulers and `ulama'` discussed above, held true except in cases in which a ruler claimed special spiritual powers—i.e., declared himself a *mahdi*—a divinely guided ruler who would restore Islam to its original perfection.

34. Horster 1935, 42–43; Ibn `Abidin (d. 1252/1836) 1966, vol. 4, 388–89.

35. The history of cash endowments is dealt with in detail in Mandaville 1979. What follows is based on this article.

36. Ibid., 290, n. 3.

37. See Heyd 1973, 185–87.

38. Mandaville 1979, 298.

39. On Baba Bali and his views as quoted above see ibid., 301–4.

40. On `urf` see Libson 1997; Ibn `Abidin (d. 1252/1836) 1883–1884; Johansen 1993a.

41. For the opposition in Syria to a number of changes introduced by the Ottomans, on the grounds of these changes being based on local custom prevalent in Anatolia and Rumeli but not in Syria see Rafeq 1994.

42. For a short description of the various leases see Baer *EI²*.

43. Many of the examples cited in this part are taken from the Ottoman Empire. I believe, however, that the general conclusions hold true for other periods and regions of the premodern Islamic world as well.

44. Actually, quite a number of urban studies, particularly in the past few decades, are mainly based on *waqf* documents. For some of the more recent studies pertaining to the subject under discussion see Hoexter 1998b, 482, n. 25.

45. For further details, examples, and literature on endowments for these purposes see Baer 1997, 279–85, 288, 291–97; Hoexter 1998b, 481, n. 22.

46. For further details, examples, and bibliography see Baer 1997, 265–69; Hoexter 1998b, 481, n. 22. On endowments, particularly for *madrasas* by the patrician class in Iran see Arjomand 1998; 1999 and further bibliography there.

47. For further details, examples, and bibliography see Baer 1997, 273–75.

48. For further details and literature see Hoexter 1998b, 476–77, nn. 6, 7, 8. For the use of endowments as an instrument of public policy see Arjomand 1998.

49. Veyne 1990, 418.

50. See above.

51. For further details see Hoexter 1998a, chapter 5.

52. Contrary to what has been the accepted wisdom, *ahli* endowments reached their *khayri* stage quite often and within a relatively short span of time. See ibid., esp. 90–91; Baer 1983, 21–22; Ben Achour 1992, 61; Yerasimos 1994, 45.

53. For details see Hoexter 1995.

54. Kindi (d. 350/961) 1912, 346. See also Tyan 1960, 380 and n. 3.

55. The exact date is not clear. See Devoulx 1863, 104–5.

56. Féraud 1868, 121–25.

57. Hoexter 1998a, esp. 22–23, 83–86.

58. Peri 1983, 32–36; Gerber 1988, 164–66; Marcus 1979; 1989, 307.

59. See Hoexter 1998a, chapter 3.

60. Peri 1983, 42–45.

61. See Raymond 1973–1974, vol. 2, 794; Crecelius 1995, 257–58. Both relate to the eighteenth century—a particularly corrupt period in Egypt.

62. Thompson 1971.

63. On voice and exit see Hirschman 1970.

64. For an example of how this worked in Ottoman Algiers see Hoexter 1998a.

CHAPTER EIGHT

CONCLUDING REMARKS: PUBLIC SPHERE, CIVIL SOCIETY, AND POLITICAL DYNAMICS IN ISLAMIC SOCIETIES

SHMUEL N. EISENSTADT

I

The chapters collected in this volume were presented and discussed in a workshop that took place in Jerusalem at the Van Leer Jerusalem Institute. The workshop constituted part of a program on "Collective Identity, Public Sphere, and Political Order," under the auspices of the Van Leer Jerusalem Institute, the Swedish Collegium for Advanced Study in the Social Sciences in Uppsala, and the Max Weber Kolleg at Erfurt University, its major aim being to reexamine critically some of the basic assumptions of recent studies of the topic as they bear on the dynamics of different civilizations and contemporary societies.

II

Notions of civil society were proposed and elaborated in different European contexts in the course of the seventeenth and eighteenth centuries, especially within the intellectual tradition of what came to be termed the Scottish Enlightenment, but also earlier by such scholars as Pufendorf. However the revival of interest in this concept in contemporary social science has been largely and somewhat curiously limited to the rather particular conceptualization of civil society, formulated mainly by Hegel, in a continental European setting in the period of transition from absolutist monarchies to nations and states. This conceptualization certainly did not apply to other European societies, such as the Scandinavian countries, Holland, or even England, where, in the relations between "state" and "society," the influence of the latter on the former was much greater than in the German states or even in France.[1]

Whatever its strengths and limitations, the discourse on civil society was for a long period dormant in the social science literature—to be revived again only after the breakdown of the Soviet Empire and the promulgation of the concept of civil society as a norm for Middle and East European societal reconstruction. This revived discourse was connected with greater attention to the concept of "public spheres" in the period after World War II—a concept presented in Jürgen Habermas's *Structural Transformation of the Public Sphere*, a book that gained additional recognition in the contemporary discourse.[2] In this discourse, the concepts of public sphere and civil society tended to be coupled, overlapped, almost conflated, often without any clear distinction between them. Moreover, in this contemporary discourse a very strong assumption emerged that the development of a public sphere and a civil society constitutes a critical condition for the formation and continuity of constitutional and democratic regimes.[3]

The available historical and contemporary evidence shows these assumptions to be very problematic. First, the relations between civil society, public sphere, and the political arena are much more variable than is implied in these assumptions. The concept of a public sphere entails that there are at least two other spheres—the official sphere and the private sphere—from which the public sphere is more or less institutionally and culturally differentiated. It is, therefore, a sphere located *between* the official and the private spheres. It is a sphere where collective improvements, the common good, are at stake. This holds also for the official sphere; but in the public sphere such business is carried out by groups that do not belong to the ruler's domain. Rather, the public sphere draws its membership from the private sphere. It expands and shrinks according to shifting involvements of such membership, as Albert O. Hirschman has demonstrated with regard to modern development.[4]

The public sphere is the place of voice rather than of loyalty, to use Hirschman's famous distinction. Its strength depends on its institutional locus, whether it is dispersed or unified, whether it is close to the center or on the periphery. It is based on oral or written communication. Its influence rests on interpretations of the common good vis-à-vis the ruler on the one hand and the private sphere or spheres of different sectors of the society on the other.

The term *public sphere* therefore denotes the existence of arenas that are not only autonomous from the political order but are also public in the sense that they are accessible to different sectors of society. Public spheres are constructed through several basic processes—namely, those of framing, communicating, and institutionalizing. The first process is one of categorization; it defines a discourse beyond face-to-face interaction. The second process is one of reflexivity; it invites a debate on problems of the common good, on criteria of inclusion and exclusion, on the permeability of boundaries, and on the recognition of the "other." The third process stabilizes this sphere. Public spheres tend to develop dynamics of their own, which, while closely related to those of the political arena, are neither coterminous with nor governed by the dynamics of the latter. They develop in different ways in different societies, and they differ in their relations not only to the rulers but also to what has been often designated as civil society.

Hence, second, these two concepts—public sphere and civil society—should not be conflated. Public sphere must be regarded as a sphere between the official and the private. And it must be regarded as a sphere that expands and shrinks according to the constitution and strength of those sectors of society that are not part of the rulership. Civil society entails a public sphere, but not every public sphere entails a civil society, whether of the economic or political variety, as defined in the contemporary discourse, or as it developed in early modern Europe through direct participation in the political process of corporate bodies or a more or less restricted body of citizens in which private interests play a very important role. We do indeed expect that in every civilization of some complexity and literacy a public sphere will emerge, though not necessarily of the civil society type.[5]

Even this broad definition of the public sphere seems to be culturally bound, however. As Benjamin Schwartz once remarked in a rejoinder to Hannah Arendt's distinction between the public and the private, a number of important societies such as the Chinese "had long done quite well without any conception at all of the public as distinct from the private good."[6] And indeed, the notion of private interests as distinct from public interests—especially the idea that private interests could serve as a solid base for the pursuit of public interests—seems to be European. It is tied to a legal tradition that endows the individual with subjective rights and defines many associations as corporate bodies with legal rights, to an economic tradition that relies on the rational pursuit of self-interest; and it belongs to an institutional tradition that emphasizes the separation between state and civil society.

But whatever the differences with respect to the relations between public sphere, civil society, and the political arena, in all societies these relations have entailed continual contestation about power and authority, their legitimation and accountability.

In recognition of the very complex and variable relations among public sphere, civil society, and the political arena, one central focus of the program within whose framework the Jerusalem workshop was undertaken was, first, the reexamination of these concepts—especially, but not only, as they apply to non-Western societies; second, the ways in which the contestations about power and its legitimation have crystallized in different civilizations and shaped their dynamics; and third, a possible reassessment of the dynamics of Western societies themselves.

III

Such a critical appraisal of the concepts of public sphere and civil society as they developed in contemporary scholarship is closely related to the "Orientalist" debate—that is, criticism of the analysis, in Western and Western-inspired scholarship, of non-Western, especially Asian, societies.

Critics of so-called Orientalism, from Edward Said on, have shown that many of the analyses of "Oriental" (above all Asian) societies undertaken by Western and Western-inspired scholarship have imposed concepts and categories rooted in the cultural program of modernity that developed in the West.[7] In particular, the conceptions of world history implicit in such scholarship have viewed the modern nation state as the epitome of progress.

On the analytical level, this approach often entailed, as Talal Asad has shown, the transposition of certain concepts—for instance, "religion"—that were rooted in Western thought and in the distinct Western historical experience, to the analysis of non-Western societies, often giving rise to the misinterpretation of many crucial aspects of the latter.[8]

On the conceptual level, the imposition of these concepts on the analysis of "Oriental" societies was often connected with a view that depicted Asian societies as being a mixture of stagnation and Oriental despotism. Truly enough, this view of Asian societies was not the only one prevalent in modern European historiographical discourse. Indeed, a strong current in this discourse as it developed in the Enlightenment promulgated a very positive view of some of these societies (e.g., the Chinese) as exhibiting civilizing features not to be found in the West. Yet the negative "Orientalist" view of these societies has become predominant in large parts of Western, especially European, scholarship and in public discourse.[9] Many studies have been guided by the implicit—and often also explicit—assumption to be found already in Marx's discussion on the "Asian mode of production."[10] The assumption was that these civilizations, even when initially dynamic, became static, stagnant—one major manifestation of such stagnation being that "modernity," whether in the economic or in the political sphere, and rationality did not develop in them. In the case of Muslim societies, such decline was seen to have set in already early in the thirteenth century, with the victory of orthodoxy over the more open trends oriented to "Western" Greek philosophy.[11]

Concomitantly, many such societies—including most of the Muslim societies, especially Middle Eastern ones, as well as China—were often portrayed as epitomizing Oriental despotism; all power was seen as concentrated in the hands of the rulers, with the various sectors of society granted no autonomy beyond purely local affairs and even these affairs often tightly regulated by the great despots.[12]

IV

The critique of Orientalism gave rise, as is well known, to intensive discussion and controversy—with highly ideological overtones. It became closely connected with the many criticisms of the models—predominant in the social sciences of the 1950s and early 1960s—of the structural-framework approach, in particular studies of modernization.[13] One of the major foci of these criticisms was that no institutional or organizational setting was taken as "given," nor was the extent to which different parts or components thereof contributed to its continuity considered. Instead, the very construction of any such setting was seen as problematic—and as always taking place through continual power contestations and negotiations among the different actors, through which, to follow Gramsci's terminology, hegemonies were established.[14] These intensive discussions and controversies opened up the problem of the relations between agency and social structure and between social structure and culture.[15]

The criticism of Orientalism was indeed closely interrelated with general developments in the social sciences and humanities. Such criticism has shown that much of the research that was guided by "Orientalist" conceptions neglected many aspects of non-Western societies—especially those related to power contestations and the relations between power and culture, which are crucial for understanding their contours and dynamics. At the same time the researches that burgeoned in conjunction with these broad controversies highlighted the extent to which the crystallization of different hegemonies has influenced many aspects of social life, among them constructs of sexuality and gender, conceptions of the human body, or the shaping of collective memory and rituals of commemoration.[16]

Within the broad spectrum of such studies, two major lines of research developed that directly challenged what they perceived as the "Orientalist" assumption. One was the so-called subaltern studies,[17] developed first in India, which emphasized above all the continual development of different forms of opposition, or more accurately resistance, to the Western political and also intellectual hegemony, especially on different local levels. The other, more recent line of research, rooted far more than the subaltern studies in Western "postmodern" scholarship, criticized the emphasis on the modern nation-state as defined in Western terms as the model and the major unit of analysis, with the concomitant neglect of regional, occupational, gender, and other social sectors and networks.[18]

But interestingly enough, the critics of "Orientalist" scholarship did not take up the most important and potentially most constructive challenge opened up by the "Orientalist" debate—namely, how to account for the internal dynamics of these non-European modern civilizations in their own terms, possibly also putting them in a comparative framework that would not bestow a privileged position on the Western experience.

It is paradoxical that many of the studies of Asian societies criticizing the Orientalist approach in many ways accepted the assumption that in most of these societies, in some crucial period of their development, a process of stagnation had set in; that the impact of colonialization and imperialism had, at least partially, stifled their transformation into modern capitalist societies. One fascinating illustration of such an approach is the debate on the potentialities for capitalist development in seventeenth- to early nineteenth-century India, presumably stifled by British colonialism.[19]

Marshall Hodgson's ideas, as expressed in his *Venture of Islam* and some of his very incisive articles, many published posthumously, could have served as a starting point for going in such directions beyond the "Orientalist" debate had they been more fully developed by Hodgson himself before his untimely death. He had as yet taken only the very first steps in analyzing the Muslim societies, and their encounter with modernity, which of course later became the point of departure for much of "Orientalist" critique and scholarship.[20] Moreover, Hodgson was not followed, at least until quite recently, in the mainstream studies of Islamic societies, even if references to him abounded.

V

The failure of these studies to analyze the internal dynamics of Asian societies was possibly rooted in a certain analytical blindness or blockage connected with the general ideological ambience of the intellectual and academic discourse of the 1970s. The central analytical point of much of such discourse— possibly the point most emphasized in the Orientalist debate and certainly one that was greatly influenced by Foucault[21] and to a smaller extent by Gramsci[22]—was the close relation between power and culture; indeed, Foucault saw an almost complete identity between the two. Most of the criticism focused on the ways in which the cultural program of modernity was imposed on these societies through the exercise of power—especially colonial or imperial power. Yet, until recently, most of these studies did not address the problem of the extent to which the relation between power and culture developed in the dynamics of these civilizations prior to the impact of the West. They did not take up the problem of how relations between culture and power— and the challenges to the hegemonic relations and discourses that developed in these societies—differed from or were comparable to Western ones, much less how these relations and challenges differed among various non-Western societies.

With the interesting exception of some studies of early Mesoamerican societies,[23] an important outcome of this analytical blindness was the fact that these studies, with their strong emphasis either on subaltern resistance or on the autonomy of various social sectors (regional, professional, economic, gender), barely touch on a problem central to Weber's analysis. That problem relates to the various broad symbolic and institutional frameworks of these civilizations—whether of the Brahminic or Sanskritist or Confucian cosmopolis, or of the Islamic *umma*—and its dynamics. It is Sheldon Pollock's singular merit to be probably the first among the critics of Orientalism to raise this problem. In his central statement as well as his later work on the vernacular millennium, he pointed out the importance of the relations among the carriers of these broad frameworks and the various groups—especially various local political elites and groups—and the specific dynamics generated by these relations.[24] Further research would indicate how such dynamics—which included both resistance and a quest for autonomy, but also potential challenges to the legitimation of such hegemonies and patterns of power—crystallized in different societies.

It is interesting that most of these studies did not refer to Weber; and insofar as they did, they adopted that interpretation of Weber that tended to see him as a Eurocentric preoccupied with analyzing the origin of modern capitalism and demonstrating the superiority of the West.[25] They neglected the other side, or other reading, of his work—namely, the reading of the *Gesammelte Aufsätze zur Soziologie und Sozialpolitik* as studies of the internal dynamics of the various great civilizations in their own terms, with a special emphasis on the role of heterodoxies and sectarian movements in these dynamics.[26]

The comparison between Weber and Foucault is indeed of great interest from the point of view of our analysis. As is well known, Foucault and his followers focused on the ways in which the concrete institutional patterns, patterns of life, and basic conceptions of order have been shaped by the interweaving of culture in the exercise of power. The relation between power and knowledge is also a central focus of Weber's analysis in the *Gesammelte Aufsätze*—probably best illustrated in his analysis of the place of the Confucian literati in the construction of the Chinese imperial order. Needless to say, Foucault's own work—as well as the many more contemporary historical, sociological, and anthropological studies influenced in one way or another by Foucault—provides far more detail than can be found in Weber's analysis, even if many details of Foucault, especially his analysis, have recently been subjected to far-reaching criticism.[27]

This can perhaps be best seen in Foucault's reluctance to face two broad problems. There is the problem of agency and its place in the constitution of different social and political orders, different orders of power and culture. And there is the closely related problem of the historical roots of different orders, and of continuities or discontinuities between historical periods and the concomitant difficulty in explaining the possible place of resistance in the generation of processes of social change.

As T. B. Hansen has indicated, the term *parrhesia* is used by Foucault for the courageous act of disrupting dominant discourses, thereby opening a new space for another truth to emerge—not a discursive truth but rather a "truth of the self," an authentication of the courageous speaker in this "eruptive truth-speaking."[28] But while this term goes beyond the simple emphasis on resistance as simply due to the inconvenience of being confined within the coercive frameworks of an order, it does not systematically analyze the nature of the agency through which such other truth may emerge,[29] or how the emergence of such "truth of the self" may become interwoven with processes of social change and transformation.

In contrast to Foucault, Weber's analysis focused on the way in which institutional patterns are constructed by human agency as well as on the problems of continuity and discontinuity between different historical periods.[30] Weber did not conflate power and culture; he attempted to specify the distinct aspects or dimensions of culture. For instance, he tried to clarify how the basic ontological premises, conceptions of salvation, and the like prevalent in a society influence specific institutional patterns—such as the structure of rulership or configurations of strata—as well as the mechanism through which such influence is exerted. Second, he emphasized that the contours of such patterns constitute a continual focus of contention among various groups among which of special importance are the various heterodoxies that potentially develop and continually challenge the existing hegemonies. The strong emphasis on the importance of heterodoxies in crystallizing such challenges indicates that such challenges are influenced not only by pure "power" contestation but also by the basic premises of the different religions or systems of belief and knowledge that become hegemonic in their respective societies, and that such premises, especially when institutionalized, contain within them seeds of potential challenge—and transformation.[31]

VI

It is indeed with respect to analyzing the relation between culture and power that the analysis of public spheres is of central importance. Public spheres—and of course social movements, especially heterodoxies, sectarianisms, and collective identities (for example, those that crystallized in the vernacular age)—constituted the most important institutional arena in all these societies, for it was in this arena that the rulers, different elites, and various social groups in the centers and peripheries continually negotiated with, contested, and confronted one another about the definition of the common good, as well as about the legitimation and accountability of authorities and the concomitant possible challenges to the existing hegemonies..

But the concrete ways in which such negotiations or contestations develop differ greatly among different civilizations—attesting to the different ways in which power and culture are interwoven—and shape their distinct dynamics. Analyzing the dynamics of different societies may help in facing the challenge of how on the one hand to recognize the dynamics specific to particular civilizations, and on the other to confront the problem of the fruitfulness—and limits—of applying concepts developed in the Western social science discourse to the analysis of non-Western societies.

VII

The essays presented in this volume will hopefully help to resolve some of these problems and take up some of these challenges. To no small degree the chapters build on some of Hodgson's powerful insights and clearly indicate the inadequacy of the approaches that have promulgated the view of Muslim societies as stagnant and of their political regimes as epitomizing Oriental despotism. They clearly demonstrate, as Hoexter, Levtzion, and Eickelman succinctly indicate in their introduction and foreword, that there crystallized in Muslim society a very vibrant and autonomous public sphere that was of crucial importance in shaping the dynamics of Muslim societies.

This public sphere crystallized out of the interaction of the `ulama' (the interpreters of the religious sacred law), the shari`a (the religious law), various sectors of the broader community, and the rulers. The basic framework within which such interaction took place was that of the shari`a, which was the main overall framework of Islamic societies, the regulator of the moral and religious vision, the cohesive and boundary-setting force of Muslim communities.

In the words of Hoexter and Levtzion in their introduction:

> Umma and shari`a are central conceptions running through the discussion in virtually all the chapters included in the present volume. The umma—the community of believers—was accorded central importance in Islamic political thought. Not only were the protection and furthering of its interests the central concern of the ruler, the individual Muslim and the `ulama'; the umma's consensus (ijma`) on the legitimacy of the ruler as well as on details concerning the development of social and cultural norms was considered infallible. The community of believers was thus placed as the most significant group in the public sphere, and above the ruler. (see Miriam Hoexter).
>
> The shari`a—the sacred law, or the rules and regulations governing the lives of Muslims, derived in principal from the Qur'an and hadith—was developed by fuqaha' (jurists) and was basically an autonomous legal system, independent from the ruler's influence. Above and beyond a legal system, the shari`a embodied the values and norms of the social order proper to the community of believers and became its principal cultural symbol. The sacred nature of the shari`a is deeply entrenched in the public sentiment of Muslim societies. The sanction of the sacred law has contributed to the formation of a Muslim public opinion and endowed institutions and social groupings based on the shari`a—such as the qadi, the mufti, the schools of law (madhabib)—with a high degree of autonomy vis-à-vis the ruler. It has also accorded moral authority to the `ulama'—the shari`a specialists—who have asserted the position as authorized interpreters of the shari`a law and custodians of the moral values underlying the ideals of social order of the umma.

Among the many organizations that developed in Muslim societies, it was mainly in the schools of law, the waqf, and the different Sufi orders that reconstitution of the public sphere continually took place. As the essays presented here indicate, the relative importance and scope of these institutions did change in different historical settings and periods; but some combination of them seems to have existed in all cases. Many aspects of the institutional arenas constituting the public sphere varied in different societies and periods; though regulated by the ruler, they were yet autonomous and could exert far-reaching influence on the ruler—an influence that went far beyond simple subservience to official rule or attempts to evade it.

VIII

The overall pattern of the public sphere (or spheres) that developed in Muslim societies, the mode of interaction between the `ulama', the different sectors of society, and the rulers, was rooted in the basic premises and conceptions of Islam. The specific constellations, the concrete institutional arenas thereof, on the other hand, were shaped by the historical experience of the various Islamic societies.

Most important among the factors bearing on the construction of public spheres in Islam was the ideal of the *umma*—the community of all believers—as the major arena for the implementation of the moral and transcendental vision of Islam; the strong universalistic component in the definition of this Islamic community; and the closely connected emphasis on the principled political equality of all believers.

This pristine vision of the *umma*, probably implicit only in the very formative period of Islam, entailed a complete fusion of political and religious collectivities, the complete convergence or conflation of the sociopolitical and religious communities.[32] Indeed, the very conceptual distinction between these two dimensions, rooted as it is in the Western historical experience, is probably not entirely applicable to the concept of the *umma*.

In the implementation of these basic premises of Islamic vision, Islamic societies evinced, as Maxime Rodinson has put it,[33] the characteristics of a "totalitarian movement," as if it were a political party strongly oriented to the reconstruction of the world and very militant in this pursuit—albeit needless to say without having all the modern technological and administrative means of totalitarianism. Such implementation, however, was to be realized not in the establishment of one continual political regime but through the *shari`a*, the law, which from early on in Islamic history became the main framework of the overall moral and transcendental visions of Islam and the regulator of the modes of its implementation. It was only in the early phase of Islamic conquest and then in some of the "renovated" regimes to be discussed later that these "totalitarian"-like tendencies became predominant.

The emphasis on the construction of a political-religious collectivity was connected in Islam with the development of a principled ideological negation of any primordial element or component within this sacred political-religious identity. Indeed, of all the Axial Age civilizations in general, and the monotheistic ones in particular, Islam was, on the ideological level, the most extreme in its denial of the legitimacy of such primordial dimensions in the structure of the Islamic community—although de facto of course the story was often markedly different, as Bernard Lewis has shown.[34] In this it stood in opposition to Judaism, with which it shared such characteristics as an emphasis on the direct, unmediated access of all members of the community to the sacred. It differed, however, from Judaism in its basic conception of the relations between man and God, in the strong emphasis—as the name Islam connotes—on the total submission to God and in the lack of any possible contractual or covenantal relationship between God and the community of believers.[35]

Two primordial aspects have very forcefully persisted in very central areas of Islam: first, the strong emphasis, in the initial historical phase of Islam, then to a large extent in Shi`i Islam, and in its Moroccan version, on descent from the Prophet as a source of legitimation of rulers; second, the emphasis on Arabic as the sacred language of Islam, of the Qur'an, of prayer, and also to a large degree of the legal exegesis. This was in contrast to Judaism, where the Bible was read in Greek in Alexandria (and in English in many synagogues in the United States); and to Christianity, where the liturgy was naturally read in Greek (or other languages) in the East, and later on in Europe after the Reformation not only in Latin but in the various vernacular languages. But beyond these two primordial elements or emphases, there developed in Islam no sanctification of any "ethnic" primordial-communal elements or symbols, and it was the universalistic ideology of the *umma* that became predominant.

Yet from the very beginning of Islam's history strong tensions developed between these particularistic primordial Arab components, which were natural, as it were, to the initial carriers of the Islamic vision, and the universalistic orientation—tensions that became more important with the continual conquest and incorporation of new territorial entities and ethnic groups.[36] The final crystallization of this universalistic ideology took place with the so-called `Abbasid revolution.

Paradoxically, also in this period—indeed, in close relation to the institutionalization of this universalistic vision—there developed, especially within Sunni Islam, a de facto separation between the religious community and the rulers. This separation was partially legitimized by the religious leadership, and was continually reinforced, above all by the ongoing military and missionary expansion of Islam—an expansion far beyond the ability of any single regime to sustain. This separation between the religious and political elites involved, as M. Sharon has shown,[37] a shift in the legitimation of rulers in Sunni Islam (with the partial exception of some rulers such as for instance the Moroccan sultans) from direct descent from the Prophet to the consensus of the community and the rulers' ability to maintain their power.[38] Ultimately, any persons or groups able to seize power were accepted and post facto legitimated through the influence of the *khalifa*.

In the different Muslim regimes that developed under the combined impact of the continual expansion of Islam and the Mongol invasion, a separation took place between the *khalifa* and the actual ruler, the sultan, heralding de facto separation between the rulers and the religious establishment (`ulama'). The *khalifa* often became de facto powerless yet continued to serve as an ideal figure—the presumed embodiment of the pristine Islamic vision of the *umma*, and the major source of legitimation of the sultan—even if de facto he and the `ulama' legitimized any person or group that seized power. Such separation between the *khalifa* and the sultan was closely connected with the crystallization (in close relation to the mode of expansion of Islam, especially of Sunni Islam) of a unique type of ruling group—namely, the military-religious rulers, who emerged from tribal and sectarian elements. It also produced the system of military slavery, which created special channels of mobility—such as the *gulam* system in general and the Mamluk and Ottoman *devşirme* in particular—through which the ruling groups could be recruited from alien elements.[39]

But even when some imperial components developed, as was the case in Iran, which became a stronghold of Shi`i Islam and in which relatively continual strong patrimonial regimes developed, a complete fusion between the political ruler and the religious elites and establishment did not ensue.[40]

IX

This separation between *khalifa* and sultan was most prevalent in the mainstream of Islamic (Sunni) religious thought and tended to legitimize any ruler who ensured the existence of the Muslim community and the upholding of the *shari`a*. At the same time this mode legitimated—indeed, assumed—the possible coercive nature of such rulers and their distance from the pristine Muslim ideal regarding the moral order of the community. While rulers, even oppressive ones, were legitimized in the seemingly minimalistic tone necessary for the maintenance of public order and of the community, they were not seen as the promulgators, guardians, or regulators of the basic norms of the Islamic community. But whatever the extent of the acceptance of their legitimation, it usually entailed the rulers' duty to uphold the social order and to implement *shari`a* justice—and hence also the possibility of close scrutiny of their behavior by the `ulama'—even if such scrutiny did not usually have clear institutional effects. It was indeed the `ulama', however weak their organization, who were the guardians of the pristine Islamic vision, upholders of the normative dimensions of the *umma*, and keepers and interpreters of the *shari`a*.

It was the central place of the `ulama'—their relatively high symbolic standing despite small organizational autonomy—that distinguishes the Muslim regimes from other traditional patrimonial regimes in South or Southeast Asia or the early Near East. Truly enough, this highly autonomous religious elite did not develop into a broad, independent, and cohesive ecclesiastic organization, and the religious groups and functionaries were not organized as a distinct, separate entity; nor did they constitute a tightly organized body—except, and even then only partially, in the Ottoman Empire,[41] where large sectors of the `ulama' were organized by the state or in different modes in Shi`i Islam.[42] Yet the `ulama' were largely autonomous in that they were constituted according to distinctive—even if highly informal—criteria of recruitment and were, at least in principle, independent of the rulers.

It was these religious leaders, the `ulama'—even the relatively controlled `ulama' of the Ottoman Empire, as Haim Gerber shows, who were the custodians of the law, of shari`a, and through it of the boundaries of the Islamic community, and hence performed important juridical functions. It was the `ulama' who created major networks that brought together, under one religious—and often also social-civilizational—umbrella, varied ethnic and geopolitical groups, tribes, settled peasants, and urban groups, creating mutual impingement and interaction among them that otherwise would probably not have developed. And it was the `ulama', acting through different, often transstate, networks, who were the crucial element forming the distinctive characteristics of public spheres in Islamic societies. As M. Hodgson has indicated, and as is fully illustrated in the chapters in this volume, it was the `ulama' who, through their activities in schools of law, the waqfs, and the Sufi orders constituted the public spheres in Islamic societies and provided arenas of life not entirely controlled by the rulers. These public spheres were arenas in which different sectors of the society could voice their demands in the name of the basic premises of Islamic vision. Indeed, the dynamics of these public spheres cannot be understood without taking into account the crucial importance in them of the place of the community, rooted also in the basic premise of Islam, that of the equality of all believers and of their access to the sacred—conceptions that have necessarily given members of the community a right to participate, if not in the political arena, certainly in the communal and religious ones, in the promulgation and voicing of norms of public order.

X

The continual interaction between the `ulama', the rulers, and the different sectors of the community, then, were crucial to the constitution of an autonomous public sphere in Islamic societies. To quote Hoexter and Levtzion's introduction once more:

> The picture that emerges from the contributions to this volume is that of a vibrant public sphere, accommodating a large variety of autonomous groups

and characterized by its relatively stable but very dynamic nature. The community of believers was the center of gravity around which activity in the public sphere revolved. Its participation in the formation of the public sphere was a matter of course; its well-being, customs, and consensus were both the motives and the main justifications for the introduction of changes in social and religious practices, in the law and policies governing the public sphere. The independence of the *shari`a* and the distribution of duties toward the community between the ruler and the `*ulama'*, established very early in Islamic history, were crucial factors in securing the autonomy of the public sphere and putting limits on the absolute power of the ruler.

The relative strength of these actors varied of course, as the essays in this volume attest, in different periods and in different Muslim societies; and these differences greatly influenced the specific contours of the major institutions of the public sphere.

In some cases, as Said Arjomand has shown in his analysis of the emergence of the academics in medieval Islamic societies, they could indeed be greatly dependent on the ruler; he could exercise strong control—based on patronage—over the appointment of personnel to the institutions and hence limit their independence.[43] But in all cases the rulers retained the basic parameters of public spheres as constituted in Islamic societies. In cases where the rulers were weak, as for instance in Malaka, as Robert Heffner has shown, strong merchant groups could become not only autonomous in their own milieu but also major players in the political arena vis-à-vis the ruler.[44]

XI

The autonomy of the `*ulama'*, the hegemony of the *shari`a*, and the continuous yet variable vitality of the public spheres in Muslim society do not however imply direct autonomous access to the domain of rulership. Notwithstanding what might have been deduced from some of the more recent discussions about civil society and democracy, these factors did not result in the decision-making process of rulers, as they did in European parliaments and corporate urban institutions. Needless to say, some—often very strong—attempts to exert such influence did develop in many Muslim societies. But in concrete matters, especially foreign or military policy, as well as in such internal affairs as taxation and the keeping of public order and supervision of their own officials, the rulers were quite independent from the various actors in the public sphere.

It was this rather limited access of the major actors in the public sphere to concrete policy making that gave rise to the wrong perception of the rulers of Muslim societies as Oriental despots. This image is wrong because in fact the scope of the decision making of these rulers was relatively limited. Even if the rulers could behave in despotic ways in their relations to the officials most close to them, in internal affairs beyond taxation and the keeping of public order, they were limited, and not only because of the limits of technology. Their power was also limited because, unlike the European experience, rulership ("politics") in these above all Sunni Islamic societies did not constitute—contrary to the pristine image of the Muslim ruler as the embodiment of a transcendental vision of Islam—a central ideological component in the upholding of the *moral* order, even if pragmatically it constituted a necessary condition for the implementation of *shari`a*. Paradoxically enough, the fact that political problems constituted a central focus of Muslim theology was to no small extent rooted in this disjunction between the ideal of the Islamic ruler as the upholder of the pristine transcendental vision of Islam and the reality of his rulership. Moreover, the "political" weakness of many of the major organizations in the public sphere, as Said Arjomand has shown, is to be attributed not to the despotic tendencies of the ruler but to the absence of legal concepts and of corporations.[45]

Thus, in Muslim, especially Sunni, societies a very interesting decoupling developed between the makeup of the public sphere and access to the decision making of the rulers. This decoupling was manifest in the combination, on the one hand, of granting to large sectors of the society, to the major actors in the public sphere, rather limited autonomous access to concrete policy making; on the other hand the upholding of the moral order of the community was vested in the `ulama' and in the members of the community, with the rulers playing a secondary role.

This decoupling of a vibrant public sphere, autonomous from the political arena—or to be more precise from the realm of rulership, which differed greatly from its counterparts in Europe, especially Western and Central Europe—constituted one of the distinctive characteristics of Muslim civilization. It was distinctive, too, from the relations between the public sphere and the political rulership arena that developed in other non-Muslim Asian civilizations. It differed from India, where the political order did not constitute a major arena for the implementation of the predominant transcendental and moral vision; where sovereignty was highly fragmented; and where rulership was to a large extent embedded in the very flexible caste order,[46] giving rise to a vibrant public sphere with relatively strong access to the rulers. And it differed from China, where the political order in fact constituted the major arena for the implementation of the transcendental vision and where it was the rulers who, together with the Confucian literati, constituted the custodian of this order, leaving very limited scope for an autonomous public sphere.[47]

XII

From the point of view of the contemporary discourse on civil society, constitutionalism, and democracy, this specific combination of a vibrant public sphere with highly limited access of the major actors to the rulers' decision making gave rise in Muslim societies to a very paradoxical situation with respect to the impact of these main actors on changes in the political arena. The most important fact here—one that seemingly strengthened the view of these regimes as despotic—is that despite the potential autonomous standing of members of the `ulama', fully institutionalized effective checks on the decision making of the rulers did not develop in these societies, and there was no machinery other than rebellion through which to enforce any far-reaching "radical" political demands.

And yet in contrast to other patrimonial regimes, the potential not just for rebellion but also for principled revolt and possible regime changes was endemic in Muslim societies. True, as Bernard Lewis has shown,[48] a concept of revolution never developed within Islam. But at the same time, as Ernest Gellner indicated in his interpretation of Ibn Khaldun's work,[49] a less direct yet very forceful pattern of indirect ruler accountability and the possibility of regime changes did arise. This pattern was closely connected with a second type of ruler legitimation and accountability in Muslim societies—that embodied in the ruler being seen as the upholder of the pristine, transcendental Islamic vision.

Yet the possibility of implementing that pristine vision of Islam, of achieving that ideal fusion between the political and the religious community, of constructing the *umma*, was actually given up relatively early on in the formation and expansion of Islam. Indeed, the fact that political issues constituted a central focus of Muslim theology was to no small extent rooted in this disjunction between the ideal of the Islamic ruler as the upholder of the pristine transcendental vision of Islam and the reality of rulership in Islamic religion.[50] Yet although never fully attained, it was continually promulgated, as Aziz al-Azmeh has shown, with very strong utopian orientation, by various scholars and religious leaders, in the later periods.[51] Given the ongoing perception of the age of the Prophet as an ideal, even utopian model, the idea of restoration constituted a perennial component of Islamic civilization, promoted above all by some of the extreme reformist movements. Muhammad's community in Medina became—in the apt phrase of Henry Munson Jr., the Islamic "primordial utopia."[52] Many of the later rulers (the `Abbasids, Fatimids, and others) came to power on the crest of religious movements that upheld this ideal and legitimized themselves in just such religious-political terms.

XIII

The impact of this enduring utopian vision of the original Islamic era, of the fact that this ideal was neither ever fully implemented nor ever fully given up, became evident in some specific characteristics of the political dynamism of Islamic regimes and of Islamic sects—or rather movements with sectarian tendencies. One has of course to be very careful in using the term *sect*—with its Jewish and especially Christian roots—with respect to Islam, or even with respect to Hinduism. Other than the fundamental break between the Shi'is and the Sunnis, the distinctive characteristic of Christian sectarianism—the tendency to schism—has barely been applicable to Islam. But sectarian-like tendencies have existed in the recurring social movements in Muslim societies; and one of their distinctive characteristics has been the importance of their political dimensions, frequently oriented toward the restoration of that pristine vision of Islam, which has never been given up. Such renovative orientations were embodied in the different versions of the tradition of reform— the Mujaddid tradition.[53]

These radical reform movements could be focused on the person of a *mahdi* and/or be promulgated by a Sufi order or in a tribal group such as the Wahhabis, or in a school of law. As Emanuel Sivan has pointed out:

> Islamic Sunni radicalism was born out of the anti-accommodative attitude towards political power which had always existed within this tradition as a vigilante-type, legitimate, albeit secondary strand. Its most consistent and powerful paragon over the last seven centuries was the neo-Hanbalite school of Islamic law. When modern Sunni radicals looked in the 1920s and 1960s for a tradition to build upon, they turned quite naturally, like their predecessors in the late eighteenth century (the founders of Saudi Arabia), to neo-Hanbalism.[54]

Such restorative protofundamentalist tendencies were often connected with strong utopian eschatological orientations. In the words of Aziz al-Azmeh:

> The Medinan Caliphate can thus be regarded, with Laroui, as a utopia. What Laroui omits is an important complement without which consideration of this matter would remain incomplete: this is eschatology. Unlike activist, fundamentalist utopia, this finalist state of felicity and rectitude associated with the future reigns of the Mahdi (the Messiah) and of 'Isa b. Maryam (Jesus Christ) is not the result of voluntaristic action! Like the Medinan regime and the prophetic example, it is a miraculous irruption by divine command onto the fact of history, although it will be announced for the believers by many cosmic and other signs. Not only is the End a recovery of the Muslim prophetic experience, it is also the recovery of the primordial Adamic order, of the line of Abel, of every divine mission like those of Noah, Abraham, Moses, David, Solomon, Jesus and Muhammad, who incorporates, transcends and consummates them all in the most definitive form of primeval religiosity, Islam. The End, like the beginning and like the periodic irruptions of prophecy, is really against nature; it is the calque of the beginning so often repeated in history, and is the ultimate primitivism.[55]

Political and/or renovative orientations could be oriented toward active participation in the political center, or its destruction or transformation, or toward a conscious withdrawal from it. But even such withdrawal, which developed in both Shi'ism and Sufism, often harbored tendencies to pristine renovation, leading potentially to political action.

XIV

The fullest development of the political potential of such renovative tendencies took place in Islamic societies where such tendencies became connected with the resurgence of tribal revival against "corrupt" or weak regimes, rooted in the mode of Islamic expansion. Here the political impact of such movements became connected with processes attendant on the expansion of Islam and especially with the continuous impingement on the core Islamic polities of relatively newly converted tribal elements who presented themselves as the carriers of the original ideal Islamic vision and of the pristine Islamic polity. Many tribes (e.g., some of the Mongols), after being converted to Islam, transformed their own "typical" tribal structures to accord with Islamic religious-political visions and presented themselves as the symbol of pristine Islam, with strong renovative tendencies oriented to the restoration of pristine Islam.[56]

This tendency became closely related to the famous cycle depicted by Ibn Khaldun—namely, the cycle of tribal conquest, based on tribal solidarity and religious devotion, giving rise to the conquest of cities and settlement in them, followed by the degeneration of the ruling (often the former tribal) elite and then by its subsequent regeneration out of new tribal elements from the vast—old or new—tribal reservoirs. Ibn Khaldun emphasized above all the possibility of such renovation from within the original, especially Arab, tribal reservoir, and not from reservoirs acquired as it were through the expansion of Islam. Moreover, he focused more on the dilution of internal tribal cohesion as an important factor in the decline of Muslim dynasties and paid less attention to the "dogmatic" dimensions of Islam. But the overall strength of Ibn Khaldun's approach is that it provides an important analytical tool for understanding the dynamics of Islamic societies beyond the geographical scope of his own vision. Such new "converts"—along with the seemingly dormant tribes of the Arabian peninsula, of which the Wahhabis constituted probably the latest and most forceful illustration—became a central dynamic political force in Islamic civilization.

By virtue of the combination of this expansion with such sectarian, renovative orientations, Islam was probably the only Axial civilization within which sectarian-like movements—together with tribal leadership and groups—often led not only to the overthrow or downfall of existing regimes but also to the establishment of new political regimes oriented, at least initially, to the implementation of the original pristine, primordial Islamic utopia.

XV

It was indeed the Wahhabis who constituted, as John Voll has indicated, the last—and very forceful—case of a "traditional" Islamic, renovative proto-fundamentalist movement:

The vision of creating a society in which the Qur'an is implemented means that Ibn `Abd al-Wahhab's mission would inevitably entail political conse-quences. It was the local rulers who forced him to leave the town where he began teaching, and it was another local ruler, Ibn Sa`ud, who provided nec-essary support. The political system created by the Wahhabis did not place the inspirational teacher in a position of political rule. Instead, the Wahhabi state was based on the close cooperation of a learned ruler (shaykh) and an able commander (emir). The combination reflected a long-standing percep-tion of the proper relations between the institutions of the scholars and those of the commanders. Such a system of institutionalization reflected a reduced emphasis on charismatic leadership among Sunni fundamentalists and was also an important aspect of the great Sunni sultanates of the medieval era.

"Wahhabism" is thus a term used today for the type of reformism elucidated in `Abd al-Wahhab's opposition to popular religious superstitions and inno-vations, his insistence on informed independent judgment rather than the rote reliance on medieval authorities, and his call for the Islamization of society and the creation of a political order that would give appropriate recognition to Islam. Wahhabism represents an important type of funda-mentalism, one that continues to operate within the modern world but was not initiated as a result of conflict with the modernized West. The Wah-habis succeeded in establishing a state that, while imperfect, has nonethe-less been recognized by many in the Islamic world as consonant with the fundamentalist vision to create an Islamic society. It is the most enduring experiment within the broader mission, and as such it has provided a stan-dard against which other movements and states could be measured.[57]

In such "renovative" regimes a concept of rulership, and of its legitimation, was promulgated that presented the ruler as the upholder of the pristine, tran-scendental vision. Such regimes constituted probably the most widespread illus-tration of at least a partial transformation of the "usual" conception of rulership in Sunni Islam. Such transformation could be found also in cases where the rulers, the sultans, were also recognized as being *khalifas*—or at least as having many of the attributes of *khalifas*—by virtue of some charismatic qualities of *baraka* (blessing) attached to them. This was the case among the Moroccan rulers. For instance, the Moroccan sultans Sidi Muhammed and Mowlay Suley-man based their claim to represent the pristine vision largely on *baraka*, derived from the fact that they could claim to be descendants of the Prophet—to be challenged by different sectors of the `ulama' and various popular sectarian-like movements.[58] Such rulers could be recognized—in John Waterbury's felicitous characterization—as "Commanders of the Faithful" by wide-ranging groups over whom they would not impose their sultanic rulership.[59]

The most extreme case of such transformation of the usual Sunni con-ception of rulership was to be found within Shi`i Islam, where a strong poten-tial for the implementation of such visions by the ruler continually existed, even if in a subterranean fashion, in the image of the hidden *imam*. When combined with messianic or eschatological orientations it came to embody, in the *mahdis*, messianic-like renovators who appeared in Muslim societies—first in Sunni then in Shi`i ones—throughout history. Their transformed conception of rulership and of its legitimation was connected with a public sphere that differed greatly from the one analyzed above. With the possible exception of the *mahdi* regimes, the `ulama' continued to constitute a very important element in those *waqf* institutions that were fully developed, although the Sufi orders were suppressed by the "puritan" renovative regimes. In the latter regimes, the public sphere was much less autonomous, and the ruler constituted the major—possibly the dominant—actor in the public sphere, at least in the regulation of the moral consensus of the community.

XVI

Insofar as such movements did not create, in the Ibn-Kahldunian mode, new regimes, the impact of such movements on Muslim societies indeed continually constituted their organizational foci. Such construction of autonomous public spheres gave rise to some of the distinct patterns of pluralism characteristic of these societies. This pluralism was characterized by very strongly *patrimonial* features—such as the existence of segregated—regional, ethnic, and religious—sectors perhaps best illustrated by the Ottoman millet. It also resulted in a relative blurring as between the center and the periphery, as well as the prevalence—especially in these sectors—of multiple patterns of legitimation. But in contrast to more classical patrimonial regimes that developed in such non-Axial civilizations as those of Mesoameria, the ancient Near East, and (Hinduized) South Asia, the Muslim patrimonial regimes were in constant tension with the more sectarian "totalistic" tendencies and they could be undermined by the more extreme proto-fundamentalists, who could attempt, as was the case with the Wahhabis, to establish new "pristine" regimes.

XVII

It is only natural that these tensions and confrontations between pluralistic and totalistic tendencies became intensified in Muslim societies with the establishment within them of regimes rooted in the ideological premises of modernity, with their strong emphasis on relatively homogeneous territorial states. The rise of modern nation states, with their claim to homogeneity, has greatly undermined the autonomy of the public sphere—with the state attempting to appropriate, control, and even monopolize it. Although, as Dale Eickleman has shown,[60] a vibrant public sphere did develop in these regimes—and its very development attests to a growing democratization—this trend did not necessarily broaden the scope of autonomous political participation and of pluralism. These problems became even more acute with the rise of contemporary fundamentalist movements, which often combined the control mechanisms of the modern states with strong Jacobin tendencies, legitimized in terms of an essentialist tradition.

Contemporary Muslim societies can be seen as moving between two poles: attempts to establish territorial states with some elements of pluralism that build on their earlier historical experience; and strong antipluralistic tendencies in the form of either extreme secular oppressive—often military—regimes or extreme Jacobin fundamentalist ones. But these problems are beyond the scope of this volume.

XVIII

The above analysis of the characteristics and dynamics of public spheres in Islamic societies illustrates how one might account for the internal dynamics of these non-European modern civilizations at least to some extent in their own terms; how one might analyze the ways in which power and culture are interwoven in different societies and shape also the distinct dynamics of these societies; how to put them in a comparative framework that does not bestow a privileged position on the Western experience.[61]

Additionally, the analysis of public spheres in Islam provides some clues as to the applicability of Western social scientific concepts to non-Western societies. We cannot avoid Western concepts, but we can make them more flexible, so to speak, through differentiation and contextualization. The use of such concepts as public sphere, civil society, and collective identity is helpful as long as we do not assume that the way in which these components were put together in Europe constitutes an evaluative yardstick for other modernizing societies. These components can develop in many different ways, depending, among other factors, on the major symbols available, especially the relative importance of their religious, ideological, primordial, and historical aspects; the conception of the political order and its relation to other societal orders; the conception of political authority and its accountability; the conception of the subject; and the modes of center-periphery relations.

We need to avoid the pitfalls of both Western- and Eastern-centeredness. Such a fallacious position can be found, for instance, in the Nihonjinron literature, with its claims about the incomparable uniqueness of Japan. We cannot identify uniqueness without making some comparisons. The attitude of "inverted Orientalism," sometimes to be found among the more critical Western and Japanese scholars, developed in reaction to the Nihonjinron literature and led to a denial of the validity of certain Japanese categories of thought as applied to the analysis of Japanese historical and contemporary experience. Such an approach turns out to be rather paradoxical, as it goes against the exploration of those categories emphasized by the critics of the "Orientalist" approach.

The existence of debates on these issues attests to the intricacies of comparative research. The root of the problems lies not only in the fact that, at least until recently, most of the scholars who addressed these issues came from the West, but also in that this type of research has developed almost entirely—Ibn Khaldun notwithstanding—as part of the Western modern discourse. The adoption of various critical stances toward the earlier "Orientalist" literature—in the West, in India, in Japan, and elsewhere—has remained part of this discourse. The continuous reconstruction of this discourse by intellectuals in non-Western countries has greatly transformed it, but for the most part these interventions have not gone beyond the confines of this discourse.

NOTES

1. Eisenstadt and Schluchter 1998; this is partly based on a research proposal by S. N. Eisenstadt, W. Schluchter, and B. Wittrock, entitled "Collective Identity, Public Sphere, and Political Order: Cultural Foundations and the Formation of Contemporary Societies."

2. Habermas 1989.

3. Cohen 1999; Galston 1999; Mardsen 1999; Barber 1999.

4. Hirschman 1982; 1970.

5. Eisenstadt 1987; 2000.

6. As quoted in Hirschman 1982, 63; see also Eisenstadt and Schluchter 1998, 10–12.

7. Said 1978; Hussain, Olson, and Qureshi 1984, esp. the chapter by Turner; Breckenridge and Van der Veer 1993; Dirks 1995.

8. Asad 1993.

9. Stauth 1993.

10. See Vidal-Naquet 1996, esp. chapter 11, 267–76 and chapter 12, 277–318.

11. Grunebaum 1976; Grunebaum and Hartner 1960.

12. Springborg 1987.

13. Eisenstadt 1973; 1995 chapter 11, 280–305; Vidal-Naquet 1996; Dirks, Eley, and Ortner 1996.

14. Gramsci 1991.

15. Eisenstadt 1995.

16. Gorski 1993.

17. Guha and Spivak 1988.

18. Duara 1988.

19. Chandra 1968; Matsui 1968; Morris 1968.

20. Hodgson 1974; 1993.

21. Foucault 1973; 1988; 1975; 1965.

22. Gramsci 1991.

23. Pollock 1993; Brown 1991; Tedlock 1992.

24. Pollock 1998a; 1998b.

25. Stauth 1993.

26. Eisenstadt 2000; Schluchter 1989, esp. part II, 83–279.

27. O'Neill 1986; Van Krieken 1990.

28. Hansen 1999, 243 (note 3 to chapter 2).

29. It is only in his reportages of the Iranian revolution that Foucault went beyond these limitations; but in these reportages he did not take up the analytical challenge of reconciling such different portrayals.

30. Weber 1924; 1968; 1951; 1958; 1952.

31. Eisenstadt 1995, chapter 12, 306–27.

32. Cook 1983; Hodgson 1974; Turner 1974; Lapidus 1988; 1982; Shahid 1970; Schluchter 1987; Pipes 1981; Crone 1980.

33. Rodinson 1971.

34. Lewis 1973; al-Azmeh 1997, esp. part II, chapters 6–8.

35. Eisenstadt 1992a.

36. Lapidus 1975; 1996.

37. Sharon 1983.

38. Gibb 1968; Lapidus 1988; 1996; Pipes 1981; Crone 1980.

39. Ayalon 1951; 1996.

40. Arjomand 1999; 1988a; 1984; 1988b.

41. Gibb 1968; Inalcik 1973.

42. Arjomand 1988a.

43. Arjomand 1988a; 1999.

44. Heffner 1998.

45. Arjomand 1999.

46. Goodwin Raheja 1988; Rudolph and Rudolph 1987; Wink 1994.

47. Balazs 1964; Chang 1955; Van der Sprenkel 1958; Wakeman 1998; Woodside 1998; Eisenstadt 1992b.

48. Lewis 1973.

49. Ibn Khaldun (d. 808/1406) 1958; Gellner 1981

50. al-Azmeh 1997; Rosenthal 1958; Rosenthal 1968.

51. al-Azmeh 1997; 1993.

52. Munson 1988.

53. Landau-Tasseron 1989; Lazarus-Yafeh 1986; Levtzion 1986; Levtzion and Voll 1987; Levtzion and Weigert 1995; Voll 1991.

54. Sivan 1995, 16.

55. al-Azmeh 1993, 98

56. Lewis 1973, chapter 18, 253–66; Gellner 1981; Ibn Khaldun 1958.

57. Voll 1991, 351.

58. Munson 1988.

59. Waterbury 1970.

60. Eickelman and Piscatori 1996; Eickelman 1993; Eickelman and Anderson 1999.

61. This follows Eisenstadt and Schluchter 1998.

WORKS CITED

al-`Abbadi, A. `U. 1988. *Al-Qada' `inda al-`Asha'ir al-Urduniyya. Silsila Man Hum al-Badw?* 4. Ph.D. dissertation, Cambridge University.

Abu-Lughod, J. 1987. "The Islamic City—Historic Myth, Islamic Essence, and Contemporary Relevance." *International Journal of Middle Eastern Studies* 19: 155–76.

Abu-Manneh, B. 1990. "Khalwa and Rabita in the Khalidi Suborder." In *Naqshabandis*, ed. M. Gaborieau, A. Popovic, and T. Zarcone. Istanbul-Paris: Institut Français d'Études Anatoliennes d'Istanbul, 289–302.

Abun-Nasr, J. 1965. *The Tijaniyya.* London: Oxford University Press.

Abu Shama (d. 665/1268). 1947. *Tarajim Rijal al-Qarnayn al-Sadis wa'l-Sabi`.* Ed. M. Z. al-Kawthari. Cairo: Dar al-Kutub.

———. 1990. *Kitab al-Ba`ith `ala Inkar al-Bida` wa'l-Hawadith,* Ed. M. S. Riyad. Riyad: Dar al-Raya.

———. 1991–1992. `*Uyun al-Rawdatayn fi Akhbar al-Dawlatayn,* 2 vols. Ed. A. al-Baysumi. Damascus: Manshurat Wizarat al-Thaqafa.

Abu Yusuf, Ya`qub b. Ibrahim (d. 182/798). 1969. *Kitab al-Kharaj,* vol. 3. Trans. A. Ben Shemesh. Leiden: Brill.

Abu Zahra, M. 1953. *Ibn Taymiyya.* Cairo: Dar al-Thaqafa al-`Arabiyya.

Aksan, V. H. 1993. "Ottoman Political Writing, 1768–1808." *International Journal of Middle East Studies* 25: 53–69.

al-Albani, M. N. 1960–1961. *Musajala `Ilmiyya bayn al-Imamayn al-Jallalayn al-`Izz b. `Abd al-Salam wa-Ibn al-Salah.* Damascus: Manshurat al-Maktab al-Islami.

Algar, H. 1976. "Silent and Vocal *Dhikr* in the Naqshabandi Order." *Akten des VII. Kongresses für Arabistik und Islamwissenschaft. Abhandlungen der Akademie der Wissenschaften in Göttingen, Philologisch-Historische Klasse.* Göttingen: Vandenhoeck and Ruprecht, 3rd ser. 98: 39–46.

———. 1990. "A Brief History of the Naqshabandi order." In *Naqshabandis*, ed. M. Gaborieau, A. Popovic, and T. Zarcone. Istanbul-Paris: Institut Français d'Études Anatoliennes d'Istanbul, 13–19.

Amin, H. 1965. *Ta'rikh al-`Iraq fi'l-`Asr al-Saljuki.* Baghdad: n. p.

Anderson, J. N. D. 1951a. "Homicide in Islamic Law." *Bulletin of the School of Oriental and African Studies* 13: 811–28.

———. 1951b. "The Religious Element in Waqf Endowments." *Journal of the Royal Central Asian Society* 38: 292–99.

———. 1970. *Islamic Law in Africa.* London: Frank Cass.

———. 1976. *Law Reform in the Muslim World*. London: Athlone Press.

Ansari, S. 1992. *Sufi Saints and the State Power: the Pirs of Sind, 1843–1947*. Cambridge: Cambridge University Press.

Arjomand, S. A.1984. *From Nationalism to Revolutionary Islam*. Albany: State University of New York Press.

———. 1988a. ed., *Authority and Political Culture in Shi`ism*. Albany: State University of New York Press.

———. 1988b. *The Turban for the Crown: The Islamic Revolution in Iran*. New York: Oxford University Press.

———. 1998. "Philanthropy, the Law, and Public Policy in the Islamic World before the Modern Era." In *Philanthropy in the World's Traditions*, ed. W. F. Ilchman, S. N. Katz, and E. L. Queen II. Bloomington and Indianapolis: Indiana University Press, 109–32.

———. 1999. "The Law, Agency, and Policy in Medieval Islamic Society: Development of the Institutions of Learning from the Tenth to the Fifteenth Century." *Comparative Studies in Society and History* 41: 263–93.

Asad, T. 1993. *Genealogies of Religion: Discipline and Reason of Power in Christianity and Islam*. Baltimore: The Johns Hopkins University Press.

Aubin, F. 1990. "En Islam Chinois? quels Naqshabandis." In *Naqshabandis*, ed. M. Gaborieau, A. Popovic, and T. Zarcone. Istanbul-Paris: Institut Français d'Études Anatoliennes d'Istanbul, 491–572.

Ayalon, D. 1951. *L'esclavage du Mamelouk*. Jerusalem: Israel Oriental Society.

———. 1996. *Le phénomène mamelouk dans L'Orient islamique*. Paris: Presses Universitaires de France.

al-Azmeh, A. 1993. *Islams and Modernities*. London: Verso.

———. 1997. *Muslim Kingship: Power and the Sacred in Muslim, Christian and Pagan Politics*. London: I. B. Tauris.

Baer, G. 1964. *Population and Society in the Arab East*. London: Routledge and Kegan Paul.

———. 1969. *Studies in the History of Modern Egypt*. Chicago: Chicago University Press.

———. 1981. "The Muslim *Waqf* and Similar Institutions in Other Civilizations." Paper presented at the Workshop on Economic and Social Aspects of the Muslim *Waqf*, Jerusalem, 1–20 February 1981.

———. 1983. "Women and Waqf: An Analysis of the Istanbul Tahrir of 1546." *Studies in the Social History of the Middle East in Memory of Professor Gabriel Baer, Asian and African Studies* 17: 9–27.

———. *EI²* "Hikr." In *Encyclopaedia of Islam*, new edition, supplement.

———. 1997. "The *Waqf* as a Prop for the Social System (Sixteenth-Twentieth Centuries)." *Islamic Law and Society* 4: 264–97.

Balazs, E. 1964. *Chinese Civilization and Bureaucracy: Variations on a Theme*. New Haven: Yale University Press.

Barber, B. 1999. "Civil Society: Getting Beyond the Rhetoric. A Framework for Political Understanding." In *Civic Engagement in the Atlantic Community*, ed. J. Janning, C. Kupchan, and D. Rumberg. Gütersloh: Bertelsmann Foundation Publishers, 115–42.

Barkan, Ö. L., and E. H. Ayverdi. 1970. *Istanbul Vakıfları Tahrir Defteri 953 (1546) Tarihli*. Istanbul: Baha Matbaası.

Ben Achour, M. 1992. "Le habous ou waqf: l'institution juridique et la pratique tunisoise." In *hasab wa nasab: Parenté, Alliance et Patrimoine en Tunisie*, ed. S. Ferchiou. Paris: Éditions du CNRS, 51–78.

Bennigsen, A. 1964. "Un mouvement populaire au Caucase au 18e siècle: la guerre sainte du sheikh Mansur, 1785–1791." *Cahiers du Monde Russe et Sovietique* 2: 159–205.

Berkey, J. P. 1992. *The Transmission of Knowledge in Medieval Cairo*. Princeton: Princeton University Press.

———. 1995. "Tradition, Innovation, and the Social Construction of Knowledge in the Medieval Islamic Near East." *Past and Present* 146: 38–65.

———. 2000. "Storytelling, Preaching, and Power in Mamluk Cairo." *Mamluk Studies Review* 4: 53–73.

Berque, J. *EI²* "'Amal." In *Encyclopaedia of Islam*, new edition.

Bill, J. A., and C. Leiden. 1979. *Politics in the Middle East*. Boston: Little, Brown.

Birge, J. K. 1937. *The Bektashi Order of Dervishes*. London: Luzac.

Black, H. C., et al. 1990. *Black's Law Dictionary*, 6th ed. St. Paul: West Publishing Co.

Blanc, H. 1974. "The *nekteb-nektebu* Imperfect in a Variety of Cairene Arabic." *Israel Oriental Studies* 4: 206–26.

Bosworth, C. E. 1973. "Barbarian Incursions: The Coming of the Turks into the Islamic World." In *Islamic Civilization, 950–1150*, ed. D. S. Richards. Oxford: Cassirer, 1–16.

———. 1976. *The Medieval Islamic Underworld. The Banu Sasan in Arabic Society and Literature*. Leiden: Brill.

Breckenridge, C. A., and P. Van der Veer, eds. 1993. *Orientalism and the Postcolonial Predicament: Perspectives on South Asia*. Philadelphia: University of Pennsylvania Press.

Brenner, L. 1988. "Concepts of *Tariqa* in West Africa: the Case of the Qadiriyya." In *Charisma and Brotherhood in African Islam*, ed. D. C. O'Brien and C. Coulon. Oxford: Clarendon, 33–52.

Brown, C. 1991. "Hieroglyphic Literacy in Ancient Mayaland: Inferences from Linguistic Data." *Current Anthropology* 32: 489–96.

Brown, P. 1981. *The Cult of Saints: Its Rise and Function in Latin Christianity*. Chicago: University of Chicago Press.

Bulliet, R. 1972. *The Patriciate of Nishapur: A Study in Medieval Islamic Social History*. Cambridge: Harvard University Press.

———. 1973. "The Political-Religious History of Nishapur in the Eleventh Century." In *Islamic Civilization, 950–1150*, ed. D. S. Richards. Oxford: Cassirer, 71–91.

———. 1994. *The View from the Edge*. New York: Columbia University Press.

Cahen, C. 1937–1938. "Une chronique syrienne du VIe/XIIe siècle: le Bustan al-Jami'." *Bulletin d'Études Orientales* 7–8: 113–58.

———. 1961. "Réflexions sur le *waqf* ancien." *Studia Islamica* 14: 37–56.

———. *EI²* "Ayyubids." In *Encyclopaedia of Islam*, new edition.

Cahen, C., and M. Talbi. *EI²* "Hisba." In *Encyclopaedia of Islam*, new edition.

Calder, N. *EI²* "Shari'a." In *Encyclopaedia of Islam*, new edition.

Calhoun, C. 1992, 1994. "Introduction." In *Habermas and the Public Sphere*, ed. C. Calhoun. Cambridge: MIT Press, 1–48.

———. 1993. "Civil Society and the Public Sphere." *Public Culture* 5: 267–80.

Chamberlain, M. 1994. *Knowledge and Social Practice in Medieval Damascus, 1190–1350*. Cambridge: Cambridge University Press.

Chandra, B. 1968. "Reintrepretation of Nineteenth-Century Indian Economic History." *The Indian Economic and Social History Review* 5: 35–75.

Chang Chung-li. 1955. *The Chinese Gentry: Studies on Their Role in Nineteenth-Century Chinese Society*. Seattle: University of Washington Press.

Chartier, R. 1991. *The Cultural Origins of the French Revolution*. Trans. L. G. Cochrane. Durham and London: Duke University Press.

Çizakça, M. 1995. "Cash Waqfs of Bursa, 1555–1823." *Journal of the Economic and Social History of the Orient* 38: 313–54.

Clancey-Smith, J. A. 1994. *Rebel and Saint: Muslim Notables, Populist Protest, Colonial Encounters (Algeria and Tunisia, 1800–1904)*. Berkeley: University of California Press.

Clayer, N. 1994. *Mystiques, état et société: les Halvetis dans l'aire balkanique de la fin du 15ᵉ siècle à nos jours*. Leiden: Brill.

Cohen, J. 1999. "Trust, Voluntary Association, and Workable Democracy: The Contemporary American Discourse of Civil Society." In *Democracy and Trust*, ed. M. Warren. Cambridge: Cambridge University Press, 208–48.

Cohen, J. L., and A. Arato. 1992. *Civil Society and Political Theory*. Cambridge: MIT Press.

Cohen, M. 1997. "Jewish Communal Organization in Medieval Egypt: Research, Results and Prospects." In *Studies in Muslim-Jewish Relations: Judeo Arabic Studies*, ed. N. Galb. New York: Harwood Academic Press, 73–86.

Colas, D. 1997. *Civil Society and Fanaticism: Conjoined Histories*. Stanford: Stanford University Press.

Colucci, M. 1927. "Il diritto consuetudinario della tribù della Cirenaica." *Revista Coloniale* 22: 24–37.

Cook, M. 1983. *Mohammad*. Oxford: Oxford University Press.

Cornell, V. J. 1998. *Realm of the Saint: Power and Authority in Moroccan Symbolism*. Austin: University of Texas Press.

Coulson, N. J. 1957. "The State and the Individual in Islamic Law." *The International and Comparative Law Quarterly* 6: 49–60.

———. 1964. *A History of Islamic Law*. Edinburgh: Edinburgh University Press.

———. 1971. *Succession in the Muslim Family*. Cambridge: Cambridge University Press.

Crecelius, D. 1995. "Introduction." *Journal of the Economic and Social History of the Orient* 38, 3: 247–61.

Crone, P. 1980. *Slaves on Horses*. Cambridge: Cambridge University Press.

———. 1987. *Roman, Provincial, and Islamic Law*. Cambridge: Cambridge University Press.

Crone, P., and M. Hinds. 1986. *God's Caliph*. Cambridge: Cambridge University Press.

Davis, J. 1987. *Libyan Politics: Tribe and Revolution*. London: I. B. Tauris.

———. 1998. "A Social Perspective." In *Legal Documents on Libyan Tribal Society in Process of Sedentarization*, ed. A. Layish. Wiesbaden: Harrassowitz, 7–13.

Deegan, H., ed. 1994. *The Middle East and Problems of Democracy*. Boulder: Lynne Rienner Publishers.

Desan, S. 1989. "Crowds, Community and Ritual in the Work of E. P.Thompson and Natalie Davis." In *The New Cultural History*, ed. L. Hunt. Berkeley: University of California Press. 47–71.

Devoulx, A. 1863. "Les édifices religieux de l'ancien Alger." *Revue Africaine* 7: 102–13.

DeWeese, D. 1993. "Review of Jurgen Paul." *Journal of Asian History* 27: 66–67.

Dhahabi, Shams al-Din (d. 748/1348). 1984-1985. *Siyar A'lam al-Nubala'*, vols. 21–23. Ed. B.'A. al-Ma'ruf and M. H. Sirhan. Beirut: Mu'asasat al-Risala.

Dirks, N. B., ed. 1995. *Colonialism and Culture*. Ann Arbor: University of Michigan Press.

Dirks, N. B., G. Eley, and S. Ortner, eds. 1996. *Culture, Power, History: A Reader in Contemporary Social Theory*. Princeton: Princeton University Press.

Drory, J. 1988. "Hanbalis of the Nablus Region in the Eleventh and Twelfth Centuries." *Asian and African Studies* 22: 93–112.

Duara, P. 1988. *Culture, Power, and the State: Rural North China, 1900–1942*. Stanford: Stanford University Press.

Duben, A., and C. Behar. 1991. *Istanbul Households: Marriage, Family, and Fertility, 1880–1940*. Cambridge: Cambridge University Press.

Eaton, R. M. 1978. *Sufis of Bijapur: Social Roles of Sufis in Medieval India*. Princeton: Princeton University Press.

———. 1993. *The Rise of Islam and the Bengal Frontier, 1204–1760*. Berkeley: University of California Press.

Eddé, A.-M. 1999. *La principauté Ayyoubide d'Alep (579/1183–658/1260)*. Stuttgart: Steiner.

Eickelman, D. F. 1964. "Is There an Islamic City? The Making of a Quarter in a Moroccan Town." *International Journal of Middle East Studies* 5: 274–94.

———, ed. 1993. *Russia's Muslim Frontiers: New Directions in Cross-Cultural Analysis*. Bloomington and Indianapolis: Indiana University Press.

———. 1996. "Forward." In *Civil Society in the Middle East*, vol. 2, ed. A. R. Norton. Leiden: Brill.

Eickelman, D. F., and J. W. Anderson, eds. 1999. *New Media in the Muslim World: The Emerging Public Sphere*. Bloomington and Indianapolis: Indiana University Press.

Eickelman, D. F., and J. Piscatori. 1996. *Muslim Politics*. Princeton: Princeton University Press.

Eisenstadt, S. N. 1973. *Tradition, Change and Modernity*. New York: Wiley.

———. 1987. *European Civilization in a Comparative Perspective*. Oslo: Norwegian University Press.

———. 1992a. *Jewish Civilization: The Jewish Historical Experience in Comparative Perspective*. Albany: State University of New York Press.

———, ed. 1992b. *Kulturen der Achsenzeit II: Ihre Institutionelle und Kulturelle Dynamik. Teil I: China, Japan*. Frankfurt: Suhrkamp.

———. 1995. *Power, Trust, and Meaning: Essays in Sociological Theory and Analysis*. Chicago: University of Chicago Press.

———. 2000. *Die Vielfalt der Moderne*. Berlin: Velbruck Wissenschaft.

Eisenstadt, S. N., and W. Schluchter. 1998. "Introduction: Paths to Early Modernities— A Comparative View." *Daedalus* 127: 1–18.

Elisséeff, N. 1949. "Les monuments de Nur al-Din." *Buletin d'Études Orientales* 13: 5–43.

———. 1972. "Un document contemporain de Nur al-Din. Sa notice biographique par Ibn 'Asakir." *Bulletin d'Études Orientales* 25: 125–40.

Ephrat, D. 2000. *A Learned Society in a Period of Transition: The Sunni 'Ulama' of Eleventh-Century Baghdad*. Albany: State University of New York Press.

Ernst, C. E. 1993. "An Indo-Persian Guide to Sufi Shrine Pilgrimage." In *Manifestations of Sainthood in Islam*, ed. G. M. Smith and C. E. Ernst. Istanbul: Isis Press, 43–67.

Evans-Pritchard, E. E. 1949. *The Sanusi of Cyrenaica.* Oxford: Clarendon Press.

Faroqhi, S. 1976. "The Tekke of Haci Bektaş, Social Position and Economic Activities." *International Journal of Middle East Studies* 7: 183–205.

———. 1981. "Seyyid Gazi Revisited: The Foundation as Seen through Sixteenth-Century Documents." *Turcica* 13: 90–122.

———. 1986. "Political Initiatives 'from the Bottom Up' in the Sixteenth- and Seventeenth-Century Ottoman Empire: Some Evidence for their Existence." In *Osmanische Studien zur Wirtschafts- und Sozialgeschichte,* ed. H. G. Majer. Wiesbaden: Harrassowitz, 24–45.

———. 1993. "Sainthood as Means of Self-Defense in Seventeenth-Century Ottoman Anatolia." In *Manifestations of Sainthood in Islam,* ed. G. M. Smith and C. E. Ernst. Istanbul: Isis Press, 193–208.

Féraud, C. 1868. "Province de Constantine: Les anciens établissements religieux musulmans de Constantine." *Revue Africaine* 12: 121–32.

Fernandes, L. 1988. *The Evolution of a Sufi Institution in Mamluk Egypt: the Khanqah.* Berlin: Klaus Schwarz Verlag.

Fierro, M. I. 1985. "Los Malikies de al-Andalus y los Dox Árbitros (*al-hakaman*)." *Al-Qantara* 6: 79–102.

———. 1992. "The Treatises Against Innovation (*Kutub al-Bida`*)." *Der Islam* 69: 204–46.

Fleischer, C. H. 1992. "The Lawgiver as Messiah: The Making of Imperial Image in the Reign of Suleyman." In *Soliman le Magnifique et son Temps,* ed. G. Veinstein. Paris: École des Hautes Études en Sciences Sociales, 159–77.

Foucault, M. 1965. *Madness and Civilization: A History of Insanity in the Age of Reason.* New York: Pantheon Books.

———. 1973. *The Birth of the Clinic: An Archaeology of Medical Perception.* Trans. A. M. Sheridan Smith. New York: Vintage Books.

———. 1975. *Surveiller et punir: naissance de la prison.* Paris: Gallimard.

———. 1988. *Technologies of the Self: A Seminar with Michel Foucault.* Ed. L. H. Martin et al. Amherst: University of Massachussetts Press.

Frenkel, J. 1992. "The Endowment of al-Madrasa al-Salihiyya in Jerusalem by Saladin." In *Palestine under the Mamluks,* ed. J. Drory. Jerusalem: Ben Zvi Institute, 72–77 (in Hebrew).

Galston, W. 1999. "Social Capital in America: Civil Society and Civil Trust." In *Civic Engagement in the Atlantic Community,* ed. J. Janning, C. Kupchan, and D. Rumberg. Gütersloh: Bertelsmann Foundation Publishers, 67–78.

Gardet, L. *EI²* "*Dhikr.*" In *Encyclopaedia of Islam,* new edition.

Geertz, C. 1979. "Deep Play: Notes on the Balinese Cockfight." In *Interpretive Social Science,* ed. W. M. Sullivan and P. Rainbow. Berkeley: University of California Press, 181–224.

Gellner, E. 1969. *Saints of the Atlas.* Chicago: Chicago University Press.

———. 1981. *The Muslim Society.* Cambridge: Cambridge University Press.

———. 1984. "Doctor and Saint." In *Islam in Tribal Societies,* ed. S. A. Akbar and D. M. Hart. London: Routledge and Kegan Paul, 21–38.

———. 1994. *Conditions of Liberty: Civil Society and Its Rivals.* London: Hamish Hamilton.

Gerber, H. 1983. "The Waqf Institution in Early Ottoman Edirne." *Studies in the Social History of the Middle East in Memory of Professor Gabriel Baer, Asian and African Studies* 17: 29–45.

———. 1987. *The Social Origins of the Modern Middle East*. Boulder: Lynne Rienner Publishers.

———. 1988. *Economy and Society in an Ottoman City: Bursa 1600–1700*. Jerusalem: The Hebrew University.

———. 1994. *State, Society, and Law in Islam: Ottoman Law in Comparative Perspective*. Albany: State University of New York Press.

———. 1998. "Rigidity versus Openness in Late Classical Islamic Law: The Case of the Seventeenth-Century Palestinian Mufti Khayr al-Din al-Ramli." *Islamic Law and Society* 5: 165–95.

———. 1999. *Islamic Law and Culture, 1600–1840*. Leiden: Brill.

Gibb, H. A. R. 1968. *Studies in the Civilization of Islam*. Boston: Beacon Press

Gibb, H. A. R., and H. Bowen. 1957. *Islamic Society and the West*, vol. 2. London: Oxford University Press.

Gilbert, J. E. 1977. "The `Ulama' of Medieval Damascus and the International World of Islamic Scholarship." Ph.D diss., University of Michigan, Ann Arbor.

———. 1980. "Institutionalization of Muslim Scholarship and the Professionalization of the `Ulama' in Medieval Damascus." *Studia Islamica* 52: 105–35.

Ginat, J. 1987. *Blood Disputes among Bedouin and Rural Arabs in Israel: Revenge, Mediation, Outcasting, and Family Honor*. Pittsburgh: University of Pittsburgh Press.

Goitein, S. D. 1967. *A Mediterranean Society: The Jewish Communities of the Arab World as Portrayed in the Documents of the Cairo Geniza*. Vol. 1: *Economic Foundations*. Berkeley: University of California Press.

———. 1970. "Minority Self-Rule and Government Control in Islam." *Studia Islamica* 31: 101–16.

———. 1971. *A Mediterranean Society. The Jewish Communities of the Arab World as Portrayed in the Documents of the Cairo Geniza*. Vol. 2: *The Community*. Berkeley: University of California Press.

Goldziher, I. 1967, 1971. *Muslim Studies*, 2 vols. Ed. and trans. S. M. Stern and C. R. Barber. London: George Allen and Unwin.

———. 1981. *Introduction to Islamic Theology and Law*. Trans. A. Andras and R. Hamori. Princeton: Princeton University Press.

Goodwin, G. 1994. *The Janissaries*. London: Saqi Books.

Goodwin, Raheja G. 1988. "India: Caste, Kingship, and Dominance Reconsidered." *Annual Review of Anthropology* 17: 497–522.

Gorski, P. 1993. "The Protestant Ethic Revisited: Disciplinary Revolution and State Formation in Holland and Prussia." *American Journal of Sociology* 99: 265–316.

Gramsci, A. 1991. *Selections from Cultural Writings*. Cambridge: Harvard University Press.

Grandin, N. 1990. "À propos des *asanid* de la Naqshabandiyya dans les fondements de la Khatmiyya du Soudan oriental: stratégies de pouvoir et relation maître/disciple." In *Naqshabandis*, ed. M. Gaborieau, A. Popovic, and T. Zarcone. Istanbul-Paris: Institut Français d'Études Anatoliennes d'Istanbul, 621–55.

Gross, J. A. 1988. "The Economic Status of a Timurid Sufi Shaykh: a Matter of Conflict or Perception." *Iranian Studies* 21: 84–104.

———. 1990. "Multiple Roles and Perceptions of a Sufi Shaykh: Symbolic Statements of Political and Religious Authority." In *Naqshabandis*, ed. M. Gaborieau, A. Popovic, and T. Zarcone. Istanbul-Paris: Institut Français d'Études Anatoliennes d'Istanbul, 109–21.

Grunebaum, G. E. 1976. *Islam and Medieval Hellenism*. London: Variorum Reprints.

Grunebaum, G. E., and W. Hartner, eds. 1960. *Klassizismus und Kulturverfall*. Frankfurt.

Guha, R., and G. Spivak, eds. 1988. *Selected Subaltern Studies*. Oxford: Oxford University Press.

Haarman, U. W. 1988. "Ideology and History, Identity and Alterity: the Arab Image of the Turk from the `Abbasids to Modern Egypt." *International Journal of Middle East Studies* 20: 175–96.

Habermas, J. 1989, 1992. *The Structural Transformation of the Public Sphere: An Inquiry into a Category of Bourgeois Society*. Trans. Th. Burger. Cambridge: Polity Press.

Hallaq, W. B. 1994. "From *Fatwas* to *Furu*`: Growth and Change in Islamic Substantive Law." *Islamic Law and Society* 1: 29–65.

Halpern, M. 1963. *The Politics of Social Change in the Middle East and North Africa*. Princeton: Princeton University Press.

Hammoudi, A. 1997. *Master and Disciple: The Cultural Foundations of Moroccan Authoritarianism*. Chicago: University of Chicago Press.

Hann, C., and E. Dunn, eds. 1996 *Civil Society: Challenging Western Models*. London: Routledge.

Hansen, T. B. 1999. *The Saffron Wave: Democracy and Hindu Nationalism in Modern India*. Princeton: Princeton University Press.

Al-Harawi, `Ali (d. 611/1215). 1953. *Kitab al-Isharat fi Ma`rifat al-Ziyarat*. Ed. J. Sourdel-Thomine. Damascus: Institut Français de Damas.

Hart, D. M. 1996. "Murder in the Market: Penal Aspects of Berber Customary Law in Precolonial Moroccan Rif." *Islamic Law and Society* 3: 343–71.

Hartmann, A. *EI²* "al-Mansur, al-Malik Muhammad b. `Umar b. Shahnshah." In *Encyclopaedia of Islam*, new edition.

Heffening, W. *EI* (1931) "*Wakf*." In *Encyclopaedia of Islam*.

Heffner, R. 1998. "A Muslim Civil Society? Indonesian Reflections on the Conditions of Possibility." In *Democratic Civility: The History and Cross-Cultural Possibility of a Modern Political Ideal*, ed. R. Heffner. New Brunswick, N. J.: Trescoton Publishers, 285–323.

Henninger, J. 1959. "La religion bédouine préislamique." *L'antica Società Beduina. Studi Semitici* 2: 115–40.

Heyd, U. 1973 *Studies in Old Ottoman Criminal Law*. Ed. V. L. Ménage Oxford: Clarendon Press.

Hinds, M. *EI²*. "Mihna." In *Encyclopaedia of Islam*, new edition.

Hirschman, A. 1970. *Exit, Voice, and Loyalty: Responses to Decline in Firms, Organizations, and States*. Cambridge: Harvard University Press.

———. 1982. *Shifting Involvement: Private Interest and Public Action*. Princeton: Princeton University Press.

Hiskett, M. 1975. A *History of Hausa Islamic Verse*. London: School of Oriental and African Studies.

Hodgson, M. G. S. 1974. *The Venture of Islam* 3 vols. Chicago: University of Chicago Press.

———. 1993. *Rethinking World History: Essays on Europe, Islam, and World History*. Cambridge: Cambridge University Press.

Hoexter, M. 1984. "Le contrat de quasi-aliénation des *awqaf* à Alger à la fin de la domination turque: étude de deux documents d'`ana'." *Bulletin of the School of Oriental and African Studies* 47: 243–59.

———. 1987. "The Idea of Charity: A Case Study in Continuity and Flexibility of an Islamic Institution." In Wissenschaftskolleg zu Berlin, *Jahrbuch 1985/6.* Berlin: Sideler Verelag, 179–89.

———. 1995. "*Huquq Allah* and *Huquq al-'Ibad* as Reflected in the *Waqf* Institution." *North African, Arabic, and Islamic Studies in Honor of Pessah Shinar, Jerusalem Studies in Arabic and Islam* 19: 133–56.

———. 1997. "Adaptation to Changing Circumstances: Perpetual Leases and Exchange Transactions in *Waqf* Property in Ottoman Algiers." *Islamic Law and Society* 4: 319–33.

———. 1998a. *Endowments, Rulers, and Community: Waqf al-Haramayn in Ottoman Algiers.* Leiden: Brill.

———. 1998b. "*Waqf* Studies in the Twentieth Century: The State of the Art." *Journal of the Economic and Social History of the Orient* 41: 474–95.

Hofheinz, A. 1990. "Encounters with a Saint: al-Majdhub, al-Mirghani, and Ibn Idris as Seen through the Eyes of Ibrahim al-Rashid." *Sudanic Africa* 1: 19–59.

Horster, P. 1935 *Zur Anwendung des islamischen Rechts im 16. Jahrhundert.* Stuttgart: W. Kohlhammer.

Humphreys, R. S. 1977. *From Saladin to the Mongols: The Ayyubids of Damascus, 1193–1260.* Albany: State University of New York Press.

———. 1989. "Politics and Architectural Patronage in Ayyubis Syria." In *Essays in Honor of Bernard Lewis,* ed. C. E. Bosworth et al. Princeton: Princeton University Press, 151–75.

———. 1994 "Women as Patrons of Religious Architecture in Ayyubid Damascus." *Muqarnas* 11: 35–54.

Hunt, L. ed. 1989. *The New Cultural History.* Berkeley: University of California Press.

Hussain, A., R. Olson, and J. Qureshi, eds. 1984. *Orientalism, Islam and Islamists.* Brattleboro, VT: Amana Books.

Ibn 'Abidin, Muhammad Amin (d. 1252/1836). 1883–1884. *Nashr al-'Urf fi Bina' Ba'd al-Ahkam 'ala al-'Urf.* Damascus: Matba'at Ma'arif Suriyya al-Jalila.

———. 1996. *Radd al-Muhtar 'ala al-Durr al-Mukhtar,* vol. 4. Cairo: Matba'at Mustafa al-Babi al-Halabi.

Ibn Abi al-Wafa' (d. 775/1371). 1993. *Al-Jawahir al-Mudi'a fi Tabaqat al-Hanafiyya,* vols. 1–3. Ed. 'A. al-Hulu. Cairo: Hajar.

Ibn al-'Adim, 'Umar (d. 660/1262). 1954, 1968. *Zubdat al-Halab fi Ta'rikh Halab,* vols. 2, 3. Ed. S. al-Dahhan. Damascus: Institut Français de Damas.

———. 1988–1989. *Bughyat al-Talab fi Ta'rikh Halab,* vols. 1–10. Ed. S. Zakkar. Damascus: Dar al-Fikr.

Ibn Ahmad, 'Abdallah (d. 290/903). 1986. *Kitab al-Sunna.* Dumam: Dar Ibn al-Qayyim.

Ibn Ahmad, Salih (d. 266/880). 1981. *Sirat al-Imam Ahmad b. Hanbal.* Alexandria: Mu'assasat Shabab al-Jami'a.

Ibn al-'Asakir, Thikat al-Din 'Ali (d. 571/1176). 1995. *Ta'rikh Madinat Dimashk,* vol. 2. Ed. 'A. al-'Amrawi. Beirut: Dar al-Fikr.

Ibn 'Asim, Muhammad b. Muhammad al-Maliki al-Gharnati (d. 829/1426). 1958. *Al-'Asimiyya ou Tuhfat al-Hukkam fi'l-'Uqud wa'l-Ahkam.* Ed. L. Bercher. Alger: La Typo-Litho.

Ibn al-Athir, Diya' al-Din (d. 637/1239). 1939. *al-Mathal al-Sa'ir fi Adab al-Katib wa'l-Sha'ir,* vols. 1–2. Ed. M. M. 'Abd al-Hamid. Cairo: Matba'at Mustafa al-Babi al-Halabi.

Ibn al-Athir, `Izz al-Din (d. 631/1233). 1965–1967. al-Kamil fi'l-Ta'rikh, 13 vols. Beirut: Dar Sadr and Dar Beirut.

Ibn al-Banna' (d. 471/1078). 1956. Ta'rikh. Ed. and trans. G. Makdisi as Autograph Diary of an Eleventh-Century Historian of Baghdad. Reprinted from the Bulletin of the School of Oriental and African Studies, parts 1–3, 18: 9–31, 239–60.

Ibn Fudi, `Abdallah (d. 1245/1829). 1963. Tazyin al-Waraqat. Ed. and trans. M. Hiskett. Ibadan: Ibadan University Press.

Ibn Hajar al-`Asqalani, Ahmad b. `Ali (d. 852/1449). 1984. Tahdhib al-Tahdhib. Beirut: Dar al-Fikr.

Ibn Hibban, Muhammad (d. 354/965). 1976. Kitab al-Majruhin. Aleppo.

Ibn Ishaq, Hanbal (d. 273/886). 1977. Dhikr Mihnat al-Imam Ahmad b. Hanbal. Cairo: Dar Nashr al-Thaqafa.

Ibn al-Jawzi (d. 597/1200). 1940. al-Muntazam fi Ta'rikh al-Muluk wa'l-Umam, 6 vols. [=Vols. 5–10]. Hyderabad, Deccan: Dairatu'l-Maarifi'l-Osmania.

Ibn Jubayr (d. 614/1217). 1907. Rihla. Ed. W. Wright and M. J. De Goeje. Leiden: Brill.

Ibn Kathir (d. 774/1373). 1932. Al-Bidaya wa'l-Nihaya fi'l-Ta'rikh, vols.12–13. Cairo: Dar al-Sa`ada.

―――. 1966. al-Bidaya wa'l-Nihaya, 14 vols. Beirut: Dar Sadr and Dar Beirut.

Ibn Khaldun, `Abd al-Rahman b. Muhammad (d. 808/1406). 1958. The Muqaddimah, 3 vols.. Trans. F. Rosenthal. London: Routledge and Kegan Paul.

Ibn Khallikan (d. 681/1282). 1970. Wafayat al-A`yan wa-Anba' Abna' al-Zaman, 7 vols. Beirut: Dar al-Thaqafa.

―――. 1972. Wafayat al-A`yan wa-Anba' Abna' al-Zaman. 8 vols. Ed. I. `Abbas. Beirut: Dar al-Thaqafa.

Ibn al-Nadim, Muhammad b. Abi Ya`qub (d. end of fourth century/tenth century). 1970. Kitab al-Fihrist, vol. 1. Trans. B. Dodge. New York: Columbia University Press.

Ibn Rajab (d. 795/1392-93). 1952–1953. Dhayl `ala Tabaqat al-Hanabila, 2 vols. Ed. M. H. al-Fiqi. Cairo: Matba`at al-Sunna al-Muhammadiyya.

Ibn Shaddad, `Izz al-Din (d. 684/1285). 1953. al-A`laq al-Khatira fi Dhikr Umara' al-Sham wa'l-Jazira. Ed. D. Sourdel. Damascus: Institut Français de Damas.

―――. 1956. al-A`laq al-Khatira fi Dhikr Umara' al-Sham wa'l-Jazira: Ta'rikh Madinat Dimashq. Ed. S. al-Dahhan. Damascus: Institut Français de Damas.

―――. 1991. al-A`laq al-Khatira fi Dhikr Umara' al-Sham wa'l-Jazira, vol. 1. Ed. Y. Z. al-`Abara. Damascus: Manshurat Wizarat al-Thaqafa.

Ibn Tulun (d. 953/1546). 1949. al-Qala'id al-Jawhariyya fi Ta'rikh al-Salihiyya. Ed. M. A. Duhman. Damascus: Maktabat al-Dirasat al-Islamiyya.

Ibn Wasil, Jamal al-Din (d. 697/1298). 1970–1977. Mufarrij al-Kurub fi Akhbar Bani Ayyub, vol. 3. Ed. Shayyal, S. `Ashur, and H. Rabi`. Cairo: Dar al-Qalam, vols. 4–5. Cairo: Dar al-Kutub.

`Illaysh, Muhammad b. Ahmad (d. 1299/1881–1882). n.d. Fath al-`Ali al-Malik fi'l-Fatwa `ala Madhhab al-Imam Malik, 2 vols. Cairo: Dar al-Fikr.

Imber, C. 1992. "Suleyman as Caliph of the Muslims." In Soliman le Magnifique et son temps, ed. G. Veinstein. Paris: École des Hautes Études en Sciences Sociales, 179–84.

Inalcık, H. 1973. The Ottoman Empire: The Classical Age 1300–1600. London: Weidenfeld & Nicolson.

―――. 1980–1981. "Osmanli Idare Sosyal ve Ekonomic Tarihiyle Ilgili Belgeler: Bursa Kadi Sicillerinden Seçmeler." Belgeler 10: 1–91.

————. *EI²* "Kanun—(III) Financial and Public Administration." In *Encyclopaedia of Islam*, new edition.

————. 1993. "Decision Making in the Ottoman State." In *Decision Making and Change in the Ottoman Empire*, ed. C. Farah. Kirksville, MO.: Thomas Jefferson University Press, 9–18.

al-Jabarti, `Abd al-Rahman b. Hasan (d. 1240/1825). 1879–1880. `Aja'ib al-'Athar fi'l-Tarajim wa'l-Akhbar. Cairo, Bulaq.

al-Jahiz, Abu `Uthman `Amr b. Bahr (d. 255/869). 1979. *Rasa'il al-Jahiz*, vols. 1 and 3. Cairo.

Jawad, M. 1954. "al-Rubut al-Baghdadiyya." *Sumer* 10: 218–49.

Jennings, R. C. 1986. "The Society and Economy of Maçuka in the Ottoman Judicial Registers of Trabzon, 1560-1640." In *Continuity and Change in Late Byzantine and Early Ottoman Society*, ed. A. Bryer and H. Lowry. Birmingham and Washington: The University of Birmingham, Centre for Byzantine Studies; and Dumbarton Oaks, 129–54.

————. 1990. "Pious Foundations in the Society and Economy of Ottoman Trabzon, 1565–1640." *Journal of the Economic and Social History of the Orient* 38: 271–336.

Johansen, B. 1979. "Eigentum, Familie, und Obrigkeit im hanafitischen Strafrecht." *The World of Islam* 19: 1–71.

————. 1981. "Sacred and Religious Element in Hanafite Law: Function and Limits of the Absolute Character of Government Authority." In *Islam et politique au Maghreb*, ed. J.-Cl. Vatin and E. Gellner. Paris: Éditions du CNRS, 281–302.

————. 1993a. "Coutumes locales et coutumes universelles aux sources de règles juridiques en droit musulman hanafite." *Annales Islamologiques* 27: 29–35.

————. 1993b. "Legal Literature and the Problem of Change: The Case of the Land Rent." In *Islam and Public Law*, ed. C. Mallat. London: Graham and Trotman, 29–47.

Jokisch, B. 1999. "Socio-Political Factors of Qada' in Eighth/Fourteenth Century Syria." *Al-Qantara* 20: 503–30.

Jones, W. R. 1980. "Pious Endowments in Medieval Christianity and Islam." *Diogenes* 109: 23–36.

Juynboll, G. H. A. 1983. *Muslim Tradition.* Cambridge: Cambridge University Press.

Karamustafa, A. T. 1993. "The Antinomian Dervish as Model Saint." In *Modes de transmission de la culture religieuse en Islam*, ed. H. Elboudrari. Cairo: Institut Français d'Archéologie Orientale du Caire, 241–60.

————. 1994. *God's Unruly Friends: Dervish Groups in the Islamic Later Middle Period, 1200–1550.* Salt Lake City: Utah University Press.

Karrar, A. S. 1992. *The Sufi Brotherhoods in the Sudan.* Evanston: Northwestern University Press.

al-Kasani, Abu Bakr b. Mas`ud (d.585/1189). 1910. *Kitab Bada'i` al-Sana'i` fi Tartib al-Shara'i`*, vol. 4. Cairo: Matba`at al-Jamaliyya.

al-Khatib al-Baghdadi, Ahmad b. `Ali (d. 463/1072). 1966. *Ta'rikh Baghdad.* Beirut.

Kindi (d. 350/961). 1912. *Kitab al-Wulat wa-Kitab al-Qudat. The Governors and Judges of Egypt.* Ed. R. Guest. Leyden and London: Brill.

Kister, M. 1971. "Rajab is the Month of God." *Israel Oriental Studies* 1: 191–223.

Kraemer, J. L. 1982. "Heresy Versus the State in Medieval Islam." In *Studies in Judaica, Karaitica, and Islamica*, ed. S. R. Brunswick. Ramat Gan: Bar Ilan University Press, 167–80.

Kressel, G. M. 1992. *Descent through Males. Mediterranean Language and Culture Monograph Series*, 8. Wiesbaden: Harrassowitz.

Lambton, A. K. S. 1968. "The Internal Structure of the Seljuk Empire." In *The Cambridge History of Iran*, vol. 5, ed. J. A. Boyle. Cambridge: Cambridge University Press, 203-83.

———. 1981. *State and Government in Medieval Islam*. Oxford: Oxford University Press.

———. *El²* "*Khalifa*—(II) In Political Theory." In *Encyclopaedia of Islam*, new edition.

———. 1988. *Continuity and Change in Medieval Persia: Aspects of Administrative, Economic, and Social History, 11th–14th Century*. Albany: State University of New York Press.

Landau-Tasseron, E. 1989. "The 'Cyclical Reform': A Study of the Mujaddid Tradition." *Studia Islamica* 70: 79–118.

Laoust, H. 1939. *Essai sur les doctrines sociales et politiques de Taki al-Din Ahmad b. Taimiya*. Cairo: Institut Français d'Archéologie Orientale.

———. 1959. "Le hanbalisme sous le Califat de Baghdad, 241–656/855–1258." *Revue des Études Islamiques* 27: 67–128.

———. 1965. *Les schismes dans l'Islam: introduction à une étude de la religion musulmane*. Paris: Payot.

———. 1973. "Les Agitations Religieuses à Baghdad aux IVe et Ve siècles de l'Hégire." In *Islamic Civilizatioon, 950–1150*, ed. D. S. Richards. Oxford: Cassirer, 169–85.

Lapidus, I. M. 1967. *Muslim Cities in the Later Middle Ages*. Cambridge, Mass.: Harvard University Press.

———. 1969. "Muslim Cities and Islamic Societies." In *Middle Eastern Cities: Symposium on Ancient, Medieval, and Modern Middle Eastern Urbanism*, ed. I. M. Lapidus. Berkeley: University of California Press, 47–79.

———. 1975. "The Separation of State and Religion in the Development of Early Islamic Society." *International Journal of Middle Eastern Studies* 6: 363–85.

———. 1982. "The Arab Conquest and the Formation of Islamic Societies." In *Studies on the First Century of Islamic Society*, ed. G. Juynboll. Carbondale, Ill.: Southern Illinois University Press, 49–72.

———. 1988. *A History of Islamic Societies*, 1st ed. Cambridge: Cambridge University Press.

———. 1996. "State and Religion in Islamic Societies." *Past and Present* 151: 3–27.

Layish, A. 1974. "Shari`a u-Minhag ba-Mishpaha ha-Muslimit bi-Yisra'el." *Hamizrah Hehadash* 23: 377–409.

———. 1975. *Women and Islamic Law in a Non-Muslim State*. Jerusalem: Israeli Universities Press; New York: Wiley.

———. 1980–1982. "Challenges to Customary Law and Arbitration: The Impact of Islamic Law upon Settled Bedouin in the Judaean Desert." *Tel Aviv University Studies in Law* 5: 206–21.

———. 1984a. "The Islamization of the Bedouin Family in the Judaean Desert, as Reflected in the *Sijill* of the *Shari`a* Court." In *The Changing Bedouin*, ed. E. Marx and A. Shmueli. New Brunswick, NJ: Transaction Books, 39–58.

———. 1984b. "'*Ulama*' and Politics in Saudi Arabia." In *Islam and Politics in the Modern Middle East*, ed. M. Heper and R. Israeli. London: Croom Helm, 29–63.

———. 1987. "Legal Reform in Saudi Arabia as a Mechanism to Moderate Wahhabi Doctrine." *Journal of the Amerian Oriental Society* 107: 279–92.

————. 1989. "Islamic Law in the Contemporary Middle East." *Occasional Papers* 3, Centre of Near and Middle Eastern Studies, University of London. London: School of Oriental and African Studies.

————. 1991. *Divorce in the Libyan Family*. New York: New York University Press; Jerusalem: Magnes Press.

————. 1995a. *"Dar `Adl*—Symbiosis of Custom and *Shari`a* in Tribal Society in Process of Sedentarization." *Jerusalem Studies in Arabic and Islam* 19: 198–213.

————. 1995b. *"Shari`a* and Custom in Libya: Was Tajdida Married to Two Husbands?" *Archiv Orientální* 63: 488–503.

————. 1996. "The Fatwa as an Instrument of Accommodation." In *Islamic Legal Interpretation. Muftis and Their Fatwas*, ed. M. K. Masud, B. Messick, and D. S. Powers. Cambridge: Harvard University Press, 270–77.

————. 1998. *Legal Documents on Libyan Tribal Society in Process of Sedentarization. Pt. 1: The Documents in Arabic. Mediterranean Language and Culture Monograph Series* 14. Wiesbaden: Harrassowitz.

————. *EI²a* "Mahkama." In *Encyclopaedia of Islam*, new edition.

————. *EI²b* "Mirath." In *Encyclopaedia of Islam*, new edition.

————. *EI²c* "Talak." In *Encyclopaedia of Islam*, new edition.

Layish, A., and J. Davis. 1988. *Libyan Society: A Selection of Documents from the Sijills of the Shari`a Courts of Ajdabiya and Kufra*. Jerusalem: Academon.

Layish, A., and R. Shaham. *EI²a* "Nikah." In *Encyclopaedia of Islam*, new edition.

————. *EI²b* "Tashri`." In *Encyclopaedia of Islam*, new edition.

Layish, A., and A. Shmueli. 1979. "Custom and *Shari`a* in the Bedouin Family according to Legal Documents from the Judaean Desert." *Bulletin of the School of Oriental and African Studies* 42: 29–45.

Lazarus-Yafeh, H. 1981. "Muslim Festivals." In idem. *Some Religious Aspects of Islam*. Leiden: Brill, 38–47.

————. 1986. "Tajdid al-Din: A Reconsideration of Its Meaning, Roots and Influence in Islam," *The New East* 31: 1–10.

Leder, S. 1997. "Charismatic Scripturalism. The Hanbali Maqdisis of Damascus." *Der Islam* 74: 279–303.

Leiser, G. 1986. "Note on the Madrasa in Medieval Islamic Society." *The Muslim World* 56: 16–23.

Levtzion, N. 1979a. "Toward a Comparative Study of Islamization." In *Conversion to Islam*, ed. N. Levtzion. New York and London: Holmes and Meier, 1–23.

————. 1979b. "The `Ulama' as Officials and as Popular Leaders." Paper submitted to the conference on Hierarchy and Stratification in the Middle East, under the auspices of the Joint Committee on Near and Middle East Social Science Research Council, and the American Council of Learned Societies, Mt. Kisco, New York, 9–12 May 1979.

————. 1981. "Shari`a u-Minhag be-Tahalikhei Hit'aslemut ve-Hitnahalut." *Cathedra* 20: 78–80.

————. 1986. "Eighteenth-Century Renewal and Reform Movements in Islam." *The New East* 31: 48–70.

————. 1987. "The Eighteenth Century: Background to the Islamic Revolutions in West Africa." In *Eighteenth-Century Renewal and Reform Movements in Islam*, ed. N. Levtzion and J. O. Voll. Syracuse: Syracuse University Press, 21–38.

————. 1997. "Eighteenth-Century Sufi Brotherhoods: Structural, Organizational and Ritual Changes." In *Islam: Essays on Scripture, Thought, and Society, A Festschrift in Honour of Anthony H. Johns*, ed. P. R. Riddel and T. Street. Leiden: Brill, 147–60.

Levtzion, N., and J. O. Voll eds. 1987. *Eighteenth-Century Renewal and Reform Movements in Islam*. Syracuse: Syracuse University Press.

Levtzion, N., and G. Weigert. 1995. "Religious Reform in Eighteenth-Century Morocco." *Jerusalem Studies in Arabic and Islam* 19: 173–97.

Lewis, B. 1973. *Islam in History*. London: Alcove Press.

————. 1993. "The Significance of Heresy in Islam." In idem, *Islam in History*, new ed., rev. and expanded. Chicago: Open Court, 275–94.

Lewis, I. M. 1984. "Sufism in Somaliland: A Study in Tribal Islam." In *Islam in Tribal Societies*, ed. S. A. Akbar and D. M. Hart. London: Routledge and Kegan Paul, 127–68.

Libson, G. 1997. "On the Development of Custom as a Source of Law in Islamic Law." *Islamic Law and Society* 4: 131–55.

Lindholm, Ch. 1996. "Despotism and Democracy: State and Society in the Premodern Middle East." In *The Social Philosophy of Ernest Gellner*, ed. J. A. Hall and I. Jarvie. Amsterdam and Atlanta: Rodopi, 329–55.

Madelung, W. F. 1974. "The Origins of the Controversy Concerning the Creation of the Koran." In *Orientalia Hispanica sive studia F.M. Pareja Octogenario Dicata*, vol. I/1, ed. J. M. Barral. Leiden: Brill.

————. 1985. *Religious Schools and Sects in Medieval Islam*. London: Variorum Reprints.

Makdisi, G. 1959. "The Topography of Eleventh-Century Baghdad." *Arabica* 6: 178–97.

————. 1961. "Muslim Institutions of Learning in 11th Century Baghdad." *Bulletin of Oriental and African Studies* 24: 1–56.

————. 1963. *Ibn `Aqil et la resurgence de l'Islam traditionaliste au XIe siècle*. Damascus: Institut Français de Damas.

————. 1971. "Law and Traditionalism in the Institutions of Learning of Medieval Islam." In *Theology and Law in Islam*, ed. G. E. von Grunebaum. Wiesbaden: Harrassowitz, 75–88.

————. 1973. "The Sunni Revival." In *Islamic Civilization 950–1150*, ed. D. S. Richards. Oxford: Cassirer, 155–68.

————. 1975. Review of R. Bulliet, *The Patricians of Nishapur, Journal of American Oriental Society* 95: 491–95.

————. 1981a. *The Rise of Colleges: Institutions of Learning in Islam and the West*. Edinburgh: Edinburgh University Press.

————. 1981b. "Hanbalite Islam." In *Studies on Islam*, ed. M. L. Swartz. New York: Oxford University Press, 216–74.

————. 1990. *The Rise of Humanism in Classical Islam and the Christian World*. Edinburgh: Edinburgh University Press.

Malik, Abu `Abd Allah b. Anas (d. 179/796). 1989. *al-Muwatta of Imam Malik Ibn Anas*. Trans. Aisha Abdurrahman Bewley. London: Kegal Paul International.

Mandaville, J. E. 1979. "Usurious Piety: The Cash *Waqf* Controversy in the Ottoman Empire." *International Journal of Middle East Studies* 10: 289–308.

Marcus, A. 1979. "Piety and Profit: The *Waqf* in the Society and Economy of Eighteenth-Century Aleppo." Paper presented at the International Seminar on Social and Economic Aspects of the Muslim *Waqf*, Jerusalem, 24–28 June 1979.

———. 1989. *The Middle East on the Eve of Modernity: Aleppo in the Eighteenth Century.* New York: Columbia University Press.

Mardin, S. 1988. "The Ottoman 'Tacit' Contract." In *State, Democracy, and the Military in Turkey in the 1980s,* ed. M. Heper and A. Evin. Berlin and New York: Walter de Gruyter.

———. 1995. "Civil Society and Islam." In *Civil Society, Theory, History, Comparison,* ed. J. A. Hall. Cambridge: Polity Press, 278–300.

Mardsen, R. 1999. "Community, Civil Society, and Social Ecology." In *Civic Engagement in the Atlantic Community,* ed. J. Janning, C. Kupchan, and D. Rumberg. Gütersloh: Bertelsmann Foundation Publishers, 97–114.

Marshal, G. 1994. *Oxford Dictionary of Sociology.* Oxford: Oxford University Press.

Martin, B. G. 1969. "Notes sur l'origine de la *tariqa* des Tijaniyya et sur ler débuts d'al-hajj `Umar." *Revue des Études Islamiques* 37: 267–90.

Masud, M. K., B. Messick, and D. S. Powers, eds. 1996a. *Islamic Legal Interpretation. Muftis and Their Fatwas.* Cambridge: Harvard University Press.

———. 1996b "Muftis, Fatwas, and Islamic Legal Interpretation." In *Islamic Legal Interpretation. Muftis and Their Fatwas,* ed. M. K. Masud, B. Messick, and D. S. Powers. Cambridge: Harvard University Press, 3–32.

Matsui, T. 1968. "On the Nineteenth-Century Indian Economic History: A Review of a 'Reinterpretation'." *The Indian Economic and Social History Review* 5, no. 1: 17–33.

Mayer, A. E. 1987. "Law and Religion in the Muslim Middle East." *The American Journal of Comparative Law* 35: 127–84.

Melchert, C. 1992. "Sectaries in the Six Books: Evidence for their Exclusion from the Sunni Community." *The Muslim World* 82: 287–95.

Meron, Y. 1971. *L'obligation alimentaire entre époux en droit musulman hanéfite.* Paris: R. Pichon et R. Durand-Auzias.

Milliot, L. 1953. *Introduction à l'étude du droit musulman.* Paris: Recueil Sirey.

Mir-Hosseini, Z. 1999. *Islam and Gender: The Religious Debate in Contemporary Iran.* Princeton: Princeton University Press.

Mohsen, S. K. 1975. *Conflict and Law among Awlad `Ali of the Western Desert.* Cairo: National Center for Social and Criminological Research.

Moore, B. 1966. *The Social Origins of Dictatorship and Democracy.* Boston: Beacon Press.

———. 1978. *Injustice: The Social Bases of Obedience and Revolt.* New York: Sharpe.

Morray, D. 1994. *An Ayyubid Notable and his World. Ibn al-`Adim and Aleppo as Portrayed in his Biographical Dictionary of People Connected with the City.* Leiden: Brill.

Morris, M. D. 1968. "Towards a Reinterpretation of Nineteenth-Century Indian Economic History." *The Indian Economic and Social History Review* 5: 1–15.

Morsy, M. 1984. "Arbitration as a Political Institution: An Interpretation of the Status of Monarchy in Morocco." In *Islam in Tribal Societies,* ed. S. A. Akbar and D. M. Hart. London: Routledge and Kegan Paul, 39–65.

Mottahede, R. P. 1973. "Administration in Buyid Qazwin." In *Islamic Civilization, 950–1150,* ed. D. S. Richards. Oxford: Cassirer, 33–45.

———. 1980. *Loyalty and Leadership in an Early Islamic Society.* Princeton: Princeton University Press.

Mouton, J.-M. 1994. *Damas et sa principauté sous les Saljoukides et les Bourides 468–549/1076–1154.* Cairo: Institut Français d'Archéologie Orientale.

Munson, H. Jr. 1988. *Islam and Revolution in the Middle East*. New Haven: Yale University Press.

Natur, A. 1991. "Shari`a u-Minhag ba-Mishpaha ha-Bedevit ba-Negev `al pi ha-Pesiqa shel Beit ha-Din ha-Shar`i bi-Be'ersheva." *Hamizrah Hehadash* 33: 94–111.

Nawas, J. A. 1994. "A Reexamination of Three Current Explanations for al-Ma'mun's Introduction of the Mihna." *International Journal of Middle Eastern Studies* 26: 615–29.

al-Nawawi (d. 676/1277). 1999. *Fatawa al-Imam al-Nawawi*. Ed. M. al-Arna'ut. Damascus: Dar al-Fikr.

Norris, H. T. 1993. *Islam in the Balkans: Religion and Society between Europe and the Arab World*. Columbia: University of South Carolina.

Norton, A. R., ed. 1995. *Civil Society in the Middle East*. Leiden: Brill.

Ocak, A. Y. 1993. "Kalenderi Dervishes and Ottoman Administration from the Fourteenth to the Sixteenth Centuries." In *Manifestations of Sainthood in Islam*, ed. G. M. Smith and C. E. Ernst. Istanbul: Isis Press, 239–55.

Olson, R. W. 1974. "The Esnaf and the Patrona Halil Rebellion of 1730: A Realignment in Ottoman Politics?" *Journal of the Economic and Social History of the Orient* 17: 329–44.

O'Neill, J. 1986. "The Disciplinary Society from Weber to Foucault." *British Journal of Sociology* 37, no. 1: 42–60.

Ongan, H. 1974. *Ankaranın Iki Numaralı Şeriye Sicili*. Ankara: Türk Tarih Kurumu.

Oweidi [al-`Abbadi], A. S. S. 1982. "Bedouin Justice in Jordan." Ph.D. dissertaion, Cambridge University.

Patton, W. 1897. *Ahmed Ibn Hanbal and the Mihna*. Leiden: Brill.

Paul, J. 1991. "Forming a Faction: The *himaya* system of Khwaja Ahrar." *International Journal of Middle East Studies* 23: 533–48.

Pavlin, J. 1996. "Sunni *kalam* and the Theological Controversies." In *The History of Islamic Philosophy*, ed. S. H. Nasr and O. Leaman. London: Routledge.

Pedersen, J. 1948. "The Islamic Preacher: wa`iz, mudhakkir, qass." In *Ignaz Goldziher Memorial Volume*, ed. S. Löwinger and J. Smogyi. Budapest: Globus vol. 1, 226–51.

———. 1953. "The Criticism of the Islamic Preacher." *Die Welt des Islams* n.s. 2: 215–31.

Peri, O. 1983. "The Ottoman State and the *Waqf* Institution in Late Eighteenth-Century Jerusalem." M.A. Thesis, The Hebrew University of Jerusalem (in Hebrew).

Peters, E. L. 1980. "Aspects of the Bedouin Bridewealth among Camel Herders in Cyrenaica." In *The Meaning of Marriage Payments*, ed. J. L. Comaroff. London: Academic Press, 125–60.

Peters, R. 1996. "Islamic Criminal Law: A Survey for the Course 'Introduction to Islamic Law'." Amsterdam: University of Amsterdam, Department of Arabic Studies.

Pines, S. 1996. "An Early Meaning of the Term *Mutakallim*." In *Studies in the History of Arabic Philosophy*, ed. S. Stroumsa. Jerusalem: The Magnes Press.

Pipes, D. 1981. *Slave Soldiers and Islam*. New Haven: Yale University Press.

Pollock, S. 1993. "Deep Orientalism? Notes on Sanskrit and Power beyond the Raj." In *Orientalism and the Postcolonial Predicament*, ed. C. A. Breckenridge and P. Van der Veer. Philadelphia: University of Pennsylvania Press, 76–133.

———. 1998a. "The Cosmopolitan Vernacular." *Journal of Asian Studies* 57: 6–37.

———. 1998b. "India in the Vernacular Millennium: Literary Culture and Polity, 1000–1500." *Daedalus* 127: 41–75.

Pouzet, L. 1986. *Damas au VIIe/XIIIe siècle—Vie et structures religieuses d'une métropole islamique*. Beirut: Dar al-Machreq.

Powers, D. S. 1990. "*Fatwas* as Sources for Legal and Social History: A Dispute over Endowment Revenues from Fourteenth-Century Fez." *Al-Qantara* 11: 295–341.

———. 1994. "Kadijustiz or Qadi-Justice? A Paternity Dispute from Fourteenth-Century Morocco." *Islamic Law and Society* 1: 332–66.

Pruett, G. E. 1984. "Islam and Orientalism." In *Orientalism, Islam, and Islamists*, ed. A. Hussain, R. Olson, and J. Qureshi. Brattleboro, VT: Amana Books, 43–87.

al-Qusus, `A. 1972. *al-Qada' al-Badawi*, 2nd ed. Amman: al-Matba`a al-Urduniyya.

Rafeq, A. 1994. "The Syrian `Ulama', Ottoman Law and Islamic Shar`ia." *Turcica* 26: 9–29.

Rahman, F. 1979. *Islam*, 2nd ed. Chicago: University of Chicago Press.

al-Ramli , Khayr al-Din (d. 1081/1670). 1893-94. *Al-Fatawa al-Khayriyya li-Naf` al-Bariyya*, 2 vols. Istanbul: Matbaa-i Uthmaniyye.

Raymond, A. 1973–1974. *Artisans et commerçants au Caire au XVIIIe siècle*, 2 vols. Damascus: Institut Français de Damas.

RCEA. 1931–1943. *Répertoire Chronologique d'Épigraphie Arabe*, 17 vols. Ed. E. Combe, J. Sauvaget, and G. Wiet. Cairo: Institut Français d'Archéologie Orientale.

Roded, R. 1989. "Quantitative Analysis of Waqf Endowment Deeds." *Osmanlı Araştırmaları* 9: 51–76.

Rodinson, M. 1971. *Mohammed*. New York: Pantheon Books.

Rosen, L. 1989. *The Anthropology of Justice*. Cambridge: Cambridge University Press.

———. 1995. "Law and Custom in the Popular Legal Culture of North Africa." *Islamic Law and Society* 2: 194-208.

Rosenthal, E. I. J. 1958. *Political Thought in Medieval Islam*. Cambridge: Cambridge University Press.

Rosenthal, F. 1968. *A History of Muslim Historiography*, 2nd ed. Leiden: Brill.

Roy, A. 1984. *The Islamic Syncretistic Tradition in Bengal*. Princeton: Princeton University Press.

Rudolph, S., and L. Rudolph. 1987. *In Pursuit of Lakshmi: The Political Economy of the Indian State*. Chicago: University of Chicago Press.

Saadeh, S. 1977. "The Development of the Position of the Chief Judge during the Buyid and Seljuk Periods." Ph.D. dissertation, Harvard University.

Sadowski, Y. 1997. "The New Orientalism and the Democracy Debate." In *Political Islam*, ed. J. Beinin and J. Stork. Berkeley: University of California Press, 33–50.

Said, E. 1978. *Orientalism*. New York: Vintage Books.

Sauvaget, J. 1941. *Alep: essai sur le développement d'une grande ville syrienne des origines au milieu du XIXe siècle*. Paris: P. Geuthner.

al-Sawi, Ahmad (d. 1241/1825–1826). 1806. *Bulghat al-Salik li-Aqrab al-Masalik*, 2 vols. [Cairo]: al-Maktaba al-Tijariyya al-Kubra.

Schacht, J. 1953. "Early Doctrines on *Waqf*." In *Mélanges Fuad Köprülü*. Istanbul: Osman Yalçın Matbaası, 443–52.

———. 1964. *An Introduction to Islamic Law*. Oxford: Clarendon Press.

———. 1974. "Law and the State." In *The Legacy of Islam*, ed. J. Schacht and E. C. Bosworth. 2nd edition. Oxford: Clarendon Press, 392–403.

Schimmel, A. 1973. *Islamic Literatures of India*. Wiesbaden: Harrassowitz.

———. 1975. *Classical Urdu Literature from the Beginning to Iqbal*. Wiesbaden: Harrassowitz.

————. 1976. *Pain and Grace: A Study of Two Mystical Writers in Eighteenth-Century Muslim India*. Leiden: Brill.

Schluchter, W. 1987. "Einleitung: Zwischen Welteroberung und Weltanpassung. Überlegungen zu Max Webers Sicht des frühen Islams." In *Max Webers Sicht des Islams. Interpretation und Kritik*, ed. W. Schluchter. Frankfurt: Suhrkamp, 11–124.

————. 1989. "Towards a Comparative Sociology of Religion." In idem, *Rationalism, Religion, and Domination: A Weberian Perspective*, Part II. Trans. N. Solomon. Berkeley: University of California Press, 83–279.

Schwarz, K., and H. Kurio. 1983. *Die Stiftungen des osmanischen Grosswesirs Koğa Sinan Pascha (gest. 1596) in Uzungaova/Bulgarien*. Berlin: Klaus Schwarz Verlag.

Serrano [Ruano], D. S. 1996. "La práctica legal (`amal) en al-Andalus a través de los *Madhahib al-Hukkam fi Nawazil al-Ahkam* de Muhammad Ibn `Iyad." *Qurtuba* 1: 171–92.

Shackle, C. 1993. "Early Vernacular Poetry in the Indus Valley: its Contexts and its Character." In *Islam and Indian Religions*, ed. A. L. Dallapicola and S. Zingel-Ave Lallemant. Stuttgart: Steiner, 259–89.

Shaham, R. 1993. "A Woman's Place: A Confrontation with Bedouin Custom in the Shari`a Court." *Journal of the American Oriental Society* 111: 192–97.

————. 1997. *Family and the Court in Modern Egypt*. Leiden: Brill.

Shahar, I. 1997. "Trilemma be-Diyunei Beit ha-Din 'al-Mahkama al-Shar`iyya' bi-Be'ersheva ki-Nequdat Mifgash shel Shalosh Ma`arachot Hoq: Huqei ha-Medina, ha-Hoq ha-Shar`i veha-`Urf ha-Bedevi." *Jama`a* 1: 11–35.

Shahid, I. 1970. "Pre-Islamic Arabia." In *Cambridge History of Islam*, vol. 1, ed. P. Holt, A. Lambton, and B. Lewis. Cambridge: Cambridge University Press, 3–29.

Shalabi, M. M. 1973. *Ahkam al-Usra fi'l-Islam. Dirasa Muqarana bayna Fiqh al-Madhahib al-Sunniyya wa'l-Madhhab al-Ja`fari*. Beirut: Dar al-Nahda al-`Arabiyya.

Sharon, M. 1983. *Black Banners from the East*. Jerusalem: Magnes Press.

al-Shaybani (al-Khassaf), Abu Bakr Ahmad b.`Amr (d. 261/875). 1904. *Kitab Ahkam al-Waqf*. Cairo: Bulaq.

Sibt b. al-Jawzi (d. 654/1256). 1951, 1951–1952. *Mir'at al-Zaman fi Ta'rikh al-A`yan*. Printed edition of the Jewett text. Part. 8, vol. 1 [Events in the years A.H. 495–589] (1951), vol. 8 (1951–1952). Hyderabad, Deccan: Dairatu'l-Maarifi'l-Osmania.

————. 1968. *Mir'at al-Zaman fi Ta'rikh al-A`yan*. Partial edition by A. Sevin. Ankara: Türk Tarih Kurumu. (Events connected with the Seljuks, A.H. 448–480).

Siegman, H. 1964. "The State and the Individual in Sunni Islam." *The Muslim World* 54: 14–26.

Sivan, E. 1968. *L'Islam et la croisade: idéalogie et propagande dans les réactions musulmanes aux croisades*. Paris: Librairie d'Amérique et d'Orient.

————. 1985. *Interpretations of Islam Past and Present*. Princeton: The Darwin Press.

————. 1995. "In God's Cause." In *The Limits of Pluralism: Neo-Absolutisms and Relativism*. Amsterdam: Praemium Erasmianum Foundation, 9–27.

Skocpol, T. 1973. "A Critical Review of Barrington Moore's Social Origins of Dictatorship and Democracy." *Politics and Society* 1: 1–34.

Smith, W. C. 1963. *Islam in Modern History*. New York: New American Library.

Somers, M. R. 1995. "What's Political or Cultural About Political Culture and the Public Sphere? Towards an Historical Sociology of Concept Formation." *Sociological Theory* 13: 113–44.

Sourdel, D. 1953. "Ruhin. Lieu de pèlerinage musulman de la Syrie du nord au XIIIe siècle." *Syria* 30: 89–107.

———. 1972. "Deux documents relatifs à la communauté hanbalite du Damas." *Bulletin d'Études Orientales* 25: 141–52.

Springborg, P. 1987. "The Contractual State: Reflections on Orientalism and Despotism." *History of Political Thought* 8: 395–433.

———. 1992. *Western Republicanism and the Oriental Prince*. Cambridge: Polity Press.

Stauth, G. 1993. *Islam und westlicher Rationalismus: Der Beitrag des Orientalismus zur Entstehung der Soziologie*. Frankfurt: Campus Verlag.

Stewart, F. H. 1987. "A Bedouin Narrative from Central Sinai." *Zeitschrift für arabische Linguistik* 16: 44–92.

———. 1988. *Texts in Sinai Bedouin Law. Pt. 1: The Texts in English Translation*. Mediterranean Language and Culture Monograph Series 5. Wiesbaden: Harrassowitz.

———. 1990. *Texts in Sinai Bedouin Law. Pt. 2: The Texts in Arabic*. Mediterranean Language and Culture Monograph Series 5. Wiesbaden: Harrassowitz.

al-Subki, Taj al-Din (d. 771/1370). 1966–1967. *Tabaqat al-Shafi`iyya al-Kubra*, 6 vols. Cairo: Dar al-Kutub al-Khidiwiyya.

———. 1970–1971. *Tabaqat al-Shafi`iyya al-Kubra*, vols. 7–8. Ed. `A. M. al-Julu and M. M. al-Tanahi. Cairo: Matba`at Mustafa al-Babi al-Halabi.

al-Sulami, `Izz al-Din (d. 660/1262). 1996. *Fatawa*. Ed. M. J. Kurdi. Beirut: Mu'asasat al-Risala.

al-Suri, Salah al-Din Hasan. 1984. "Libya wa'l-Ghazw wa'l-Thaqafa al-Itali." In *Buhuth wa-Dirasat fi'l-Ta'rikh al-Libi 1911–1943*, ed. al-Suri and H. Wada`a al-Husnawi. vol. 2. Tripoli: n. p., 393–431.

Swartz, M. L. 1982. "The Rules of Popular Preaching in Twelfth-Century Baghdad according to Ibn al-Jawzi." In *Prédication et propagande au Moyen Age. Islam, Byzance, Occident*, ed. G. Makdisi et al. Paris: Presses Universitaires de France.

al-Tabari, Muhammad b. Jarir (d. 310/923). 1987. *The History of al-Tabari*, vol. 32. Trans. C. E. Bosworth. Albany: State University of New York Press.

Talmon-Heller, D. 1994. "The Shaykh and the Community: Popular Hanbalite Islam in 12th-13th Century Jabal Nablus and Jabal Qasyun." *Studia Islamica* 79: 103–20.

———. 1999. "Society and Religion in Syria from the Reign of Nur al-Din to the Mamluk Occupation (1154–1260)." Ph.D. dissertation, The Hebrew University of Jerusalem (in Hebrew).

———. 2001. "Preachers and Prayer Leaders in Ayyubid Syria." *Israel Oriental Studies* (forthcoming).

Taylor, C. 1990. "Modes of Civil Society." *Public Culture* 3: 95–132.

Taylor, C. S. 1998. *In the Vicinity of the Righteous: Ziyara and the Veneration of Saints in Late Medieval Egypt*. Leiden: Brill.

Tedlock, D. 1992. "On Hieroglyphic Literacy in Ancient Mayaland: An Alternative Interpretation." *Current Anthropology* 33: 216–17.

Thompson, P. E. 1971. "The Moral Economy of the English Crowd in the Eighteenth Century." *Past and Present* 50: 76–136.

Tibawi, A. L. 1962. "The Origins and Character of al-Madrasa." *Bulletin of the School of Oriental and African Studies* 25: 225–38.

Trimingham, J. S. 1971. *The Sufi Orders in Islam*. Oxford: Clarendon Press.

Turner, B. 1974. *Weber and Islam*. London: Routledge and Kegan Paul.

——. 1984. "Orientalism and the Problem of Civil Society in Islam." In *Orientalism, Islam, and Islamists*, ed. A. Hussain, R. Olson, and J. Qureshi. Brattleboro, VT: Amana Books, 23–42.

Tyan, E. 1960. *Histoire de l'organisation judiciaire en pays d'Islam*. Leiden: Brill.

——. *EI*² "*Kadi*." In *Encyclopaedia of Islam*, new edition.

Van der Sprenkel, B. O. 1958. *The Chinese Civil Service: The Nineteenth Century*. Canberra: Australian National University.

Van Ess, J. 1992. *Theologie und Gesellschaft im 2. und 3. Jahrhundert Hidschra*, vol. 3. Berlin and New York: Walter de Gruyter.

Van Krieken, R. 1990. "The Organization of the Soul: Elias and Foucault on Discipline and the Self." *Archives Européennes de Sociologie* 31: 353–71.

Vatikiotis, P .J. 1987. *Islam and the State*. London: Croom Helm.

Veinstein, G. 1992. "La voix du maître à travers les firmans de Soliman le Magnifique." In *Soliman le Magnifique et son Temps*, ed. G. Veinstein. Paris: École des Hautes Études en Sciences Sociales, 127–44.

Venske, M. L. 1986. "Special Use of the Tithe as a Revenue-Raising Measure in the Sixteenth Century *Sanjaq* of Aleppo." *Journal of the Economic and Social History of the Orient* 24: 239–323.

Veyne, P. 1990. *Bread and Circuses: Historical Sociology and Political Pluralism*, abridged, with an introduction by O. Murray. Trans. B. Pearce. London: Allen Lane, Penguin.

Vidal-Naquet, P. 1996. *La démocratie grecque vue d'ailleurs*. Paris: Flammarion.

Vikør, K. S. 1994. "The Concept of *Ijtihad* in a Nineteenth Century Debate: Muhammad b. `Ali al-Sanusi's *Iqaz al-Wasnan*." Paper submitted to EURAMES Inaugural Conference, Warwick, 8–11 July 1994.

——. 1995. *Sufi and Scholar on the Desert Edge: Muhammad b. `Ali al-Sanusi and His Brotherhood*. London: Hurst.

Vogel, F. E. 1999. *Islamic Law in the Modern World: The Legal System of Saudi Arabia*. Leiden: Brill.

Voll, J. 1991. "Fundamentalism in the Sunni Arab World: Egypt and the Sudan." In *Fundamentalism Observed*, ed. M. Marty and R. S. Appleby. Chicago: University of Chicago Press, 345–403.

Wakeman F. Jr. 1998. "Boundaries of the Public Sphere in Ming and Qing China." *Daedalus* 127: 167–90.

Waterbury, J. 1970. *The Commander of the Faithful: The Moroccan Political Elite—A Study in Segmented Politics*. London: Weidenfeld & Nicolson.

Watt, M. W. 1968. *Islamic Political Thought*. Edinburgh: Edinburgh University Press.

Weber, M. 1924. *Gesammelte Aufsätze zur Soziologie und Sozialpolitik*. Tübingen: Mohr.

——. 1951. *The Religion of China: Confucianism and Taoism*. Glencoe: Free Press.

——. 1952. *Ancient Judaism*. Glencoe: Free Press.

——. 1958. *The Religion of India: The Sociology of Hinduism and Buddhism*. Glencoe: Free Press.

——. 1964. *The Theory of Social and Economic Organization*. New York: The Free Press.

——. 1968. *On Charisma and Institution Building: Selected Papers*. Chicago: University of Chicago Press.

——. 1969. *On Law in Economy and Society*. Cambridge: Harvard University Press.

Weckman, G. 1986–1987. "Community." In *The Encyclopedia of Religion*, vol. 3, ed. M. Eliade. New-York: Macmillan, 566–71.

Weigert, G. 1989. "The Khalwatiyya in Egypt in the Eighteenth Century." Ph.D. dissertation, The Hebrew University of Jerusalem.

Wensinck, A. J. *EI "Tarawih."* In *Encyclopaedia of Islam.*

———. *EI²* "Sha`ban." In *Encyclopaedia of Islam,* new edition.

Wheatley, P. In press. *The Places Where Men Pray Together: Cities in Islamic Lands, 7th-10th Centuries.* Chicago: University of Chicago Press.

Wink, A. 1994. "Al-Hind: The Making of the Indo-Islamic World." Paper presented at the International Symposium on Indian Studies, Kovalam, 28 November-2 December 1994.

Winkelhane, G., and K. Schwarz. 1985. *Der osmanische Statthalter Iskender Pascha (gest. 1571) und seine Stiftungen in Ägypten und am Bosporus.* Bamberg: Verlag Aku GmBh.

Winter, M. 1982. *Society and Religion in Early Ottoman Egypt: Studies in the Writings of `Abd al-Wahhab al-Sha`rani.* New Brunswick, NJ: Transaction Books.

Woodside, A. 1998. "Territorial Order and Collective Identity Tensions in Confucian Asia: China, Vietnam, Korea." *Daedalus* 127: 191–220.

Al-Ya`qubi (d. 897/1491). 1892. *Kitab al-Buldan,* ed. M. J. de Goeje. 2nd edition. Leiden: Brill.

Yazici, T. *EI²* "Qalandariyya." In *Encyclopaedia of Islam,* new edition.

Yerasimos, S. 1994. "Les waqfs dans l'aménagement urbain d'Istanbul au XIXᵉ siècle." In *Le waqf dans le monde musulman contemporain (XIXᵉ-XXᵉ siècles): fonctions sociales, économiques et politiques,* ed. F. Bilici. Actes de la Table Ronde d'Istanbul, 13–14 novembre 1992. Istanbul-Paris: Institut Français d'Études Anatoliennes d'Istanbul, 43–49.

Zaman, M. Q. 1997. *Religion and Politics Under the Early `Abbasids.* Leiden: Brill.

Zarcone, T. 1993. *Mystiques, philosophes, et franc-maçons en Islam: Riza Tevfik, penseur ottoman (1868–1949), du soufisme à la confrérie.* Istanbul-Paris: Librairie d'Amérique et d'Orient.

Ze'evi, D. 1996. *An Ottoman Century: The District of Jerusalem in the 1600s.* Albany: State University of New York Press.

Zettersteen, K. V., and Ch. Pellat. *EI²* "Ahmad b. Abi Du'ad." In *Encyclopaedia of Islam,* new edition.

Ziai, H. *EI²* "Al-Suhrawardi, Shihab al-Din Yahya b. Habash." In *Encyclopaedia of Islam,* new edition.

Zilfi, M. C. 1983. "The Ilmiye Registers and the Ottoman Medrese System Prior to the Tanzimat." In *Collection Turcica III: Contributions à l'histoire économique et sociale de l'Empire ottoman,* ed. J. L. Bacqué-Grammont and P. Dumont. Louvain: Peters, 309–27.

———. 1988. *The Politics of Piety: The Ottoman Ulema in the Postclassical Age (1600–1800).* Minneapolis: Bibliotheca Islamica.

CONTRIBUTORS

Dale F. Eickelman is Ralph and Richard Lazarus Professor of Anthropology and Human Relations at Dartmouth College. Among his publications are *Muslim Politics* (co-authored with James Piscatori), *The Middle East and Central Asia: An Anthropological Approach*, and *New Media in the Muslim World: The Emerging Public Sphere* (co-edited with Jon W. Anderson).

Shmuel N. Eisenstadt is Professor Emeritus of Sociology, The Hebrew University of Jerusalem and Senior Fellow, Van Leer Jerusalem Institute. His recent publications include: *Japanese Civilization: A Comparative View; Paradoxes of Democracy: Fragility, Continuity and Change; Fundamentalism, Sectarianism and Revolutions.*

Daphna Ephrat is Lecturer in the Department of History, Philosophy, and Judaic Studies at The Open University of Israel and teaches undergraduate courses in the Department of Middle Eastern and African History at Tel Aviv University. Her publications include: *A Learned Society in a Period of Transition: the Sunni `Ulama' of Eleventh-Century Baghdad* and articles on related subjects. She is co-author of an introductory course on Islam taught at the Open University of Israel.

Haim Gerber is Professor of Islamic and Middle Eastern Studies at The Hebrew University of Jerusalem. His publications include: *Social Origins of the Modern Middle East* and other books and articles on the legal and social history of the region.

Miriam Hoexter is Associate Professor of Islamic and Middle Eastern Studies at The Hebrew University of Jerusalem. Her publications include: *Endowments, Rulers and Community: Waqf al-Haramayn in Ottoman Algiers* and articles on the social history of Ottoman and Colonial Algeria, Ottoman Palestine, and the Islamic endowment institution.

Nimrod Hurvitz is Lecturer at the Department of Middle Eastern Studies, The Ben-Gurion University of the Negev. His recent publications include: "Biographies and Mild Asceticism: A Study of Islamic Moral Imagination" and "Schools of Law and Historical Context: Re-examining the Formation of the Hanbali *Madhhab*."

Aharon Layish is Professor of Islamic and Middle Eastern Studies at The Hebrew University of Jerusalem. He is Executive Editor of *Islamic Law and Society*. His recent publications include: *Divorce in the Libyan Family; Legal Documents on Libyan Tribal Society in Process of Sedentarization*. Books in progress: The Reinstatement of Islamic Law in Sudan under Numayri (with Gabriel Warburg); The Mahdi's Legal Methodology in Sudan, 1881–1885.

Nehemia Levtzion is Fuld and Bamberger Professor of History of the Muslim Peoples at the Hebrew University of Jerusalem. He served as Dean of Humanities at the Hebrew University and as President of the Open University of Israel. He is currently the Chair of the Council for Higher Education's Planning and Budgeting Committee. Among his publications: *Muslims and Chiefs in West Africa*; *Ancient Ghana and Mali*; *Conversion to Islam*; with J. F. P. Hopkins *Corpus of Early Arabic Sources for West African History*; editor with J. O. Voll, *Eighteenth Century Renewal and Reform in Islam*; *Islam in West Africa: Religion, Society and Politics to 1800*; editor with Randall Pouwels, *The History of Islam in Africa*.

Daniella Talmon-Heller, is Lecturer at the Department of Middle Eastern Studies, The Ben-Gurion University of the Negev. She is co-author of an introductory course on Islam taught at the Open University of Israel. She is presently working on a book on Society and Religion in twelfth- and thirteenth-century Syria.

INDEX

Abu Hanifa. *See* Hanafi

`ada. *See* custom

ahl al-hadith, muhaddithun (traditionists, advocating exclusive authority of hadith), 3, 17–29, 34, 37, 40, 41

ahl al-ra'y (rationalists, advocating the right of jurists to reason for themselves), 26, 40, 41

`alim. *See* `ulama'

`amal (judicial practice), 86, 91

`amma. *See* commoners

ashab al-ra'y. *See* ahl al-ra'y

Ash`ari, 34, 37, 38, 40, 41, 42, 48nn. 45, 46; 50, 51, 62n. 42

ashraf (sing. sharif) (descendants of the Prophet), 12, 35, 128, 149, 157

awqaf. *See* waqf

baraka (divine blessing, grace), 45, 55, 107n. 87, 110, 111, 113, 116, 157
See also Sufi

bid`a (pl. bida`) (unwarranted innovation), 39, 49, 50, 51, 59, 60, 63n. 84

bid`a hasana (welcome, good innovation), 50

caliph. *See* khalifa

commoners (`amma), 13, 23, 49–63. *See also* community of believers

community of believers (umma)
active in public sphere, 12, 13, 15, 49–50, 59–60, 71, 73, 74–75, 79, 81n. 23, 126, 127, 129, 134, 151, 152
autonomous groups within (*see* ashraf; groups of origin; guilds; madhhab; neighborhoods; Sufi)

discourse with ruling authorities (*see* rulers)
place in doctrine, 10, 66, 120–22, 123–25, 144, 147, 148–49, 154
role in shaping religious practices, 6, 13, 49–50, 55, 60
See also commoners; `ulama'; waqf

cult of saints, 55, 60, 87, 96–97, 106n. 74, 107n. 87, 110, 116

custom (`ada, ta`amul, ta`aruf, `urf), 5, 13, 73, 80, 86–93, 94–97, 125–27
See also qadi

dar `adl (tribal arbitrator incorporated in the shari`a court and treated by the qadi as a shar`i notary – `adl – of the court), 90, 93, 94, 96, 106nn. 76, 81, 82; 107n. 91

dhikr (Sufi litany), 55, 113–14, 117, 129

endowments. *See* waqf

faqih. *See* fuqaha'

fatwa (legal opinion), 14, 32, 33, 43, 49, 50, 52, 53, 74, 91, 92, 126. *See also* mufti

fiqh (the science of the shari`a), 26, 85, 121, 147

fuqaha' (sing. faqih) (scholars of fiqh), 10, 43, 53, 85, 86, 91–92, 109, 120. *See also* `ulama'

groups of origin, 12, 128–29

guilds, 5, 12, 69–70, 71, 80, 81n. 18, 128–29

187

hadith (tradition deriving from the
Prophet), 10, 19, 21, 22, 25, 26, 36,
41, 43, 50, 54, 56, 59, 66, 94–95, 120
Hanafi, Abu Hanifa, 7, 12, 14, 26, 29n.
36, 32, 37, 38, 39, 41, 47n. 27, 50,
54, 59, 62n. 42, 63n. 82, 89, 90, 92,
131, 136n. 31 *See also madhhab*
Hanbali, Ibn Hanbal, 4, 11, 14, 22–24,
26, 28n. 4, 32, 34, 37, 38, 39, 40, 41,
42, 43, 44, 47n. 27, 51, 53, 54, 55,
58–59, 109, 155. *See also madhhab*

Ibn Hanbal. *See* Hanbali
ijma (consensus of community or
`ulama`), 10, 13, 120, 147
ijtihad (exercise of independent reasoning), 5, 90
`ilm (religious knowledge), 31, 40
`ilm al-rijal (branch of knowledge con-
cerning information about *hadith*
transmitters), 21–22, 25–28, 29n.
29. *See also `ulama`*
imam (leader of public prayer), 35, 38,
49, 51, 55, 58, 59

kalam (theology), 19, 22–24, 28n. 5, 41
khalifa (caliph), 66–68, 114, 150, 157.
See also rulers
khanqah (pl. *khawaniq*) (Sufi lodge), 3,
31, 54, 56, 59, 62n. 45, 111, 116
khatib (preacher of Friday sermon), 35,
37, 53, 54, 58, 59

madhhab (pl. *madhahib*) (school of law),
31, 33, 54, 88, 128, 129, 151, 155
affiliation and membership, 37–38, 39,
44
and *madaris*, 38, 39–40, 43
arena of public sphere, 3, 11, 37–41,
43–45, 147
as solidarity group, 4, 11–12, 38, 39,
40–41, 44, 46–47n. 23, 58–59, 109
autonomy in public sphere, 10, 14, 44,
58–59, 147
internal conflicts, 4, 41–44
rulers' intervention in conflicts, 14,
41–42, 43

rulers' intervention in debates among
madhahib, 14, 42, 43
social functions, 11, 38–39, 41,
47–48n. 37, 58–59
See also: Hanafi; Hanbali; Maliki;
Shafi`i; *`ulama`*
madrasa (pl. *madaris*) (college of religious
sciences), 4, 31–32, 33, 37, 38, 39,
41, 44, 45n. 6, 47n. 34, 54, 59, 74,
75, 76, 122, 128, 131, 137n. 46
autonomy of *`ulama`* heads of *madaris*,
11, 33–34
role in public sphere, 3, 43
See also `ilm; madhhab
mahdi (a divinely guided ruler who would
restore Islam to its original perfection), 14, 68, 137n. 33, 155, 158
majlis al-`ilm (assembly of learning), 54,
59
Maliki, 32, 37, 47n. 27, 86, 90, 91, 95, 97,
105n. 56, 136n. 31. *See also madhhab*
mazalim (rulers' court of justice dealing
in particular with petitions concerning abuse of power by officials),
34, 70. *See also* Ottoman law
mihna (inquisition), 3, 6, 10, 13, 14,
17–29, 28n. 4, 41, 136n. 25
mudarris (pl. *mudarrisun*) (teacher at a
madrasa), 33–34, 37
mufti (jurisconsult who issues *fatwas*), 10,
11, 14, 32, 36, 41, 50, 52, 53, 59,
72, 74, 84, 85, 86, 92, 125, 126,
136–37n. 31, 147. *See also fatwa;*
`ulama`
muhaddithun. See ahl al-hadith
muhtasib (supervisor of moral behaviour,
particularly market inspector), 35,
49, 54, 61n. 22, 70, 78, 93
mutakallimun (scholastic theologians), 3,
17–29. *See also kalam*
mutawalli, nazir (*waqf* administrator), 34,
35, 54
Mu`tazili, 19, 23, 24, 28n. 8, 29n. 20, 37,
40

nazir. See mutawalli
neighborhoods, 12, 38, 58, 77, 80, 128–29

Orientalism, 141–44, 145, 159–60
    Oriental and Ottoman despotism, 7,
        15, 78–79, 119, 142, 147
    stagnation of Oriental societies, 142,
        143–44
Ottoman law, 68–75, 80
    general characteristics, 68–69
    procedure, 71
    qanun and *shari`a*, 13, 72
    rise of *shari`a*, 13, 72
    role of sultan, 69, 70
    tribunals, 70–71, 81n. 22 (*see also*
        mazalim)
    See also guilds; *qadi*; *shari`a*

patronage, 3, 32, 33, 34, 36, 37, 38, 39,
    54, 57, 59, 62n. 40, 111, 113, 129,
    152
public opinion, 10, 11, 13, 17, 21, 27,
    126, 130, 147
public sphere
    general:
        and civil society, 9, 65, 83, 139–41
        and the new cultural history, 65,
            119
        and official sphere, 9, 140, 141
        and private sphere, 9, 140, 141
        and relations between power and
            culture, 144–46
        applicability of Western models to
            other civilizations, 9, 142, 143,
            146, 159–60
        definition, 9, 17, 119, 140, 141
        development of theory of, 1–3,
            139–41
    in Muslim societies, 1–2, 4, 9–15, 50,
        65–66, 70, 120, 121, 122, 124,
        147
        and civil society, 65-66, 72, 74,
            76–77, 77–80, 83–84, 119
        and official sphere, 35–36 (*see also*
            `ulama')
        and policy-making decisions,
            152–53, 154
        and private sphere, 7, 9, 12, 121–22
        and religion, 1–8, 49–63, 148
        applicability of Western models to,

            17, 83–84, 142, 146, 147, 159–60
        arenas of public sphere, 37-41,
            68–75, 75–77, 79–80, 84–107,
            128–29, 134, 148, 151 (*see also*
            guilds; *madhhab*; *madrasa*; neigh-
            borhoods; *qadi*; Sufi)
        autonomy of, 7–8, 15, 70, 77, 147,
            148, 151, 152, 153
        discourse in, 3, 6–7, 15 (*see also*
            waqf)
        dynamics of, 7–8, 15, 27, 151
        impact of modern territorial states,
            157–58
        impact of renovative movements,
            154–58 (*see also mahdi*)
        informality of, 3, 4, 15, 134
    in other civilizations, 139, 140, 141,
        142, 144–45, 153, 159–60

qadi (judge), 19, 22, 26, 41, 52, 53, 54,
    59, 74, 79, 136–37n. 31
    autonomy of, 5, 10, 11, 34, 70–71,
        84–86, 94–97, 109, 147
    bridging *shari`a* and social reality, 5,
        11, 90–93, 94–97
    general duties, 32, 34–35, 70–72, 84,
        93, 133
    his court as an arena of public sphere,
        5, 11, 35, 84–107
    See also custom; Ottoman law; *`ulama'*;
        waqf

ribat (pl. *rubut*) (Sufi lodge), 31, 45, 48n.
    51, 111
rulers
    and norms governing the public sphere,
        13, 123–24, 130
    and religious sphere, 14, 49–63
    and *shari`a*, 5, 10, 11, 13, 49–50,
        52–53, 60nn. 3, 7; 62n. 42, 69, 78,
        79, 86, 123–25, 131, 150
    decrees relating to the *shari`a*, 14, 126
    discourse with *`ulama'* and commu-
        nity, 73–74, 125–27, 129–34, 137n.
        33, 147
    division of responsibilities with
        `ulama', 19–20, 27, 66–67, 123–25

rulers (*continued*)
  involvement in doctrinal discussion,
    4, 13–14, 17–20, 43, 50, 126–27
  involvement in resolving conflicts in
    the public sphere, 4, 14, 41–42, 43,
    51, 80, 152
  legitimation of, 7, 13, 14, 32, 35, 43,
    67–68, 78–79, 84, 123, 124, 130,
    150, 154, 157, 158
  responsibilities towards the commu-
    nity, 123, 124, 125, 131,150, 152
  See also khalifa; madhhab; mihna;
    Ottoman law; Sufi; `ulama'; waqf

Shafi`i, 12, 14, 32, 34, 37, 38, 39, 40, 41,
  42, 43, 47n. 27, 51, 54, 59, 62n. 42,
  63n. 82, 92. *See also madhhab*
shari`a, (the sacred law of Islam) (adjec-
  tive: *shar`i*), 66, 72, 83, 122, 131,
  132
  an autonomous civic force, 5, 9, 10,
    69, 86, 109, 120, 147, 152
  and custom (*see* custom)
  and moral, cultural, and social norms,
    10, 13, 37, 121, 127, 147, 148
  and social order, 10, 109, 124, 147
  and Sufism, 5, 109–10, 111, 114, 116
  shar`i concepts, views, 85–86, 93, 123,
    124
  shar`i courts, 34, 125 (*see also qadi*)
  shar`i regulations, rules:
    dynamics of change, 4–5, 73,
      125–27, 137n. 41
    local variations, 5, 13, 69, 73–74,
      127
    social forces involved in change,
      74–75, 126–27
    violation of, 51, 124, 133–34
  symbol of cultural identity, 10, 13, 147
  tribal notrary incorporated in the
    shar`i* court (*see dar `adl)
  See also fuqaha'; mufti; Ottoman law;
    qadi; rulers; `ulama'; waqf
sharif. *See ashraf*
Shi`i, Shi`ism, 21, 25, 26, 35, 41, 50, 51,
  52, 112, 149, 150, 151, 155, 157, 158

Sufi, Sufi brotherboods (*tariqa,* pl.
  turuq), 5, 10, 13, 31, 44–45, 51, 52,
  54, 57, 59, 73, 87, 107n. 87, 120,
  122, 126, 128, 151, 155, 158
  affiliation, 4, 45, 113, 114, 117
  alliance with other social groupings,
    110, 117
  and expansion of Islam, 111, 112,
    116
  and *jihad* movements, 112, 115–16
  and the public sphere, 3, 6, 12,
    109–10, 116–17, 147
  and radicalization of Islam, 115, 117
  and `ulama', 110, 111, 116
  and use of vernacular languages, 6, 12,
    115–116, 117
  economic and political power, 112–13,
    116
  historical development and structure,
    6, 11, 12, 109–18
  relations with the ruling authorities,
    12, 111–12, 116, 117
  social functions, 4, 6, 45, 110, 113,
    116, 117
  See also baraka; dhikr; khanqah; ribat;
    shari`a; tekke; zawiya
sunna (the Prophet's sayings and doings
  established as legally binding precedents, in addition to the Qur'an),
  13, 21, 22, 24, 60, 60n. 2, 63n. 84,
  88, 91, 120
  revival of (*ihya' al-sunna*), 14, 31, 40,
    48n. 46, 50, 58, 59
Sunni, 24, 25, 28, 28n. 5, 32, 37, 41, 42,
  43, 51, 59, 149, 150, 153, 155, 157,
  158

ta`amul. See custom
ta`aruf. See custom
tariqa, (pl. *turuq*). *See* Sufi
tekke (Sufi lodge), 111, 112

`ulama' (sing. `alim) (scholars of religious
  sciences)
  articulation of religious dogma, 3, 10,
    17–29

`ulama' (continued)
   association with rulers, 36, 39, 40, 42,
      45–46n. 7, 57, 67, 74, 84
   autonomy, independece from ruling
      authorities, 5, 10, 11, 18–20, 36,
      73–74, 79–80, 85, 124, 151
   conflict with ruling authorities, 3,
      17–29, 66–67, 74, 123, 157
   cooperation with ruling authorities,
      14, 27, 43, 49–50, 51–52, 57–58,
      59, 131, 132
   custodians of social norms, 10, 59,
      123, 125, 147, 150
   discourse with ruling authorities,
      125–27, 131
   functions, 11, 32–33, 35, 55, 84, 123,
      124, 132, 151
   informal representatives of the com-
      munity of believers, 11, 32, 76, 84,
      93, 123, 124
   in official positions, 11, 32, 33–37, 52,
      54, 59, 72, 83–84
   internal discourse among, 18–29,
      125–27
   interpreters, transmitters of shari`a, 37,
      59, 85, 109, 120, 123, 124, 130–31,
      147, 150, 158
   leaders of autonomous organizations.
      (see madhhab; Sufi)
   moral authority, 7–8, 10, 32, 84, 85,
      109, 123, 147, 153
   part of the official sphere? 32–37,
      74–75, 83–84
   social status and organization, 20–21,
      44, 45n. 3, 72, 84, 123, 136n. 29,
      150, 151
   spiritual status, 19–20
   strife among. (see madhhab, mihna)
   See also fuqaha'; `ilm; `ilm al-rijal; mad-
      hhab; madrasa; mufti; qadi; rulers;
      shari`a; Sufi; waqf
umma. See community of believers
`urf. See custom

Wahhabi, 155, 156–57, 158
waqf (pl. awqaf) (Islamic endowment), 4,
   10
   administration of large public endow-
      ments, 7, 15, 35, 76, 129, 131–33
   and groups in the community, 12, 77,
      128–29, 135
   and urban public space, 12, 128
   autonomy of, 5, 6, 77, 80, 129, 130,
      131
   cash endowments, 13, 73, 126–27
   endowments by rulers and retinue, 7,
      14, 32, 34, 53, 54, 55, 58, 75–77,
      121, 130, 131, 132, 135
   focus of discourse or tacit bargaining
      in public sphere, 6–7, 12, 15,
      125–27, 129–34, 135,147
   ideology, 7, 12, 121–22, 124, 130,
      134–35
   involvement of community, 7, 76, 77,
      131–32, 133–34, 135
   involvement of qadis, 7, 15, 76, 77,
      132, 133
   involvement of ruling authorities, 7,
      45n. 6, 77, 124, 129–34, 135
   involvement of `ulama', 7, 76, 77, 123,
      124, 129–34, 135, 151, 158
   See also mutawalli; shari`a; `ulama'
wa`z, wa`iz (pl. wu`az) (deliverer of
   wa`z, admonition or sermon), 34,
   54, 57, 59, 63n. 67, 68

zawiya (Sufi lodge), 87, 111, 128, 129

Printed in the United States
70979LV00003B/85